How to Clear the Negative Ego

How to Clear the Negative Ego

Dr. Joshua David Stone

Marcia Dale Lopez, Ph.D.
Rev. Linda L. Schweke

Writers Club Press
San Jose New York Lincoln Shanghai

How to Clear the Negative Ego

Writers Club Press
an imprint of iUniverse.com, Inc.

For information address:
iUniverse.com, Inc.
5220 S 16th, Ste. 200
Lincoln, NE 68512
www.iuniverse.com

ISBN: 0-595-16932-5

Printed in the United States of America

Contents

Preface

You are about to read a book that bears the title *How To Clear the Negative Ego*. The preface for this book, however, is of a genuinely unique nature.

This particular book is geared to helped you, my beloved readers, to learn to understand the nature of "the Negative Ego" itself, and by the understanding thereof, to learn how to replace thinking and processing life from it's point of view to that of God's Point of View! The "Negative Ego" 'sees through a glass darkly', processing both the inner and outer world through a separate, lower-self centered, fear-based and isolated lens. It "sees" through a Godless mind, which by it's very nature anchors itself in separation, manipulation, greed, and selfishness.

Understanding how the Negative Ego functions, one can then make use of the God-given quality of free will, and doing so, choose to see the world through the polar opposite of the negative ego, which is that of the Higher Self, and/or Monadic Realm. The nature of the Higher Self/Monad/Mighty I Am Presence, is the nature of God or the Christ/Buddha/Spiritual Mind, which both "sees" and processes the inner and outer world through the Lens of Pure Love, Unity and Oneness! The Christ/Buddha/Spiritual or God Mind is "the mind in you which was in Christ Jesus." It is, therefore, "At One With The Father/Mother God Who Art In Heaven," and is, in the ultimate sense, the only "True Seeing," for it "sees by the nature of that which in reality is our "Essential Self"!!! It is the mind that is in all Saints and Sages, from all religions and spiritual paths that have achieved liberation.

For this very reason, the Masters wish me to make clear at the outset of your venture through this book, to Be Vigilantly On Guard That You

"Do Not" Pursue The Study of It From The Point of View of The Negative Ego! I realize that this is quite a request, for as you have not yet begun to read the book. I am told to ask you to read it from the point of view of God Awareness and the Christ/Buddha/Spiritual Mind and not that of the Negative Ego!

The question then arises, how to do this. The answer is surprisingly simple. All you need to do, beloved readers, is to let go of the idea that you need to hold onto any judgments of Self, others, or the material contained herein, and to link up with your own Divine I Am Presence or Higher Self to whatever degree you are able. This does not mean that you "blindly believe" every word that you read, for no Advanced Initiate or Master would ask another to throw away their faculty of "discrimination." It does mean, however, that you set the Intent to read this material from within your own Christ/Buddha/Spiritual Consciousness, letting the intuitive faculty of the Highest within you discern the "true" from the "not true."

Following this simple process, I am sure that you will then understand that it is the Negative Ego Itself which is the false and separate "lens" and that it is the Christ/Buddha/Spiritual Mind that "sees things *as they are.*" This book is designed to bring you into the full understanding of how the faulty belief system with which we may at any time view the world keeps us in a state of isolation, separateness, fear, doubt, greed, bondage, bewilderment and ultimately "pain." The pain I speak of here is the pain of separation, or more aptly put, "the false belief" that we are separate and alone.

The goal of this book is to help you lift yourself out of this miasma of faulty thinking, into that of the realm of "the Divine Thinker," who knows themselves to be the Higher Self, Christ/Buddha Consciousness, God, "One With The One." All that I ask, therefore, is that you do the very best that you are able at any given point to keep yourself "hooked up" to the Christ Principle, the Spiritual Mind, the Ultimate Truth of Unity and Oneness, and to venture forward in the study of this material with "The

Highest of Your God-Self Ever In the Fore of Your Consciousness."

In essence, what I am saying or asking you to do is to read this material As the Christ or Buddha, and not as the isolated separate self, which is in its isolation the "Negative Ego." Therefore, call upon your Higher Self and Monad, center your Mind within the Christ/Buddha Mind, and share with me the journey of purification, cleansing, balancing, harmonizing and synthesizing all that still needs further purification, cleansing and clarity in order to be the Full and Total Expression of the Christed God Being Which You and All of Us Ultimately Are!

The Negative Ego, caught in the delusion of needing to feel superior or inferior, will tell you that you mastered this material in the "Spring of '72." Alternatively, it will tell you that you can't allow yourself to admit a mistake, for that makes you inferior which, of course, is delusion also. The Negative Ego will also tell you that it is more interested in other celestial and esoteric matters dealing with the Ascended Masters and such a book is not necessary for you to read. I am here to tell you myself and on behalf of the inner plane Ascended Masters of the Spiritual Hierarchy, that there is no subject on planet Earth in dealing with your spiritual life more important than this. The transcendence of Negative Ego is the core foundation of Ascension and all spiritual development no matter what spiritual path you are on.

I conclude this preface with the famous quote from His Holiness, the Lord Sai Baba, defining God in the following statement: "God equals man minus ego." You may be a seventh degree initiate and may be holding 98% light quotient, however, until the Negative Ego is transcended and the Christ/Buddha/Spiritual consciousness replaces the deluded and illusionary thought system, God has not yet been realized!

Introduction

The conception of this book came about in a very interesting manner. About four months ago during a very accelerated spiritual period in our collective growth cycle, my friend had a dream that I came to her, entered her office and firmly placed two books on her desk with a loud thump. She was sitting at her desk in the dream, and I said to her that if we really want to make spiritual progress, this is what we need to focus on. My friend looked down at the books and they read "How to Clear the Negative Ego Archetypes."

My friend shared the dream with me the next morning. I was deeply moved for this is a subject I am very impassioned about as can be witnessed by reading my second book *Soul Psychology: Keys to Ascension.* In my personal opinion, the issue of releasing the negative ego is the single most important spiritual practice bar none. This is why I so often quote Sai Baba who says the definition of God is, "God equals man minus ego."

In our next collective meditation, I explored this dream. We were told that these were books that I (Joshua) had written on the inner plane, and the Masters wanted me to bring them forth into material reality. I was very excited about this prospect, however Wesak 1995 was three weeks away, and I was extremely busy. So I put the manifestation of this idea on the shelf and let it incubate.

The importance of this particular book cannot be over-estimated. One of the key insights in the ascension process that has deeply startled me is the degree to which the negative ego is still in control of lightworkers, although they have taken initiations as high as the fifth, sixth and seventh degree. This is obviously not true of all lightworkers, but is true of a great many. In my opinion, the inability to master and clear the negative ego is the number one weak area of lightworkers generally. This book was inspired to remedy and help in this regard!

Sanat Kumara recently told me that one of the dangers of the period of history that we live in is that lightworkers are advancing spiritually at an awesome rate of speed; however their mental, emotional and physical selves are not keeping pace.

The key insight here is that ascension, and the passing of the seven levels of initiation has more to do with spiritual development and light quotient increase than it does with mental, emotional or psychological development. I personally was shocked to find this out. I began meeting extremely high level initiates, some who had completed their seven levels of initiation, who were egomaniacs, emotional victims, and extremely damaged psychologically.

As more and more examples of this began to confront me, we finally approached the Masters about this. In our mediations, we were told that in the past initiates were stuck at the fifth initiation until the psychological levels were cleaned up. In this speeded up period of Earth's history, however, beginning really in and around 1990, this was changed to the seventh initiation.

Now, I am personally pleased that lightworkers are being allowed to achieve their ascension and break the wheel of reincarnation more easily. However, there must be a point of "accountability." I was firmly told that no lightworker would be allowed to fully complete their seven levels of initiation or 50 chakra anchoring, or movement to solar, galactic, and universal levels unless this level is cleaned up. They may be able to get to the seventh sublevel of the seventh initiation, but their evolution will be stopped in its tracks until the three minds and the four bodies are balanced, the negative ego is gotten under control, and the three-fold personality (mind, emotions, and body) are mastered.

You only need to master 51% of your karma to pass the initiations at the seventh initiation, however, there is a ring pass not, to further evolution. The Masters and the Powers That Be will hold you at that level no matter how much ascension activation work, light quotient building and meditation you do if your emotional body, negative ego, and inner child, are not dealt with properly. The buck stops here.

This book is written to help lightworkers master their negative ego and "Dweller on the Threshold," and to clear the fields of all the negative ego manifestations such as alien implants, negative elementals, parasites, negative imprints, astral entities, psychological disturbance, physical disease, negative ego archetypes, and fear-based programming, to name a few. This book, in truth, may be one of the most important books you ever read. The negative ego and how to clear it is definitely one of the least understood aspects of the spiritual path and yet one of the most important. I also recommend reading this book in conjunction with my book on *Soul Psychology*. *Soul Psychology* lays the entire foundation for all I will be speaking of in this book.

So what that you achieve ascension and complete your initiations if you are an egomaniac, feeling inferior all the time, an emotional victim, don't have inner peace, live in poverty, fight with your mate all the time, or are chronically physically ill. This is not meant as a judgment, but rather very directly bringing the point home that just because you are ascended or at a very high level of initiation doesn't mean that this psychological level is mastered.

This very easy-to-read and practical book has been channeled forth to help in this regard. One of the biggest reasons that lightworkers are often weak in this area is not really their fault: it is because of lack of education. There are not that many spiritual teachers, healers, psychologists, ministers, marriage, family, and child counselors, psychiatrists, or social workers that truly understand what it means to transcend negative ego consciousness in all its ramifications. It is my hope that this book will be the answer to many people's heart-felt prayers.

It has been very healing for me personally to write this book. What is the saying? "You teach what you want to learn." Even Masters such as

Sanat Kumara and Vywamus still have a little bit of negative ego left. It is probably unrealistic to get rid of it completely, but the goal is to realize Christ Consciousness as much as humanly possible at this level of existence. On this note, we will begin our in-depth discussion!

1

What is the Negative Ego and How to Clear It

Before a person can clear the negative ego, they must know what the negative ego is. This may seem elementary to some; however, I assure you to the vast majority of humanity, and even lightworkers, it isn't. As I have already stated in my introduction, it is probably the least understood lesson of the entire spiritual path. Since I have written about this extensively in my book *Soul Psychology*, I am going to be brief here and get right to the point.

Everyone has an ego or personality which the soul and spirit work through which is good. The key idea though is that people want to ideally spiritualize their ego and not have a negative ego. The key to the mastering of this lesson is to understand that there are two ways of thinking in the world and only two. This might be stated that there are two distinct philosophies of life that all of humanity fit into regardless of their spiritual beliefs or lack there of. Every person in God's infinite universe thinks with their spiritual, soul, or Christ mind or they think with the negative ego mind.

In the beginning, prior to creation and just after creation, there was no negative ego mind. God didn't create the negative ego mind, humanity did. It developed as a result of God's sons and daughters coming into matter and physical human bodies and "overidentifying" with them. In that moment when the sons and daughters of God thought they were a physical body rather than a son and daughter of God just inhabiting and visiting a physical body is when negative ego developed.

This is referenced in the Bible as the story of Adam and Eve and the eating of the forbidden fruit and the serpent or snake which was the symbol of the negative ego mind or lower self. These two philosophies could be called the philosophies of the lower self and the Higher Self. If you listen to the lower self, you live a "low life existence". If you listen to the philosophy of the Higher Self, Holy Spirit, the soul, the monad, the I Am, or the Christ mind, you live a high life existence. To realize God you must remove your attention from the lower-self interpretations and perceptions of life, and instead keep interpreting and perceiving life from the Higher Self.

Since our thoughts create our reality, which philosophy you choose will determine what you see. In truth, you don't see with your eyes, you see with your mind. This is why Sai Baba has said that "Your mind creates bondage, or your mind creates liberation." You will have negative emotions if you think with your negative ego mind. You will have positive emotions if you think with your Spiritual Mind. Your thoughts create your feelings, emotions, behavior, and physical health or lack thereof. Psychological health is nothing more than maintaining a good mental diet. As the Master Jesus said in *A Course in Miracles*, the key is to deny any thought that is not of God to enter your mind. The key is to be vigilant for God and His Kingdom at all times and never to go on automatic pilot.

Whenever a negative ego thought tries to enter your mind just deny it entrance and push it out. Switch your mind like a channel changer to a positive and/or more spiritual thought. This is the concept of denial and affirmation. It is occurring literally a million times a day. You are the executive director of your personality and it is your choice. God and the Ascended Masters will not do this for you no matter how much you ask. This is your job. By denying the negative thoughts and keeping your mind steady in the Light at all times, the negative thoughts will die from lack energy and a new positive habit will be formed in your subconscious mind. Moreover, it will become easy to be positive.

It is only hard in the beginning, although vigilance must always be retained regardless of your level of development. The essence of negative ego is fear, separation, and self-centeredness. The funny thing is that the negative ego, in truth, doesn't really exist. Jesus said in *A Course in Miracles* "the fall never really happened, we just think it did"! In other words we have all always been one with God and have always been the Christ, or Sons and Daughters of God. However, if we give into negative ego thinking in our own minds, we will live in that state of consciousness although, in truth, it is not true.

This is much like living in a negative hypnosis, or like dreaming. When we dream at night we really believe and feel that the dream is real. When we wake up in the morning from a nightmare we are so relieved and say to ourselves, "I am so glad that was just a dream." This is what I am trying to say to you now about your normal waking life. You have been dreaming with your eyes open, living your conscious life. You are living in a dream of the negative ego's interpretation of life, rather than interpreting life from your Christ Mind.

It is much like the glass of water: is it half empty or half full. This simple analogy applies to every moment of life! There is a way of interpreting life that will bring you inner peace, calmness, joy, happiness, unconditional love, evenmindedness, equanimity all the time regardless of what is going on outside of self. There is another way of interpreting life that will make you angry, upset, irritable, impatient, moody, emotional, unstable, manic-depressive, depressed, and sad! This has absolutely nothing to do with what is going on outside of yourself. It has everything to do with how you are interpreting life.

One example of this that the Masters want me to discuss on this point of how to flow with the universe instead of fighting it, is the "Blessing Method." The Holy Spirit and the Masters would have us bless and give thanks for everything that happens in our lives. Kind of like the saying in the Bible, "Not my will but thine" and thank you for the lesson.

The negative ego does not interpret things as teachings, lessons, challenges, or gifts; it curses and gets angry when its attachments and/or expectations are not met. The Christ Mind only having preferences, rather than attachments, is happy either way for its inner peace is a state of mind rather than attached to something out side of Self. Bless everything that comes into your life and welcome adversity as Sai Baba has said, for everything that comes into your area of influence happens for a reason and is God teaching you something you need to learn. This is just one example of what I am speaking of here in terms of the two distinct philosophies of life.

My book *Soul Psychology* is a master thesis explaining these two distinct ways of thinking so I am not going to repeat myself here. If you have not read the book do get it for I have explained this process in one of the most comprehensive yet easy-to-read forms that has ever been put forth in written form. It is kind of like *A Course In Miracles* made easy-to-understand.

It is essential to understand that every person on planet Earth only has one real problem and that is the negative ego. The negative ego is the cause of all negative emotions, all negative thoughts, all negative behaviors, all physical diseases, all psychological diseases, all relationship problems, poverty consciousness or lack of money. In essence, the negative ego is blocking you from God-realization. Sai Baba says, "God is hidden by the mountain range of ego"! It is the negative ego in all its infantile variations and manifestations that leaves us open to negative implants, negative elementals, parasites, negative imprints, etheric damage, etheric mucous, astral entities, core fear, gray fields, and negative archetypes. In essence, the negative ego could be defined as "imbalance".

Anytime we are getting out of balance; it is the negative ego that is causing it. This comes down to which voice you are listening to. Are you listening to the voice of separation, or the voice of oneness? Are you listening to the voice of fear or the voice of perfect love? Are you listening to the voice of self-centered-ness, or group consciousness? As *A Course in Miracles* says, "Choose once again."

Every moment of our lives we are choosing either God or ego. I challenge you to make a pact and vow with yourself and God to choose only God and the Holy Spirit no matter what, from this day forward. This vow is one I made approximately seven or eight years ago and is the number one reason I have made the progress I have made in my life. I closed the door on the negative ego and lower self for God, and made a choice I would never "consciously" choose this path again. Perfection is not ever making a mistake, but rather never making a conscious mistake. I am confronting you now with the ultimate existential choice of existence. Do you want God or do you want your ego, which is a life of overidentification with matter?

As Yogananda said, if you want God you must want Him like a drowning man wants air. You will not find God being indecisive or sitting on the fence. Jesus said the whole commandment can be summed up as, "Love the Lord thy God with all thy heart and soul and mind and might, and love thy neighbor as you love yourself." We each, in truth, are not a physical body but the "Eternal Self" living in a physical body.

We all share the same identity as the Eternal Self. Quoting from *A Course in Miracles,* "Nothing real can be threatened, nothing unreal exists. Herein lies the peace of God". In India they call this vow the "vow of the Bramacharya," or the "Vow of Purity." Gandhi took it and it was the key to his success. The taking of this vow will move you forward faster than all the ascension activations in all my books. This is the real key to Self-realization and God-realization.

Do you see my point now? Lightworkers have been focusing on the spiritual level and making great progress but if this core psychological level is not mastered, there is a cancer. This can be healed very quickly for all I am really discussing here is the science of "attitudinal healing." Just because you have achieved your ascension or taken your seventh initiation and broken the wheel of reincarnation doesn't mean your work is done and you are some God-realized Master.

Remember there are 352 levels of initiation to return to Source at the highest cosmic level and the seventh initiation although high for our planet is minuscule in the whole scheme of things. It is when you get to this level the real work begins. If you thought you were going on vacation after reaching this goal, think again. It is just the opposite.

The Masters have given much, and much is now expected. The expectation is to, number one; act like God or act like Christ at all times in all situations in all contacts with people. Secondly, the expectation is planetary world service. The form it takes is up to you but this is a requirement to move forward. You cannot move forward without helping your brothers and sisters in some capacity. In truth, this is the only reason you are here.

There are corollary lessons that are also required that emanate out from this initial lesson of denying the negative ego and choosing the Christ Consciousness. The main corollary lessons are: learning to balance the four bodies (physical, emotional, mental and spiritual), learning to integrate the three minds, (conscious, subconscious and superconscious), learning to properly parent the inner child, developing self love and self worth, learning to own your personal power at all times, learning to reprogram the subconscious mind, proper control of sexual energy, psychic self defense, right human relationships, proper care of the physical vehicle, and mastery of desire body.

Imbalances in any of these areas are, of course, because the negative ego programming is still present. Much of these areas I have focused on in my *Soul Psychology* book so I will not repeat myself here. My friend, however, had a very good metaphor for balancing the four bodies, which she received from the Masters. They suggested to look at the four-body system as four tubes filled with water. The water actually is energy, but it is easier to understand what happens if you see it as water. Many Lightworkers are top heavy. They are filtering a great deal of their water into the spiritual tube, which leaves the mental, emotional and physical tubes depleted. This creates imbalances, leakages, and a whole host of problems.

The same can be seen in the chakras. When certain chakras are overemphasized, causing over-activity in some and under-activity in others, this effects the glandular system and causes a whole other manifestation of lessons which I will explore in great detail later in this book. The idea here is to keep the water balanced in all four tubes. Other Lightworkers may be more mental, others too feeling, and emotional, some even too fixated on the physical body. The key lesson is always balance and moderation in all things.

All these issues must be addressed and mastered to truly achieve Self-realization, and complete your ascension fully. It is kind of like you can install and activate your seven levels of initiation prior to really mastering this psychological level; however, you will not fully "actualize" your ascension until you master this area also. This will allow you to become a truly Self-realized being on all levels.

The rest of this book will be dealing with some of the more esoteric and more refined levels of this process beyond just the psychological level such as how to clear the negative ego archetypes, implants, elementals, parasites, negative imprints, astral entities, psychological diseases, and physical diseases that can develop when the negative ego is not mastered, cleared and transcended.

One more word that describes the negative ego could be the word "duality." In transcending negative ego in its fullest extent, one has learned to transcend the world of duality. Another reason this is important is that as one moves into their ascension and seven levels of initiation one begins clearing not only one's own karmic stuff but also the planetary mass karma, clearing on some level the karma from all ones soul extensions from one's oversoul, and the 144 soul extensions from one's monad. As one continues to evolve this continues to the group soul level, the group monadic level, and eventually to clearing on the solar, galactic, and universal levels. If you haven't done it completely in your Self, how can you possibly consider doing it on these larger more expansive levels? In this most accelerated period in Earth's history, we are now receiving a more expanded and full understanding of what the ascension process is really about. I think you will agree it is all very exciting!

How Do You Know When You Are Out Of Balance And In Balance?

On the physical level being out of balance may manifest as fatigue, on the emotional level as mood swings, or negative emotions, on the mental level as negative thinking. Improper diet may be another example on the physical level. On the spiritual level, it may be meditating too much or too little. A balanced person is a calm person, who has inner peace. A balanced person has detachment but is also very responsive to self, other people, and life. Balancing the four bodies is not a point of stillness or non-movement but more like a gentle teeter-totter or like driving a car where you are constantly making subtle adjustments. The balanced person can feel themselves going out of that subtle appropriate range and will then be vigilant and make the appropriate correction, within an individual body or within the entire organism.

In a sense, we live within a group consciousness within our own being. We must strike a balance between our physical body, emotional body, mental body, spiritual body, inner child, inner parent, subconscious mind, conscious mind, super conscious mind, our seven major chakras, our Christ Mind over the negative ego mind, our soul, our monad and our personality. Each part has a voice and a place, except for the negative ego in the ideal state, which allows for the full merger with the soul and monad. All these other parts form a vast communication system within us that we must stay attuned to, and honor. When we don't, imbalance occurs which then can lead to a whole host of other problems, like dominoes falling.

One must be right with self, before one can be right with God and right with other people. Each of us as the conscious mind and/or president must be like an orchestra leader bringing them all together in balance like a beautiful symphony, which is called "God realization," every day. It is a good idea to do a super quick inventory of all these parts to make sure everybody is happy. All these parts really want is to be part of the team. Sometimes they can get a little greedy and it is the job of the orchestra leader, conscious mind, or inner parent to demonstrate tough love and be a strong loving president, so to speak, and to let all these parts know who is in charge.

Even though the president or conscious mind is in charge, the president and whole team is totally subservient to the dictates of the soul and Mighty I Am Presence. In Eastern religion, this is called the "satvic personality" as opposed to the tamasic or rajasic (read about this in *Hidden Mysteries* in the chapter on the teachings of the Bhagavad-Gita). It is being in tune with the rhythm of the soul. So, I say to you now my brothers and sisters, are you willing in this moment to make a commitment to maintaining this subtle synergistic balance in service of the soul and monad for the purpose of demonstrating God-realization on Earth? This is the challenge and the "Mantle of the Christ", which God wishes us all to put on in this moment, and to demonstrate as a tribute of our love and devotion to Him on Earth. Are you willing to dedicate your life to such a noble purpose? This is the path of all religions, all mystery schools, and all spiritual traditions. God is awaiting your answer!

Before such things as levitation, teleportation, and materialization can even be approached or broached this other aspect must be 100% committed to and demonstrated in your daily life. This has been called in some circles "practicing the Presence of God" in our daily life. Can there be a more noble purpose for us all? Is there anything else in the infinite universe we should be focusing our energies upon? As the Master Jesus said, "Be ye faithful unto death, and I will give thee a crown of life"!

2

Ascension Psychology

Ascension Psychology is a revolutionary new understanding in the field of the psychological movement. It has a number of premises that are completely new and cutting edge in relationship to the traditional practice of psychology in the past. The first basic premise is that in ascension psychology it is understood that one's thoughts create their reality. Our thoughts create our feelings, emotions, behavior, and what we attract, magnetize, and/or repel in our lives. The second key understanding in ascension psychology is that there are two ways of thinking in the world and only two. Every person in the world thinks with their Spiritual Mind, Positive Mind, Higher Self Mind, Christ Consciousness, Buddha Consciousness, and/or God Consciousness, or each person in the world thinks with their negative ego mind, lower self mind, fear based mind, separative mind, self-centered mind, and/or personality-level mind. People in the world don't just see with their eyes; we see also with our mind. In every situation in life, one can interpret the world and any situation through one of these two opposing attitudes, interpretations, and philosophies. By how you interpret each situation will govern how you feel. The spiritual interpretation of life always looks at everything as a lesson and a spiritual test to remain in unconditional love and oneness with Self, God, and others. Interpreting life from the spiritual mind will only create loving, positive, and harmonious feeling and emotions. Interpreting the same situation from the negative ego or lower self mind will create conditional love, judgment, fear, separation, anger, impatience, attack, upset, sadness, and depression. It is not outside things that create these emotions as some would suggest and it is not chemicals in the body that create these feelings and emotions. It is the attitude and perspective we take towards life in all situations that determine this. Every person in life is a master and cause of their reality or a victim and an effect.

To achieve God realization and inner peace His Holiness in India the Lord Sai Baba has summed it up the best in his definition of God. Sai Baba has said the definition of God is "God equals man minus ego." This is a revolutionary new concept to the field of psychology. It is the key to achieving God realization, inner peace, harmonizing relationships, ending war, stopping terrorism, ending gang violence, and ultimately curing all mental and physical disease. The source of all problems stems from only one thing: you can call this fear, you can call it separation, or you can call it negative ego thinking. It is all the same thing. Every problem in life will find its initial source and cause in this place.

Ascension psychology teaches the transcendence of negative ego thinking and the consistent on-going thinking and feeling of your spiritual Christ/Buddha attitude and perspective. As the Bible says, "Let this mind be in you that was in Christ Jesus." One could also say "Let this mind be in you that was in Lord Buddha, Lord Krishna, Rama, Moses, Mohammed and all the great prophets and saints from our religions and great mystery schools. What you choose to call it does not matter and what religion or mystery school or spiritual path you choose to follow does not matter for they all taught and teach unconditional love, forgiveness, nonjudgmental-ness, oneness, positivity and faith.

Ascension psychology also teaches the importance of balance in all things. Balancing the feminine and masculine and/or yin/yang aspects of self, balancing the heavenly and earthly aspects of self, balancing the four bodies (physical, emotional, mental, and spiritual), balancing the three-fold flame that lives within each person's heart (love, wisdom, and power), and also the importance of integrating and balancing the conscious, subconscious, and superconscious minds.

In ascension psychology it is understood that the subconscious mind is a non-reasoning mind that is the storehouse of all of our programming which also has certain abilities within it. Ascension psychology teaches that we must learn to master the subconscious mind, make it our servant, and not let it be our director. We must be our own computer programmers of the subconscious mind to utilize its abilities. Just as we must train the subconscious mind to be subservient to our conscious minds, the conscious mind must become subservient to the superconscious mind and/or to the Mighty I AM Presence within. It is through this combined process that the three minds learn to function as one integrated mind.

Ascension psychology also teaches the importance of learning to properly parent the inner child with firmness and love. When we parent our inner child by being too critical or spoiling the inner child acts out in inappropriate ways and often becomes the director of people's lives because of this lack of training. The inner child becomes either filled with feelings of being unloved and unworthy or acts out in anger and rebelliousness.

In Ascension psychology, it is understood that the two most important relationships in a person's life are the relationship to self and relationship to God. If one does not have a right relationship to self, all other relationships in a person's life will be out of harmony and balance. This even includes one's relationship to God. When we do not have a right relationship with self, we project this wrong relationship on to everything. This is why we see so much misunderstanding in many of the different traditional religions and false prophets and cults that we are all aware of.

Ascension psychology teaches that there are four levels of mastery which each must be mastered on its own plane of existence. Many consciousness seekers seek to master one level or two levels, but are weak in the others, which creates imbalance. The four levels of mastery are the spiritual level, the psychological level, the physical body level, and one's environmental and outer life level. Many people in the spiritual movement are highly developed spiritually but much less developed psychologically. Often there is high spiritual development but this does not translate into mastery of the outer world and manifestation of one's overall vision into earthly manifestation. This is not a judgment, just an important reminder that God lives in all dimensions and in all levels and all levels including one's third-dimensional reality need to be mastered, loved, sanctified, and manifested in God's Divine Image and Divine Plan. This is why it is not enough, in truth, just to achieve one's ascension, which is the achievement of one's sixth initiation. It is essential to achieve what I call "Integrated Ascension." This means not only spiritual mastery but also psychological, physical and earthly mastery as well in service of God. It also means transcending negative ego, fear-based thinking and feeling and learning to demonstrate Christ/Buddha thinking and feeling in a consistent ongoing manner.

Ascension psychology also teaches the importance of stepping forward and claiming one's spiritual leadership and commitment to planetary world service in whatever way, manner, and puzzle piece that feels comfortable and harmonious to you.

If one does not learn to transcend negative ego thinking and feeling and replace it with Christ/Buddha thinking and feeling no matter what level of initiation a person is at, this will begin to corrupt the spiritual work that one is doing. The psychological level is like the first floor of a two-story house. If the foundation of your symbolic house is not built properly on the first floor, the second floor or the spiritual level will not be supported and may ultimately collapse. Not properly addressing the psychological level will cause corruption in one's channelings and clairvoyance and inner guidance causing them to be filled with personal agendas, selfish motivations, self aggrandizement and glamour. This again is not a judgment, just a keen and insightful warning from the inner plane Ascended Masters as to the importance of developing a flawless character on the psychological level. Without this, clear channeling and clairvoyance can not take place. There is no exception to this psychological law. A person's channeling ability always flows through one's consciousness, subconscious programming, character development, subconscious information banks, and conscious attitudes and belief systems. The Masters bring this insight forward to emphasize the importance of spiritual discernment within one's self, one's channelings, and the channelings of others. Lightworkers are sometimes far too undiscerning and impressionable in these matters and need to see the enormous effect of one's psychological development on the channeling and clairvoyant abilities as a whole.

The ultimate process of full-fledged ascension and realization and merging one's total being into the light, love and power of God, which is what ascension means, cannot take place unless each of these levels is mastered and balanced in the manner and direction outlined in the above writings. For more information on this process, I would highly recommend that you also read my book *Soul Psychology*, which has just come out in a newly revised edition with new chapters and new information just published by Ballantine.

3

Who Am I?

One of the great Spiritual questions of all time is "Who Am I?" A friend of mine asked me to write an article on this subject and I think my answer here will surprise all my readers. The reason I say this is that it all depends on the lens you are answering this question from. For example, if you answer this question from the lens of a worldly, third dimensional person who is an atheist, they would say that they are their physical bodies. Strangely enough, many fundamentalist Christians would say the same thing. They think that when a person dies, it is oblivion unless they are one of the chosen few who are resurrected by Christ. They see no distinction between the soul and the physical body.

Now if you saw life through the lens of a philosopher you might say, "I think therefore I Am." Philosophers being more identified with the mind to the neglect of Spirit and the emotional and physical body.

Now if you were into Humanistic Psychology, the answer would be "I feel therefore I Am." All Humanistic Psychology thinks about is feelings.

Feelings are GOD to them. As long as you are expressing your feelings and emotions, all is well.

If you are a Freudian Psychologist, the answer to this question is you are the combination of your ego, id, and superego.

If you ask a Transactional Psychologist, the answer to this question is you are the combination of your adult, parent, and child.

If you ask a Behavioral Psychologist, the answer to this question is you are the product of all your positive and negative reinforcement of your environment.

If you ask a Cognitive Psychologist this question, he would say, you are what you think because your thoughts cause your reality.

If you asked a Family Systems Therapist this question, they would say you are a product of the Family System you grew up in.

Now if you look at life through the lens of Psychology or a Psychologist they would answer this question you are the consciousness or conscious mind that chooses which thoughts to think, which feelings to feel and how to deal with the physical body. As with all these lenses, there is a sliver of truth to them all.

Now if you were a First, Second or Third Degree Disciple or Initiate on the Path of Initiation the answer to this question would be you are the soul or Higher Self. This could also be described as the Oversoul or Superconscious Mind.

Now if you answer this question from the lens of a Fourth, Fifth, Sixth and Seventh Degree Initiate on the Path of Initiation, then the answer to this question would be, you are the Monad and/or Mighty I Am Presence.

If you answer this question from the standpoint of a completed Seventh Degree Initiate, the answer would be you are an Ascended Master.

If you answer this question from the perspective of an initiate who has completed their seven levels of initiation and integrated these initiations fully into their mental, emotional and physical bodies, then the answer to this question would be, they are an "Integrated Ascended Master."

If you ask this question of some of the well known Ascended Masters they might answer by saying they are Solar or Galactic Ascended Masters rather than Planetary Ascended Masters.

If you ask this of Sai Baba he would say, "I am a Universal Ascended Master."

Now if you ask this question to a Buddhist, they would say, "I am the Buddha."

If you ask this question to a Christian, they might say, "I am a Son or Daughter of GOD."

If you asked this question of a Hindu, they would say, I am the Atma.

If you ask this question of a person in a Western Mystery School, they might say, "I am the Eternal Self."

In other Western Mystery schools, the answer might be "I am an incarnated soul."

In other Western Traditions, the answer might be "I am Spirit."

In the Islamic religion, they might answer that they are embodiments of Allah.

In the Kabbalah, a Kabbalist might answer "embodiments of YHWH!"

Now if you asked this question of Melchizedek, the Universal Logos, he might respond that he is a Cosmic Ascended Master rather than a Planetary Ascended Master. He also might say he is the Cosmic Monad not a Planetary Monad. He might also say he is the "Cosmic Eternal Self."

If you ask this question of someone on the Path of Devotion they might respond by saying, "I am love!"

If you ask this question of someone who is a First Ray Initiate they might say, "I am the Power of GOD!"

If you ask this of a Second Ray initiate, they might say, "I am the Wisdom of GOD."

If you ask this of an initiate on the Path of Ascension they might say, "I am the balanced integration of the Love/Wisdom and Power of GOD!"

If you ask this of an astrologer, they might say they are the embodiment of their horoscope at the time of incarnation.

If you ask this of a numerologist, they might give you the numbers in their numerology configuration of their name. If you ask this question of someone who doesn't believe in GOD, they might say they are their personality.

If you asked a Biblical Prophet the answer might be, "I Am GOD!"

So, my beloved readers, as you can see this is not the easiest question to answer. It depends on your perspective and your lens. Therefore, I ask you what is the truth. I would say the truth depends on your level of Spiritual Development and the lens you wish to look through. Certainly, we each are incarnating souls. We also each are the "I" or chooser that creates our reality by the choices we make in regard to every thought, feeling, impulse, desire and piece of energy that comes to us from within or without.

It is also true, however, that we are Spirit, the Monad, the Mighty I Am Presence even if we have not realized it yet, in our path of initiation and Ascension.

In the ultimate sense the answer is, we are God! The important distinction here is, are we talking about the ultimate ideal of what we are or what we have actually realized?

There are some that have realized their Higher Self and some that have not. Some have realized their Mighty I am Presence and some have not. There is no one on Earth, including Sai Baba, who has realized the Eternal Self in the highest Cosmic sense. The most advanced realization of GOD on this Planet is Sai Baba, who has done it up to the Universal level. He has not done it to the Multiuniversal level and to the Cosmic level yet. He is the closest on Earth. However, it would not be untruthful to answer the question "Who Am I?" with the answer, "I am God or I am the Eternal Self," because in the ultimate reality this is the truth.

It is also important; however, to not claim realization of something you have not truly achieved or realized. Many, many people on Earth claim to have realized GOD in the ultimate sense. This is complete illusion and a manifestation of the negative ego and misunderstanding. They may have realized GOD on a Planetary level, however, not on a Solar, Galactic, Universal, Multiuniversal, and Cosmic level. The truth is, it is impossible to fully realize GOD on Earth. One can realize their Higher Self, Monad, Mighty I Am Presence, become a full-fledged Ascended Master and even begin realizing Solar and Galactic Ascension. No one will go beyond this level, except in the decent of an Avatar. The only true Avatar on this Planet is Sai Baba. The meaning of an Avatar means you are God Realized at birth, and need no Spiritual training at all. There are some that claim to be Avatars, however, this is a misunderstanding of the term and in some cases a massive ego trip.

So, my beloved readers, the answer to this eternal question lies in if you are looking through the lens of what you have realized or what the ultimate truth of your identity is. From another lens or perspective it would also be truthful to say that you are what you have realized and you are the Ultimate Goal you seek as well. So, in truth, all of the answers to this question are true at certain moments. Maybe the best answer is that you are a synthesis of all of these in their proper perspective, as GOD would have it be!

In conclusion, I would say the only answer that is not true is that "we are GOD," with all capital letters. As I have already stated, "we are God" with only the "G" capitalized, but we are not GOD with all capital letters. This is because GOD with all capital letters is the androgynous Being who created us. The reason that "we are not GOD" with all capital letters is because GOD created us; we did not create GOD. So a more apt answer is, we are Sons and Daughters of GOD. Another term I heard from the process of Realization point of view is that we are "Apprentice Gods." Once we realize Planetary Godhood, then we can begin working on Solar Godhood. When that is complete, we can evolve to Galactic, Universal, Multiuniversal, and Cosmic Godhood. Even when Cosmic Ascension is achieved at the 352nd level of Divinity, evolution still continues for there is always a greater level of GOD to realize and refine. This, my beloved readers, is because of the "unfathomableness of GOD!" To claim that one has fully realized GOD as we can see is faulty thinking at best, especially given that one has not even done it once one has realized all 352 levels of initiation at the 352nd level of Divinity. This understanding of the unfathomableness of GOD, I feel brings forth a healthy humbleness and humility, my beloved readers, which is good for us all. On that note, I think its time to close this chapter which I hope has enlarged your "Full Spectrum Prism Consciousness" of who you really are!

4

Why Am I Here?

This is another one of those Age-old questions which people have been asking since the beginning of time. The answer to this question is multifaceted. The first answer would be if you want to be with GOD in Heaven, then act like him on Earth. Simple but true. The second answer to this question is to be the embodiment of unconditional love on Earth. The third answer would be to complete your seven levels of initiation and become hence an Ascended Master and therefore break the wheel of reincarnation and achieve liberation.

The fourth answer is to become an integrated Ascended Master which means, embodying your Mighty I Am Presence and/or Monad on Earth not just in your Spiritual body, but also in your mental, emotional, etheric, physical bodies and in your environment and Earthly Civilization.

The fifth answer to this question is to be of service, and help others do the same, in the way and manner that you feel most guided to help; everyone has a puzzle piece in GOD's Divine Plan, and a part of our purpose is to become aware of what our puzzle piece is, and what is the best way to be of service. If any of you, my beloved readers, feel stuck in this area, I would guide you to read my book *Your Ascension Mission: Embracing Your Puzzle Piece*. This book has been written to help guide you to stimulate a greater awareness of this aspect within self.

The first stage of everyone's purpose is to become whole within self, and to become right with self and right with GOD. It is only when these are achieved that true service of others can take place. Part of this process is to become a cause of your reality rather than an effect, to become a Master rather than a victim.

The sixth purpose for being here is to demonstrate egolessness, or to demonstrate Sai Baba's famous statement, "God equals man minus ego."

The seventh reason you are here is to bring Heaven to Earth, not only within self, but to do everything you can to help manifest a fifth dimensional society on the Earthly plane.

The eighth reason you are here is not only to demonstrate Godliness and practice the Presence of GOD in big ways, but also in an infinite number of small ways. By this I mean greeting your neighbor, taking care of your garden, being kind to animals, smiling at people on the street, being friendly to the bank teller and grocery clerk, cleaning your house, helping the elderly person across the street, picking up trash off the ground even if it isn't your house. I think you catch my drift here. Your purpose in life isn't necessarily to just focus on something big. It is also all the moments in between.

The ninth answer to this question is to not compare your Spiritual Path to others, and to not embrace another person's puzzle piece. Not everyone is supposed to be a channel, public speaker, another healer, or Spiritual Teacher. Not everyone is meant to be famous and rightly so. Some people are here to raise their children and serve in what seems like a smaller way, but, in truth, is a big way.

The tenth answer to this question, and maybe most important, is to manifest and demonstrate Melchizedek/Christ/Buddha Consciousness in your every thought, word, deed and motive. If you live each moment properly, always choosing GOD and not fear, separation and lack of love then your entire life will unfold in a Godly and Divine manner!

5

Where Am I Going?

This is a most interesting topic! As with all questions in life, the answer to this question depends on the lens you are looking from. From the perspective of a Fundamentalist Christian, you are going to Heaven or Hell, depending on whether you accept Jesus. They might also say you are going into oblivion, because they think death is real, unless you accept Jesus. Now if you accept Jesus, St. Peter, will be waiting for you at the "Pearly Gates" to let you into Heaven.

If you are an atheist, then oblivion is the answer, for you are a physical body, and the physical body definitely dies. If you are someone who is more emotionally or astrally focused, then you are going to the astral worlds, probably in the medium or upper levels which looks a lot like this world, but is astral in nature and not physical.

If you are mentally focused, and below the fifth initiation, you will probably be going to the Mental Worlds on the inner plane, which again looks like this world but is a little more refined and a little higher vibration then the astral realms.

If a person is a criminal and evil person, they will be going to the lower astral plane, which is commonly referred to as hell, but in truth is just the lowest vibratory rate you can attune to in the astral realm.

If you have passed the Seventh Initiation, you vibrate and go to the Spiritual Plane on leaving this world. I should also explain here that all Souls who have not completed their Seventh Initiation will go to Planes, below the Spiritual Plane and will have to return again to Earth to complete their Initiation Process and learn the lessons they need to learn.

Those Souls who are below the Third and Fourth level of Initiation will be reincarnating on a different planet other than Earth, for the Earth is evolving to a Higher Level now, and will not be a school for Souls who have not at least reached this level. Another more suitable Planet will be made available to these other Souls that is more suitable to their level of evolution.

I should also say that all Souls no matter what level of evolution, will after death be going to a three day Bardo or death processing time, where they will review their life with Spirit's help to see if they lived a Christ/Buddha/Love filled Consciousness. In Fundamentalist Christian terms this might be called the "Last Judgement." In truth, this is Self looking at Self, with the Spiritual eye of discernment, to see how one has lived from a more fully open Spiritual perspective.

For a Buddhist, they will be going to the inner worlds and will vibrate and attune to Spiritual levels with other Buddhists. The same could be stated for Hindus, Moslems, and those of the Jewish Faith. Each soul will go to their Level of Initiation, Consciousness, and Vibratory Rate in the four-body system (Spiritually, mentally, emotionally, etherically, and physically).

For those more advanced Initiates and Ascended Beings on Earth, they have the potentiality, after completing their 12 Levels of Initiation to resurrect or dematerialize their physical bodies at death or before and transform them into Light. This is also called "Physical Ascension." Some advanced Souls do not care about bringing their physical body into Light, and do not choose to use their energies in this way and choose to leave their physical body behind, which is fine as well.

Some more advanced initiates will go and serve in one or more of the seven Inner Plane Ashrams of the Christ, headed by the Chohans of the Seven Rays (El Morya, Kuthumi, Djwhal Khul, Serapis Bey, Paul the Venetian, Hilarion, Sananda, and Saint Germain and Lady Portia). Other more advanced Initiates will very quickly continue on, onto what is called the Seven Paths to Cosmic Evolution. These Seven Paths to Cosmic Evolution are:

1. The Path of Earth Service
2. The Path of Magnetic Work
3. The Path of Training to Become a Planetary Logos
4. The Path to Sirius
5. The Ray Path
6. The Path on which The Solar Logos Himself is Found
7. The Path of Absolute Sonship

If you would like to learn more about this, please read my books *The Complete Ascension Manual* and *Beyond Ascension*.

Fundamentalist Christians say that they will go to Heaven. What they do not understand is that there are seven Heavens. These could be termed as follows:

1. The Cosmic Physical Plane
2. The Cosmic Astral Plane
3. The Cosmic Mental Plane
4. The Cosmic Buddhic Plane
5. The Cosmic Atmic Plane
6. The Cosmic Monadic Plane
7. The Cosmic Logoic Plane

A great many lightworkers claim to be one with GOD, and think at death that they will be one with GOD in Heaven. This is illusion. For, "In my Fathers House there are many Mansions." In our Universe, there are 352 levels to return to Source. This could also be termed 352 Levels of Initiation. The most advanced Souls on this Planet except for maybe Sai Baba, who is an Avatar, are not beyond the 13th or 14th Level of Initiation. You can only go to a Heavenly Realm if you have realized that level of initiation. So I think you can see that people who claim to be one with GOD and fully GOD realized are channeling their egos and have a confused understanding.

Where you are going when you die is just another plane or dimension to continue your own evolution and continue your service work. After mastering "Planetary Ascension," you will begin "Solar Ascension," then working on "Galactic Ascension," then "Universal Ascension," then "Multi-Universal Ascension," then "Cosmic Ascension." Each person must go through all 352 Levels of Initiation to return to Source. Each person must serve and demonstrate GOD at each level and must realize each level, before being allowed to move to the next.

Now here is the next kicker in the process so to speak. It is not enough to achieve each Level of Initiation. You also must integrate those initiations into your mental, emotional, etheric, and physical bodies. All initiations are taken on the Spiritual level first. Most people, who have taken their initiations even beyond the Seventh, have not integrated them fully or properly into their mental, emotional, etheric and physical bodies. If this is not done, for example, even if you have completed your Seven levels of initiation or 12 levels of initiation for that matter, you will have to reincarnate back into the Astral, or Mental Realms if those Psychological lessons have not been worked out. This means learning to completely master negative ego/fear-based/separative thinking, and learning to think only with your Spiritual/Christ/Buddha Mind! So where you go when you die is not just determined by your Spiritual Level of Initiation, but also by how you psychologically integrate those Initiations into your four-body system.

I should also mention here that the Bhagavad-Gita says, that where you go when you die is the last thought in your mind. This is true, but this must be properly understood. Every person when they die has the opportunity to merge with the "Clear Light of GOD," at death. This is what all Souls should strive to do. Earthbound concerns often cause a great many Souls to miss this opportunity. This experience does not give total GOD Realization, but does give a great boost to your Spiritual Evolutionary Process.

Now getting back to what the Bhagavad-Gita said. Our thoughts create our reality, and, in truth, we travel with our mind. So when we die if your are thinking only about the Earth, you will remain on Earth as an Earthbound Spirit. If you think death is the "Pearly Gates" you might be given this experience to help you in your passing but this won't be the true "Pearly Gates." People, in other words, will create their own visual death process according to their belief system. Angels and Spirit Guides will enter those visualizations and then bring those Souls into the true nature of reality. So if you think about GOD when you die, this is the ideal, for then your mind will help you vibrate to the highest possible plane of existence that you are capable of achieving. This is not to say, however, you can live an evil life and then just think about GOD at the last second and all is well. Because the last thought in your mind is not just one conscious thought, but the conglomeration of all your thoughts in your conscious and subconscious mind you have thought that lifetime, and for that matter all the conscious and subconscious thoughts you have thought in all your lifetimes, which is also what is meant by this statement in the Bhagavad-Gita. So the ideal is to only think GOD thoughts your entire lifetime, and at the moment of Death, and this way the place you go, will be of your highest Spiritual Potential.

Now some Souls who are less evolved who have a lot of drugs in them at death or die a violent unexpected death, may sleep for a while on the inner plane as a type of integration experience. Soon they will wake up and if they are at all Spiritually inclined will be met by Angels or Spirit Guide helpers, who will help them get back on a more efficient course.

When most people die they will go through a type of tunnel and hear a buzzing sound in the background, and they will be met by friends and relatives in this life and past lives who have served as Spirit Guides, for Love is the strongest force in the Universe.

So, in conclusion, this has been a summary of all the possible places people may go at death and beyond in their Spiritual Evolutionary Process!

6

The Three Levels of Integrated Spiritual Growth

There are three levels of integrated Spiritual growth that each person on Earth must master to truly achieve God Realization. These three levels are the Spiritual Level, the Psychological Level, and the Physical/Earthly Level. The Spiritual or Heavenly Level of God Realization deals with building one's Light Quotient and Light Body, building one's Love Quotient and Love Body and it deals with building one's Power Quotient and Power Body. This Spiritual level also deals with the anchoring, activation, and actualization of your Higher Chakras eight through three hundred thirty. It also deals with the anchoring and activation of your Higher Bodies. Some of these are the Anointed Christ Overself Body, the Zohar Body of Light, the Higher Admon Kadmon Body, the Lord's Mystical Body, the activation of the Electromagnetic Body, the activation of the Epi-Kenetic Body, the activation of the Gematrian Body, the Overself Body, the Paradise Son's Body, the

Elohistic Lord's Body, the Monadic Body, the Causal Body, the Buddhic Body, the Atmic Body, the Logoic Body, the Cosmic Astral Body, the Cosmic Mental Body, the Cosmic Buddhic Body, the Cosmic Atmic Body, the Cosmic Monadic Body, the Cosmic Logoic Body, the Light Body of Metatron, the Light Body of Melchizedek, the Light Body of the Mahatma, and the Light Bodies of the entire Planetary and Cosmic Hierarchy.

The Spiritual or Heavenly Level of growth also deals with one's ability to channel, pray, meditate, and co-create with GOD, Christ, the Holy Spirit, your own Mighty I Am Presence, your Higher Self, the inner plane Ascended Masters, the Archangels and Angels, the Elohim Masters, and the Christed Extraterrestrials. The Spiritual or Heavenly Level of growth also deals with the creation and establishment of one's Antakarana back to one's Monad and back to Source. This level also deals with many of the other forms of Spiritual practice such as chanting, repeating the names of GOD, and reciting mantras, to name a few. It also deals with the process of completing your Twelve Levels of Initiation and the fine-tuning of your Intuition and Inner Guidance. Lastly, it deals with the cleansing and integration of all your Soul Extensions from your Oversoul (Higher Self) and Monad/Mighty I Am Presence!

The Psychological Level of Spiritual Growth

The Psychological level of Spiritual growth is a totally unique level and must be mastered in its own right. Spiritual practices will not help you achieve psychological mastery. Most lightworkers on this Planet are much more developed in their Spiritual Body than they are in their Psychological Body. This often leads to massive corruption of the Spiritual Body later on the path if this is not corrected. The psychological level is your foundation of your entire Spiritual house. The reason for this is that your thoughts create your reality, hence this level of Spiritual growth enormously affects the Spiritual and Physical/Earthly Level.

The Psychological Level deals with key core issues such as owning your own personal power, self-love, self-worth, your bubble of protection, Christ/Buddha thinking rather than negative ego/fear-based thinking, balance, integration, transcending lower-self desire, proper parenting of the inner child, reprogramming the subconscious mind, mastering the subconscious mind, mastering and properly integrating your feelings and emotions, developing your inner Spiritual Higher Senses, letting go of attachments and replacing them with preferences, balancing your Threefold Flame of Love, Wisdom and Power, becoming a cause of your reality instead of an effect, balancing your Four-Body System, balancing and integrating your Conscious/Subconscious/Superconscious minds, integrating and balancing your Seven Rays, removing implants and the negative elementals, learning to make appropriate choices at all times, and developing your psychic abilities. The importance of developing a healthy and balanced psychoepistemology is one of the most important aspects of the Psychological Level. A person's psychoepistemology is the thoughts, paradigm, philosophy, and/or belief system that filter all other thoughts. For example, if a person believes their feelings and emotions are the most important thing to the neglect of their mind, intuition and physical body then they are going to not have a right relationship to self. This imbalanced psychoepistemology will cause them to be a victim of their feelings and emotions and to be psychologically and Spiritually off balanced in every thing they do. It will also knock off balance all relationships with other people for one cannot be wrong with self and right with others.

The same is true with someone who is overidentified with the mind, intuition, or the physical body. The only proper healthy psychoepistemology is to be integrated and balanced in all four aspects.

Another example of an unhealthy psychoepistemology is someone who does not understand the difference between negative ego/fear-based/separative thinking and Melchizedek/Christ/Buddha thinking. These are the only two ways of thinking in the world. This is why Sai Baba says, "God equals man minus ego." We must transcend negative ego thinking and only think with our Positive/Spiritual mind. This is why the Bible says, "Let this mind be in you that was in Christ Jesus." Most people in this world including lightworkers have not been trained in this understanding. This is why we see so much corruption and glamour in the world and in the New Age Movement. Not having this understanding causes one's psycho-epistemology, or how one filters their reality to be off center. Sai Baba has said that seventy-five percent of one's Spiritual path is the process of self-inquiry. Self-inquiry is the process of how we filter all our thoughts, feelings, emotions, and the content of one's consciousness from within and without every moment of one's life. If one does not have a healthy, balanced, well-integrated psychoepistemology or belief system that filters one's reality properly, it will cause an off-kilteredness that will cause an imbalance in every aspect of one's life. If one doesn't know that one should be Spiritually vigilant against negative ego thoughts and emotions at all times and doesn't know to replace them with Christ/Buddha Spiritual thoughts and feelings, do you see the problem that this will create. Most people in this world do not have the slightest idea what the negative ego/fear-based/separative thought system is as it relates to the Christ/Buddha thought system. This being the case they end up being run by the negative ego. This is why so many people in this world are lacking in happiness, inner peace, lack of self-love and/or self-worth, successful romantic relationships, career, and with finances, to name a few.

When one develops a healthy psychoepistemology and/or Spiritual philosophy for properly filtering their reality, they then develop the "Midas Touch." The reason for this is a healthy, balanced well-integrated Spiritual philosophy and psychoepistemology allows one to hence be right with self and right with GOD. One cannot be right with any other relationship in life if one's relationship with self is not right first. The science of developing a proper psychoepistemology is the key to learning how to properly deal with all the thoughts, feelings, impulses, desires, intuitions, subpersonalities, instincts, inner child, energies, sensations, arising from the subconscious mind and our physical bodies every moment of our lives. It also allows us to deal properly with all these aspects coming towards us from the outside world. An unhealthy psychoepistemology causes us to not filter all these energies properly, as GOD would have us process them. The slightest improper processing will cause a negative reality to manifest on a thought, feeling, or Physical/Earthly Level if you are not vigilant, clear, and centered every moment of your life.

So, the most dangerous imbalanced psychoepistemology you can have is not understanding the importance of keeping the negative ego thoughts, feelings, emotions, and behaviors out of your consciousness. Only allowing yourself to manifest Melchizedek/Christ/Buddha thoughts, feelings, emotions, and behaviors. The lack of this key understanding on the Psychological Level has corrupted more people in this world, and more lightworkers, Spiritual Teachers, Spiritual Channels, Spiritual Scientists, and Spiritual Leaders than you ever want to know. No matter how advanced you are Spiritually and no matter how good a Channel or Spiritual Teacher you are, and no matter how famous a person is, if they have not done their homework on the Psychological level, their entire Spiritual Program will become corrupted over time. It is like a cancer that spreads behind the scenes over time and spreads to every aspect of life within and without. It corrupts the channeled information, it corrupts the Spiritual teachings, and it corrupts one's motivations. Even if one has controlled it somewhat, when the true Spiritual Tests come, when a person moves into Spiritual Leadership, power, and control over others, fame, success, money, to name a few that negative ego cancer begins to spread that was not nipped at the bud. That slightly imbalanced psychoepistemology pours forth. It is like a dam with a crack in the wall, as soon as the big Spiritual Tests come and there is more stress, and the ego has tasted power, fame, money and sex, the crack in the dam moves to a crack to a major breach and gaping hole. I share this metaphor as a warning to lightworkers to be "Spiritually vigilant" against the negative ego. The number of lightworkers, Spiritual Teachers, Spiritual Channels, Spiritual Scientist, I have seen fall and become corrupted and contaminated by negative ego and glamour is astronomical. I say this with no judgement intended. I do say it with Spiritual discernment for those who have the eyes to see and the ears to hear.

Another psychoepisteomological blind spot is the over or under identification with the God/Goddess balance. Usually this manifests as a disownment of the Goddess aspect within self, and hence the inability to appreciate it within others.

Another psychoepisteomological blind spot is having too much fire, air, water, or earth in one's horoscope and psyche. People end up seeing through one lens and disowning the other aspects or being slightly imbalanced which then of course affects ones psychological and spiritual vision of oneself and their world.

Another potential psychoepisteomological imbalance is being overidentified with mastery to the diminishment of love. For some mastery is more important, and for others love is more important. In truth, both points of view are psychoepisteomological imbalances. A person who is just interested in love to the exclusion of power will make tons of mistakes all over the place and be very flighty in their energy. The person identified with power over love will be very efficient and masterful but will often lose the unconditional love connection and be prone to angry and being to critical and judgmental. Both sides of this coin are a pitfall and trap. These again are the first two rays of GOD and they both must be balanced.

Another psychoepisteomological trap is being too masculine or too feminine. This may manifest as being a workaholic or too much of a hedonist. It can also manifest as being to serious and or playful and fun loving at inappropriate times when it is really time to be focused and take care of business. It is also essential to cultivate the emotional body properly and part of this is having enthusiasm and passion, and not being too detached to properly integrate the feminine side.

Another psychoepisteomological pitfall and trap is to be overidentified with the parent and or child. The ideal is to identify with the adult and integrate the parent and child in their appropriate balance and integration.

Other imbalanced psychoepisteomologies or Spiritual philosophies are lightworkers being highly Spiritual, but not knowing how to properly parent their inner child. Another common imbalanced psychoepistemology is people not realizing and being able to demonstrate that their thoughts create their feelings and emotions. Another imbalanced Spiritual philosophy is a person or lightworker flowing with the content of their consciousness rather than choosing it every moment of their life. Another imbalanced example is someone who does not realize that the subconscious mind has no reasoning and that they have to be the master of it at all times. Another common imbalance in a person's belief system is they don't realize that they need to be the master of their thoughts, feelings, and physical body at all times. Another common imbalanced psychoepistemology is the overidentification with Heaven/Earth. This is extremely common. Another example might be the overidentification of one of the Rays instead of being balanced in all the Rays. Another example would be the overidentification to one of the twelve Major Archetypes to the neglect of the proper integration of the others. Another example is the overidentification with one of the Astrological Signs to the neglect of the others. Another classic example is the identification with a traditional form of Psychology that does not fully integrate the Soul or Spirit. Another example is a Spiritual philosophy that is highly Spiritual, but not integrated on the Psychological or Physical/Earthly Level. One other extremely common imbalanced psychoepistemology is people who try to balance negative ego thinking and feeling with Christ/Buddha thinking and feeling. They do this because they think they have to be balanced in everything. It is true that you want to be balanced in self and in life. The one thing you do not want to balance is negative ego consciousness versus Christ Consciousness. Said another way, you don't want to balance Spiritual consciousness and fear based/separative consciousness. Said one last way, you don't want to balance lower self consciousness and Higher Self Consciousness. Because of lack of Psychological training lightworkers get the crazy thought in their mind that the positive and negative should be balanced, and/or the light and dark should be balanced. Boy, does the negative ego love this psycho-epistemology. My beloved readers, you would be amazed at how many lightworkers fall into this one. This is like saying love and fear should be balanced. Unconditional love and conditional love should be balanced. Forgiveness and holding grudges should be balanced. Christ and Satan should be balanced. Anger and love should be balanced. Lower-self desires and Higher Self desires should be balanced. Judgementalness and nonjudgementalness should be balanced. I think you can see how absurd such a philosophy is, and I tell you, it is the height of negative ego corruption. Adopting such a philosophy will not only manifest massive amounts of negative energy in yourself and your life, but it will also cut you off from your Higher Self and Mighty I Am Presence. There are only two voices in the world in truth. These are the voices of negative ego and the voice of Spirit. Do you really think these should be balanced? A great many confused lightworkers will tell you so. The nature of the mind is "argue for your limitations and they are yours." Listening to counselors, psychologists, marriage and family counselors, and social workers that are steeped in traditional psychology confuses many people. They have not realized their own Soul or Monad, yet are counseling people. This is called personality level psychology and 99 percent of the books on the market and colleges and universities are steeped and stuck in it. I do not say these things as judgement, but rather I bring forward the light of Spiritual observations and discernments to help you avoid the pitfalls and traps of the negative ego. Be discerning as to the Spiritual Teachers, Channels,

Psychologists and Counselors you choose for yourself, for very few are well versed in Soul and Spiritual Psychology as opposed to Traditional Psychology or personality level psychology. Another common psychoepistemology is that similar books, counselors, and teachers will tell you that negative feelings and emotions are good. My beloved readers, "Argue for your limitations and they are yours." From the perspective of Soul and the Holy Spirit, they are not good and they are not necessary. Personality level psychology teaches victim consciousness. They do not have a clue that it is their thoughts that are creating their reality. Negative ego feelings and emotions come from negative ego thinking. Stop thinking from your lower self/fear based mind and they will disappear. Start thinking from your Christed, Higher Self mind and you will have Christed, Higher Self, positive feelings and emotions. Your anger and upset does not come from any person or situation outside yourself. It is coming from your interpretation, perception, and negative ego belief system. So, in this chapter today we are busting the negative ego's corruption of psychology. It has entered every field of Earth life including religion and the New Age Movement. Today's discussion in this section was to explore its corruption and contamination of Traditional Psychology.

My beloved readers, in conclusion, as we can see the list of imbalanced psychoepisteomologies is infinite and complex. This is why it is incredibly important to do your homework on the Psychological level and not just focus your energies on the Celestial Realms, inner plane Ascended Masters and Angels, and Spiritually Esoteric knowledge and information. I cannot tell you how many lightworkers, Spiritual Leaders, Spiritual Channels, and Spiritual Teachers have become corrupted and contaminated by negative ego and imbalanced psychoepisteomologies from focusing too much on the Spiritual level, and not enough on the Psychological Level as well as the Physical/Earthly Level.

Each one of these potentially imbalanced psychoepisteomologies I have mentioned, causes the individual to see life from not only an imbalanced and slightly skewed state of consciousness, it also causes one to have a slightly imbalanced and skewed relationship to GOD and the inner plane Ascended Masters and Angels. You cannot be wrong with self and right with GOD and the Masters. Being wrong with self will cause imbalance in every aspect of your life including your relationship to GOD and the Masters. This is an indisputable law and fact of the mind. It is a mathematical equation. I share these insights in this clear manner so there is no room for the negative ego to seduce and manipulate you into its corruption and its illusionary web of deceit.

It also must be understood that every time you buy into one of these potentially imbalanced psychoepisteomologies, it limits your Full Spectrum Prism Consciousness that GOD would have you see from. GOD would have us see life from thousands of lenses simultaneously. Each lens being an aspect of our integrated and multidimensional nature. Each time we buy into an imbalanced psychoepistemology we see life from a smaller and smaller prism. Most people on this Earth see themselves and life through an extremely limited prism. Instead of seeing themselves and life through the Full Spectrum Prism of GOD, they see themselves not through a prism but through an extremely small number of lenses. The illusionary nature of consciousness, the mind, and the negative ego thought system will cause these people to believe that they are totally centered and clear, and they will even most often believe that they are God Realized. This is at least what they tell themselves and advertise to others. When one is caught in these imbalanced psychoepisteomologies they do not realize they are seeing life from an extremely small number of lenses. The negative ego tells them they are totally clear, and clearer than anyone else is. This again is the delusionary nature of the negative ego. Do not underestimate its powers to seduce and take you over. The first second you do underestimate its powers, you will be its next victim. Very few in the world are able to escape its seduction, manipulation, and deceit. It takes enormous honesty and GOD purity to not let it take you over for a whole lifetime.

Some do it for awhile, however, as soon as they think they have mastered it, is in truth when they lost it. As the Bible says, "After pride cometh the fall." Let this be a warning to us all. No matter what level of Spiritual, Psychological, and Physical/Earthly development, and no matter what level of Initiation, Spiritual Leadership, Success, Fame, or Fortune, one must be "ever vigilant for GOD and His Kingdom." True GOD Purity through a whole lifetime is something rarely seen in this world. This section of this chapter is a "Spiritual Challenge" to each of you my beloved readers, to strive to hold this ideal. Mistakes are okay for they are just lessons. If you fall for a moment or a brief period, forgive self, learn the lesson, and get back on your "Spiritual Horse." As you do so, be ever more determined and Spiritually Vigilant to retain your "Purity in GOD."

One more interesting insight into these three levels of growth is that the physical body grows automatically. If an adolescent drinks and smokes too much, and never psychologically matures, they will still physically grow, although their physical growth could be slightly physically stunted. Spiritually, if a person focuses on the light and continues to do Spiritual activations they will continue to Spiritually grow, even if they have chronic health problems and are undeveloped and immature psychologically. The psychological level is slightly different because it does not grow automatically as the physical body does. Just because a person physically grows into an adult, it doesn't mean that they are psychologically one. Just because the Spiritual body achieves Ascension and/or the Seven Levels of Initiation doesn't mean the psychological self is evolved in the slightest. I know above and beyond seventh degree initiates who have achieved their ascension initiation and are some of the biggest egomaniacs I have ever met. I have met others in this category that are absolute victims of their emotional body. I have met ninth, tenth, and eleventh degree initiates who have been completely taken over by power and greed. I have met others who are filled with imbalanced psychoepisteomologies and are run by the negative ego thought system. So just because the physical body grows and the Spiritual body may be growing, this says absolutely nothing about their Psychological Level of development. The physical body and Spiritual body once you get tapped in can grow and evolve almost automatically. This is not true of the psychological body.

An enormous number of people on this Earth including a great number of lightworkers, are still stuck in an adolescent level of psychological development. An enormous number of Spiritual Leaders, Spiritual Teachers, Spiritual Counselors, and Spiritual Channels are extremely run by the inner child the second they get off stage. There are an enormous number of ways that this adolescent Psychology manifests. Some are victims; some are too run by the emotional body, some are too run by the negative ego, some have bizarre psychoepisteomologies. The list is endless, for there are infinite numbers of ways that the negative ego can distort and create illusion. Always remember that every thought the negative ego has, the Holy Spirit and the Christ/Buddha Consciousness has an opposite thought and attitude. Whatever your problems or dilemma, the Holy Spirit and Christ Consciousness can help you find a way out. GOD did not create the negative ego, people did. It is the misuse of free choice. So the key point here is that GOD and the Masters cannot help you develop Psychologically, and your physical body cannot help you. They cannot create a healthy psychoepistemology for you, for this is a by-product of your own thinking and GOD, the Masters, and the Angels cannot control your mind, your feelings and emotions. This is your job. So being an adult Psychologically, and becoming a Master Psychologically, will only happen when a person takes responsibility for being the cause of their reality, and becomes the Master of their thoughts and emotions, and develops a healthy, well balanced psychoepistemology and/or Spiritual Philosophy on all levels. On the Psychological Level there is no free ride. Building Light Quotient is easy, it is just a matter of calling it in from the Celestial Realms. Physically feeding the physical body is easy, and the physical body will grow even when we abuse it and feed it junk food. My beloved readers, the real "nuts and bolts" of the Spiritual Path is the Psychological Level. It again is the foundation of your Spiritual House. If you do not address this level properly it will totally corrupt the Spiritual work one has done, and it will make the physical body ill over time. Too many lightworkers are fragmented in their Spiritual growth. Too many lightworkers are falling into the glamour of the Celestial Realms and not doing their psychological homework. Because of this, a new term has had to be invented called "Fragmented Ascension." This would seem to be paradoxical. How can you Ascend and achieve the Seven Levels of Initiation and still be completely fragmented, have imbalanced psychoepisteomologies, and be run by the negative ego? My beloved readers, unfortunately this is happening and it is happening in mass. It is for this purpose that the inner plane Ascended Masters have guided me to write this chapter.

Strive with all your heart and soul and mind and might to develop a psychoepistemology that is centered, balanced, and well integrated as GOD, the Holy Spirit, your Higher Self, and your own Mighty I Am Presence would have it be. I humbly suggest that reading some of my other books on these subjects might help you refine this process a bit. The books I recommend are *Soul Psychology, How to Clear the Negative Ego, Integrated Ascension, The Golden Book of Ascension, The Golden Book of Melchizedek, Ascension and Romantic Relationships*, and *The Golden Keys to Ascension and Healing*. I have great faith and trust in you my beloved brothers and sisters to learn these lessons and to be "Pure in GOD." The main problem in this world is not that people or lightworkers are bad or have any negative intent. It is more a matter of not having the information and proper Integrated Spiritual and Psychological training they need, to avoid these traps and pitfalls. It is to this humble purpose that I have written this chapter and this series of books. It is my humble hope and prayer that you my beloved readers, will find the information and tools useful, and will help you to accelerate your path to true God Realization.

Physical/Earthly Spiritual Level

This third and final level of Spiritual growth deals with the Physical/Earthly Level. Now we have already established that the physical body will grow physically into adulthood no matter how evolved or unevolved one is Spiritually, Psychologically, or Physically. Again, if an adolescent smokes cigarettes and drinks too much alcohol and doesn't get enough exercise, that can stunt one's growth but will not stop one from growing into an adult physical body. What a lot of lightworkers do not realize is that there is an evolutionary process for the physical body as well. One aspect of this is having a healthy physical body. If the physical body is ill or chronically ill, it makes learning one's Psychological and Spiritual lessons more difficult. So part of evolving the physical vehicle is eating a good diet, physical exercise, fresh air, sunshine, drinking lots of pure water, getting enough sleep, not taking recreational drugs, work/play balance, affirming and visualizing good health, praying for good health and help from the Masters for maintaining this state.

Besides the health of one's physical body there is also the issue of bringing light quotient, love quotient and power quotient into the physical vehicle itself. The process of Ascension, in truth, would be better termed "Descension." For the ideal is to fully ground one's Mighty I Am Presence and Light/Love/Power Bodies fully into the four-body system, which includes the physical vehicle. We are meant to become embodiments of GOD in our physical bodies on Earth. We are also meant to physically ground all the Higher bodies I mentioned in the first section of this chapter from the Spiritual realm into the four-body system (Spiritual, Mental, Emotional, and Physical). We are also meant to anchor all of our 330 chakras into the physical body. So just because one has past their Seven Levels of Initiation, this does not mean they have fully integrated these initiations into their mental, emotional, and physical bodies. People are allowed to pass their initiations when it is accomplished in the Spiritual Body. This is very gracious and generous of GOD to allow this to happen. Once we pass these initiations it is then our job to make sure that we have fully integrated them into all four bodies, which includes the physical.

Another aspect of evolving the physical vehicle is building one's immune system Spiritually, Psychologically, and Physically. This is done first by mastering the Spiritual and Psychological level. This is so because every negative thought and/or negative feeling and emotions and every piece of negative energy is a toxin to the physical body, just as pesticides would be on a physical level! When you learn to master the Spiritual and Psychological Levels, this will greatly help your physical health and immune system. This is also true because the subconscious mind runs the physical body. When it is out of control and run by the negative ego it will do havoc to the physical vehicle. This is the case because it operates like a computer. It has the intelligence to create perfect health or cancer, or any other illness. It doesn't have the reasoning however to know which one to create. It needs a computer programmer, which is you, to tell it what to do. There is a natural intelligence in the body that does move towards perfect health, however it can be short circuited by giving too many negative ego orders to the subconscious mind.

The other key to evolving your immune system is removing all the physical toxins from your physical body. Your cells, organs, and glands store toxins even form childhood. These toxins also come from environmental pollution, the food we eat, the drugs we take, electrical pollution to name a few. Some of these toxins are: (pesticides, petrochemicals, heavy metals, bacteria, viruses, funguses, mercury from our silver fillings, radiation from such things as color television. Electrical pollution from the myriad of electrical appliances, phones, telephone wire, preservatives, junk food, recreational drugs, antibiotics, drugs given by traditional doctors, air, water, and Earth pollution, manufactured dead food, lead paint, dental and traditional medical x-rays, to name just a few. Part of the evolution of the physical body is to remove all negative thoughts, feelings, emotions, energy, and physical toxins from its physical and etheric cells, organs, glands, tissue, and blood stream. This is a field of endeavor that traditional Western medicine does not have a clue about. Western medicine, although extremely useful, is the cause of the great many of these toxins by all the drugs they prescribe, x-rays, invasive tests, and dyes they pump into the body for these tests. In the future energetic testing will replace this form of invasive testing.

The best way to remove all these toxins is through homeopathic medical care and herbal medicine. If you are interested in doing so I suggest you find a really good homeopathic and/or naturopathic doctor who can help guide you in a process of finding the right homeopathics to remove all these toxins. Never forget that GOD exists as much in the Material Universe as He does in the Mental, Emotional, and Spiritual Universe. Never forget the purpose of life is to bring Heaven to Earth.

When these processes that I have mentioned in this section are done, the physical vehicle will be filled with Light, Love, and Power. You will have tons of energy, you will hardly ever get sick, you will need much less sleep and your physical vehicle will be able to withstand enormous amounts of stress and not break down. Most of all, you will be filled with energy and vitality to fulfill your Spiritual Mission on Earth.

The last and highest level of evolution of the physical vehicle is the process of bringing and anchoring so much of GOD's and your own Mighty I Am Presence's Light, Love and Power into the physical vehicle itself, that there is a process of etherialization that takes place of the physical body itself. In other words, the physical body becomes fused and integrated in a sense, with the Light, Love and Power Body, so the subatomic particles begin almost to take on the nature of a more etherial-type body that is still very grounded and connected to the Earth

Mother and one's Spiritual Mission on Earth. The highest level and form of this evolutionary process is where at death, Translation or Ascension occurs and an individual can choose if they want to, Ascend the physical body as well. This means at death the physical body is translated into the Light and taken with you into the next dimension of reality that it is your destiny to magnetize and vibrate to. I need to say here that this is not required or even necessary to Ascend the physical vehicle for it does take some extra energy and training on the inner planes to do this. It is, however, every Initiate's choice as to if this is something they want to pursue. One choice is not better than another, it is just a choice, an option.

In conclusion, on this topic of the evolution of the physical vehicle, I think you can see that a great many lightworkers ignore, abuse their physical bodies by improper care and nurturing. They have a faulty belief that their physical bodies and even the Earth has nothing to do with their Spiritual evolution. They put all their energies into the Spiritual level. Others put their energy into the Spiritual and Psychological level and feel the physical body and Earth is not as important. This is illusion for all Four Faces of GOD (Spiritual, Mental, Emotional, and Physical) are equally important. It is essential to do one's "Spiritual Homework" to evolve all Four Faces of GOD within self, and within one's service work outside of Self. The Material Physical/Earthly plane is one of GOD's Seven Heavens.

The final aspect of evolving the Material Face of GOD deals with the evolution of not only the physical body of your self, but also the physical body of GOD. In our case, this is the Earth Mother, our worldly civilization, and our Solar System. Again, a great many lightworkers do not pay much attention to the Earth Mother, Worldly Civilization, Politics, Social Issues, Changing the World, and Current Events. They believe this has nothing to do with their Spiritual life. I am here to tell you that it has everything to do with Spiritual life and one will not fully Realize God, or their own Personal full-fledged Integrated Ascension, unless they integrate and realize the "Material Earthly Face of GOD." You can not hate the Earth and the Earthly world or even ignore this process and fully achieve your personal Ascension. GOD is realized through Mastery of all four levels (Spiritual, Mental, Emotional, and Physical/Earthly. The ignoring of anyone will be a blind spot and lack of Realization of GOD.

So let us now examine what the Earthly level of God Realization is about. It deals with taking care of the Earth Mother on a personal and collective level and not polluting and/or abusing her. It is to take responsibility on a personal level to do one's part in loving the Earth Mother and attuning to nature. It has to do with developing a relationship to the Kingdoms of the Earth Mother (Animal, Plant, and Mineral). It has to do with developing a relationship to the Ethereal Nature Kingdoms (Nature Spirits, Devas, Tree Spirits, Elves, Gnomes, Salamanders, Undines, Sylphs, Fairies, Pan, and the Elemental Kingdom).

Evolution of the Earthly Level has to do with grounding your physical service mission on Earth. A great many lightworkers have great visions, wonderful ideas, great love and passion, but never do anything on Earth. Their Spirituality remains on a Spiritual, Mental, and Emotional plane, and never grounds into and with the Material Face of GOD.

Evolution of the Earthly Level also deals with learning to make money and not depending on others to support you. It also has to do with maintaining self-mastery over Earth life. This means cleaning your house, doing all your errands, personal hygiene, respecting Earthly laws, and paying your taxes to name a few. It also means not only loving the Earth Mother, but also loving "Worldly Civilization." This means caring about all the problems and inequities going on in the world, such as hunger, homeless people, child abuse, spousal abuse, gang violence, equal rights, education, racism, saving endangered species, animal abuse, repairing the ozone level, stopping the destruction of our rain forests, repairing and remediating all the pollution and abuse mankind has done to the Earth Mother. My beloved readers, this is a wake-up call. Our Spiritual Paths are not separate from these issues. These issues and many more are our Spiritual Path. As Sai Baba has said, "Hands that help are holier than lips that pray." It is our job to create Heaven on Earth. Who is going to create a Utopian Society on Earth if we as the Spiritual Leaders and Lightworkers don't do it? We are the "Externalization of the Hierarchy." It is our mission to get involved with Earth life in the way and manner GOD has created us to fulfill in the "Divine Plan" of things. Each person has a puzzle piece to fulfill and this means getting your hands a little dirty in the Earth, soil, and in helping those on the Earth less fortunate who need our help. It is our job to change all the institutions of this world from negative ego based institutions to Christ/Buddha based institutions. This applies to the political system, legal system, social work, gardening, religion, the arts, sciences, economic system, business, psychology, education, traditional medicine, child care, and the list goes on and on. This also means becoming educated on all these issues and raising consciousness whenever you can. If you can't help physically or politically in certain areas then pray on these issues and make them part of your meditations. Have compassion for your brothers and sisters in other parts of the world who are being abused and mistreated. Ignoring the Earthly world and civilization is ignoring an enormous part of your Spiritual Path. I am not saying here that everyone has to go to Washington and march or write their congressman. What I am saying is that everyone must do their part as GOD guides them to. You will not realize GOD if you do not love the Earth Mother, love our Earthly World, and dedicate your life to being of service to both. To be perfectly honest, the Celestial Realms can be like a drug or glamour to some people. They believe they are being Spiritual by ignoring Earth life and in truth, what they are doing is ignoring at least one quarter of their own God Realization, if not more. Jesus taught and set an example of living in the market place.

The purpose of life is not just to achieve liberation and check out as soon as possible. It is to love the Earth Mother, Earth life, and the Material Face of GOD so much that you want to remain on Earth and help her become the shining Fifth Dimensional Civilization she is meant to realize on all levels. If you do not learn how to be happy on the Earth in truth, you have not fully learned your lessons in coming here. I am not saying that this is an easy school and I am not saying that Earth life isn't difficult at times; however, GOD lives and is in all facets of the Material Universe. If we do not love the Earth and Earth life and take responsibility for serving her and helping her heal then, in truth, we are not loving GOD fully. Remember the Earth and the Material Universe is one of GOD's Heavens and is GOD's Physical Body. We have just talked about the importance of evolving your own physical body and not ignoring and abusing it. If we are going to do this, then why would we ignore and abuse GOD's Physical body. The microcosm is like the macrocosm.

Look at the example Mother Teresa set. She got her hands dirty. Look at how Ghandi transformed India. Look at all the schools and hospitals that Sai Baba has helped set up and develop. My beloved readers, do not just let your Spirituality live in the Celestial Realm, or on the Mental and Emotional plane. Ground your Spirituality and Ascension process not only onto, but also into the Earth, and Earth life itself. Ground your Spiritual Mission onto Earth, and not just in some Spiritual Visions and Good Ideas. Do not let your negative ego go on an ego trip of having to do some glamorous super large Spiritual Vision that will, in truth, never manifest on the Earthly plane. It is time to put our actions where our visions and thoughts are. It is time to put our money where our mouth is. The two thousand year Piscean cycle never made it to the Earthly plane, and neither did very many lightworkers. The Aquarian Age and our new Seventh Ray Cycle are about grounding our Spiritual Visions and Good Ideas on Earth. Talk is cheap! It is time for physical action and demonstration on the Physical/Earthly plane. GOD is from Missouri, which is the "Show

Me" state. GOD, in truth, is from everywhere, but for this next two thousand year Cycle, He is from Missouri. The Seventh Golden Age on Earth is the complete transformation of the Earth and our Worldly Civilization into a Fifth Dimensional Society on Earth! Whatever profession or field of endeavor you are involved with in the Divine Plan, it is time now to love the Earth Mother and our Worldly Civilization, with all your Heart and Soul and Mind and Might, and to be about the "Father's and Mother's business" of healing and redeeming all aspects of our society for our children and grandchildren to come! This is the True Mantle of the Christ and Buddha Consciousness that is now being placed on each and every person reading this chapter. This is the Spiritual Leadership and Spiritual Mission of Planetary World Service that is now being placed on your shoulders. It is not a heavy load for all that is required is for you to do your puzzle piece and part. It is also not a heavy load because each of us as lightworkers and Masters on Earth stand arm-in-arm, and shoulder to shoulder in the "Great Work" of redeeming the Earth and Worldly Civilization. It is not a heavy load because GOD, Christ, the Holy Spirit, our Mighty I Am Presence, our Higher Self, the inner plane Ascended Masters, the Archangels and Angels, the Elohim Masters, the Christed Extraterrestrials, the Earth Mother, and Pan and the Nature Kingdoms both ethereal and physical, will be helping us every step of the way!

So let it be Written, So let it be Done!

7

The Personality of GOD

We have here one of the age old questions from the beginning of time, which is what is the Personality of GOD? If we could understand what the Personality of GOD was then we could really have a Golden Key to how to Realize GOD on Earth. By the Grace of GOD and the inner plane Ascended Masters, I will share with you just this in this chapter.

GOD's Personality is divided into three parts and seven parts. This is part of why the numbers three and seven are considered some of the holiest numbers. GOD is first divided into the Trinity of GOD, which, of course, is GOD, Christ, and the Holy Spirit. GOD being the Creator. The Christ being the Eternal Self we as the Sons and Daughters of GOD are, in truth, but are in the process of Realizing. The Holy Spirit, which is the Voice of GOD and the "still, small voice within," which speaks for the Atonement or the At-One-Ment. The Holy Spirit is GOD's answer to every question and ever problem. For every miscreation of the negative ego/fear-based/separative mind, the Holy Spirit is the antidote. The Holy Spirit speaks for the Christ/Buddha Consciousness, which of course is the opposite of the negative ego/fear-based consciousness. The Holy Spirit speaks for the Atonement, which is the undoing of all problems, which come from separative thinking. It can help undo everything in your personality that is not of GOD. Most people, and even lightworkers, do not take advantage of the incredible powers of the Holy Spirit.

Now, we are made in GOD's Image, as the Bible says, so we are a Trinity as well. We are a Trinity made up of the Superconscious, conscious and subconscious minds. Part of our lesson is to become as integrated as GOD is in His Triune nature. This is our first clue into the Personality of GOD.

The second clue into the Nature of the Personality of GOD is to understand GOD's seven-fold nature. GOD's Body is made up of Seven Cosmic Dimensions, with each Dimension made up of Seven subplanes or subdimensions in each of these Cosmic Dimensions. These Dimensions are called the Cosmic Physical, Cosmic Astral, Cosmic Mental, Cosmic Buddhic, Cosmic Atmic, Cosmic Monadic, and Cosmic Logoic. The Cosmic Physical Plane is made up of seven subplanes by the same names, but are the subplanes of the Cosmic Physical Plane.

This, however, explains the nature and structure of GOD's Body but does not explain GOD's Personality. GOD's Personality is divined into seven parts as well. These are the great and Holy Rays of GOD. GOD's Personality is divided into Power, Love/Wisdom/Active Intelligence, Harmony and Beauty/ New Age Science/ Devotion/ Freedom/ Transmutation/ Alchemy and Divine Structure. GOD's Personality is the Perfect Balanced and Integrated Synthesis of these Seven Attributes. This understanding is a Divine and Sanctified Gift and Map from GOD and the Masters to help us understand the proper way to balance and integrate our own personalities and psychological selves.

GOD's Personality is first made up of Power. This is the Power to be the First Cause and Creator of the Infinite Universe. It is the Power to completely cause His reality. It is also the Power and Will of GOD, rather than the will of the negative ego, lower self, fear based, separative mind. So my Beloved Readers, GOD owns His Power, and is the Embodiment of the Will of GOD and not the will of the negative ego fear-based thought system. This is the First Great Ray of GOD and Creation.

The second aspect of GOD's Personality is Love/Wisdom. GOD is Unconditionally Loving at all times towards self and His Creation and manifests and demonstrates this Unconditional Love with great Psychological Wisdom. This is the Second Great Ray of GOD and Creation.

The Third aspect of GOD's Personality is Active Intelligence. This again is a form of Wisdom, but it is not Wisdom of the Heart, or Wisdom in a Psychological Sense, as a different kind of Wisdom, that is "Wisdom to put GOD's Consciousness into Action." Without this Third Aspect of GOD's Personality, nothing would ever get done in GOD's Plan. We would have Personality/Power and Love /Wisdom; however, without this third aspect of GOD's Personality, the Power and Love would never manifest on the Material Plane of GOD's reality. This is the Third Great Ray of GOD and Creation!

The Fourth Aspect of GOD's Personality is Harmony and Beauty. GOD is not only Powerful, Loving, Psychologically Wise/Wise in Action in Material Creation but GOD is Harmonious and completely attuned to Beauty in every aspect of Creation, in the way GOD manifests his reality on the Material Plane of Creation. This is the Fourth Great Ray of GOD and Creation.

The Fifth aspect of GOD's Personality is New Age Science. GOD is not only Power, Unconditional Love/Psychologically wise, Wise in Action, Attuned to Harmony and Beauty, but GOD is very Scientific in how He has Created the Infinite Universe. Everything in GOD's Universe is governed by Laws and is very much in Divine Order. It is possible to understand and Master these Laws and hence understand the Nature of GOD on His various levels. This is why, in truth, Religion and Science blend perfectly together if properly understood. This is the Fifth Great Ray of GOD and Creation.

The Sixth Aspect of GOD's Personality is Devotion. God is not only All Powerful, All Loving, All Wise, All Wise in action on the Material plane, Attuned to Harmony and Beauty, Totally Scientific; but is also filled with Devotion and Love for His Sons and Daughters of GOD and His entire Creation. GOD is the perfect balance of Masculine and Feminine, for GOD is totally scientific yet filled with Love and Devotion for His Sons and Daughters and all Sentient Beings. This is the Sixth Great Ray of GOD and Creation.

The Seventh aspect of GOD's Personality is Freedom, Transmutation, Alchemy, Ceremonial Order and Magic. GOD is not only Powerful, Unconditionally Loving, Psychologically Wise, Wise in Action, Attuned to Harmony and Beauty, Scientific, Filled with Devotion, He is also the Embodiment of Freedom and is Divinely Structured in the process to achieve this Freedom. GOD is skilled in the process of how to Transmute and Transform energy from Fear into Love. From lower self into Higher Self, from Separation into Oneness, from negative ego into Christ/Buddha/ God consciousness. This Seventh Aspect of GOD's Personality is very skilled at setting up Structures and Systems to help His Creation achieve Freedom. Freedom from what? Freedom from glamour, illusion, maya, and negative ego thinking. As Sai Baba has said, "The mind creates bondage and the mind creates liberation." GOD is Total Freedom from limitation and from the negative ego fear based thought system. GOD knows how to set up structures to help lead His Creation back to Freedom.

There is now one last aspect to GOD's Personality and that is GOD's Personality is not just the Embodiment of these Seven Great Attributes, but is also the "Perfect Synthesis, Balance and Integration," of these Seven Great GOD Qualities and Rays. My beloved readers, listen very closely to my following words. We are made in the "Image and Likeness of GOD." We too are made up of these Seven Great Rays. For the microcosm is like the Macrocosm. "As within, So without. As above, so below." If we want to fully Realize GOD, then we too must become the perfect integration and balance of these Seven Great Rays. We must fully own our personal power, and surrender to GOD's Will and not the negative ego's will. We must learn to be unconditionally loving at all times to self and others. We must develop Active Intelligence to be wise inn learning how to manifest our conscious-ness onto the Earthly plane, and manifest our Spiritual Mission on Earth not just in our minds. We must learn to strive to be Harmonious, and Attuned to Beauty and Aesthetics in all that we do. We must learn to be very Spiritually Scientific in all that we do, and learn to understand the Laws that make up GOD's Infinite Universe. We must not only understand these laws, but we must use these Great Laws to help our selves and others. We must cultivate Devotion to GOD, to the Masters, to our fellow Brothers and Sisters in GOD, and to all GOD's Kingdoms without giving up our personal power, yet still retain the total unconditional love. We must learn to set up Divine Structure in our life and in the design of our Society and world, which will ultimately lead to Freedom for all. We must learn the process of Divine Alchemy, Transmutation, Transformation, and Spiritual Magic to change our selves and our World from just seeing our-selves as people to our true reality as Sons and Daughters of GOD living in physical bodies. Lastly, we must learn to perfectly balance and integrate these Seven Great Attributes of GOD within ourselves and develop each of them to our highest potential. In this way, we will become the living embodiment of the Mighty I Am Presence on Earth. In this way, we will become full-fledged Ascended Masters on Earth.

In conclusion, I just wanted to point out that we are all aware of the Three Fold Nature of GOD, which has also been called the Three-Fold Flame of GOD. This has been called the Love/Wisdom/Power of GOD. My beloved readers, do you not see that this embodies these First Three Rays and attributes of GOD? It contains the First Ray of Power, The Second Ray of Love/Wisdom, and the Third Ray of Wisdom. Wisdom here has two meanings. The Psychological Wisdom of knowing how to

Unconditionally Love, and the Wisdom of how to manifest GOD's Power and Unconditional love on the Material Plane. These Three Divine Attributes are the Three Key Qualities that need to be perfectly integrated to Realize GOD. I bring this up for many have not noticed the relationship of the Three Fold Flame of GOD to the First Three Rays of GOD, and I felt it was important here to make this Relationship and Tie. Add to the Three-Fold Flame of GOD, the Four Remaining Attributes of GOD, and you have the Seven-Fold Nature of GOD and of your self as an Incarnation of God. If you truly want a Map of how to Demonstrate GOD on Earth, My beloved readers, let this be your Guide and Divine Road Map for how you Create, Manifest, and Demonstrate your own Divine Personality on Earth!

8

The Glory and the Corruption of the Seven Great Rays of GOD

We have already established that the perfect integration and balance of the Seven Rays is the Personality of GOD. It is essential to understand as with all things that the Seven Rays have a higher and lower aspect. This is because the Rays although created by GOD, can be misused and corrupted by the negative ego/fear-based/separative thought system. In this chapter I would like to go through each of these aspects of GOD's Personality and clearly explain the glory and the corruption that can take place when they are used purely and when they are corrupted by the negative ego thought system.

The glory of the First Ray is when a person owns their personal power 100% in total service of GOD and Unconditional Love. It is also the glory of surrendering to GOD's Will and not the ego's self-centered, negatively selfish will. The corruption of the First Ray is when a person owns their personal power to control, hurt, and manipulate others for self-centered, narcissistic, selfish gain; not recognizing their Brother and Sister or themselves as an incarnation of GOD. The Corruption of the First Ray is also not surrendering to GOD's Will in all things and instead unconsciously or consciously following the will of the negative ego, lower-self, and self-centered mind. The glory of the First Ray is its ability to own one's personal power at all times, but be able to surrender to GOD's Will simultaneously. The negative ego/fear-based thought system completely corrupts this understanding by having the person either own their personal power and not surrender, or has them surrender to GOD's Will and not own their personal power. Both are a corruption of the negative ego/separative/lower self thought system. Hitler, Mussolini, Stalin were classic examples of historical figures who misused and misunderstood the First Ray. In the Spiritual Movement those who are on a trip of self-aggrandizement, being better than everyone else is, power trips over being a perceived Guru, and or people who are constantly angry and attacking others are classic examples.

The glory of the Second Ray is its ability to Unconditionally Love self and others at all times, and the Psychological wisdom it brings to help one do this in all situations and with all people. The corruption of the Second Ray is first off, the negative ego/fear based thought systems distortion of having the person manifest conditional love rather than Unconditional Love. The negative ego thought system has one love under certain conditions and requirements. The second main danger and corruption is becoming overly flowery, sentimental, and loving, and not having a backbone, so to speak. This might stem from not having enough of Rays One, Three and Five, which are a little more mental in nature, embodying power, intelligence, and science. The third corruption could be becoming overidentified with the teacher or guru role, and not being able to step out of it. Being a know-it-all, since the Second Ray is that of education. In the First Ray the danger would be being too political, and not speaking one's truth enough. In the case of overidentification with the Second Ray it would be speaking one's truth too much, and not knowing how to be self-controlled, tactful, Spiritually discerning, and attuned to timing. I am also reminded of a book called *Women Who Love Too Much*. This would also be an example of the imbalance of the Second Ray. A person can become obsessed, addicted and co-dependent in relationship to love, and this is in truth a negative ego thought system distortion of the true Second Ray Unconditional Love, GOD would have us learn.

The glory of the Third Ray is the Active Intelligence or Wisdom to put our God Consciousness into demonstration and action on and in the Material/Earthly world, and not just on the Spiritual, mental and emotional plane. The corruption of the Third Ray could be an over intellectual nature and lack of proper integration of one's feelings and emotions. It could also be being run by the mind, instead of being the Master of one's mind, and learning how to quiet the mind when needed. It could also be over planning and over thinking about one's mission, but never doing it. It could also be a preoccupation and overi-dentification on making money and business pursuits to the neglect of one's Spiritual Life, because the Third Ray is associated with business. It could also be a corruption of negative ego business practices based on negative ego competition instead of Spiritual cooperation. It would be the negative ego controlling one's business practices which is to make a buck at any price, and it doesn't matter who you hurt in the process. This could be summed up, "So what that you gain the whole world and lose your own Soul."

The glory of the Fourth Ray is the creation of harmony, unity, and oneness at all times with self, relationship to others and one's world. It is also the creation of the Arts in the glorification and sanctification of GOD. This could come in the form of beautiful Spiritual Paintings, beautiful Spiritual Music, Spiritual Architecture, Spiritual Poetry, Spiritual Dance, Spiritual Opera, Play, and Theatre, to name just a few. It could also be Spiritual Movies, Feng Shui, and Aesthetics in daily living. The corruption of the Fourth Ray on a psychological level would be the negative ego fear based thought system creating disharmony and conflict within self because of lack of proper integration and negative ego contamination. This Conflict within self then would manifest in conflict with others, and lack of harmony with others. The Spiritual ideal of the Fourth Ray would be to create love, harmony, oneness and peace at all times and not disharmony, conflict, separation, attack and fear. On a professional level, the corruption of the Fourth Ray would be the lower self, carnal self, and negative ego control the creation and flow of the Fourth Ray. This would manifest as maybe a great deal of the rock music these days, with very negative and dark lyrics. It could be the creation of art with images that do not Spiritually uplift, but do the opposite. Instead of Music of the Spheres and music that Spiritually inspires, it would be music that appeals to the lower-self and carnal-self. I do not think that this needs much explanation to my readers. It would be movies that appeal to violence, pornography, and horror films; instead of the use of the film or multimedia for uplifting Spiritual inspiration. We all see how many movies are playing in movie theatres that we can't even imagine that anyone would ever want to go see. These moviemakers appeal to those individuals run by the lower self, negative ego, and lower nature. When the consciousness of the masses rises enough to a more Spiritual/Christ/Buddha state, there will be no one who would even pay money to see these movies. Any form of art that is created from, and panders to the lower self and lower nature, and does not inspire and sanctify GOD by its beauty, is a corruption of the Fourth Ray of GOD.

The glory of the Fifth Ray of GOD is its focus on Spiritual New Age Science. On a Psychological level, it is the use of the mind in a scientific way; for healing all aspects of a person and our society. The proper use of this Fifth Ray leads to cutting-edge scientific breakthroughs in Medicine, Psychology, Law, Gardening, Ecology, Social Work, Religion, Business, to just name a few. In truth, the list is endless. Everything in GOD's Universe is made up of laws and by understanding and mastering these laws we can use them to help other people our world and ourselves. The corruption of the Fifth Ray could again be an over intellectual nature, that cuts off the feeling and intuitive nature if corrupted by the negative ego/fear-based thought system. It could also be a worship of science and the rejection of religion and Spirituality thinking that everything in life has to be proven by a scientific study. Or believing that nothing is real except what can be proven by scientific means. Or that nothing is real except that which can be sensed with one's five physical senses. This is a complete perversion of Spiritual Science. This is the negative ego controlling science and is not the Science of GOD. Another corruption might be the imbalanced view that Science and Religion or Spirituality do not blend and integrate perfectly together. Contrary to popular opinion, GOD is totally scientific and understandable, if one will also allow oneself to use ones intuitive mind and not just their logical mind. Another corruption of the Fifth Ray is a focus to much on what I would call the concrete mind, and not allowing oneself to tap into the abstract mind, the Higher Mind, and the Intuitive right brain mind. When the Fifth Ray is properly understood and utilized, enormous scientific ideas and inspiration will come also not only from logical thinking, which is fantastic when used properly, but also from tele-pathic Sources of Knowledge on the inner plane. Cures for Aids, Cancer, and all the ills of our Society can come. There is not one field or endeavor of life that the Fifth Ray Scientific mind can not prove useful. There is in truth a Science for everything. Even a Science for how to run an effective business, office or home. The danger and corruption of the Fifth Ray can come in being overly scientific in an intellectual dry sense and living too much in the mental body and scientific focus and not smelling the roses, enjoying and experiencing life, and not just thinking about it. Every Ray has this danger within its focus and lens; it is not just the Fifth Ray. Each Ray of GOD can be a blinder in a sense, if not balanced with the other Rays. The corruption of the Fifth Ray in a professional sense is Scientists doing animal experiments with no consideration or feeling for the animals they are experimenting upon. This is one example. Another example might be the focus on only third dimensional traditional methods as in Western medicine, and the inability to open up to the vast Spiritual Technologies that are not so invasive and poisonous to the physical body. In Psychology it is a science only focused on traditional Psychology, that does not even recognize or believe in GOD or the reality of the Soul. With no judgement intended, these people call themselves Scientists and they are seeing life through one seventh of reality and calling it science. It is a science based on seeing life through blinders. True Spiritual Science sees life through a Full Spectrum Prism lens utilizing all one's senses, not just the physical ones. Those are five of about fifty or one hundred we actually possess. For more information on this read my books *The Complete Ascension Manual, Integrated Ascension* and the *Golden Book of Melchizedek*. There are many more examples I could give of the corruption of science on a professional level; however, I think I have made my point here. You, my beloved readers, can extrapolate how this process carries over to all fields of study. I would also highly recommend that you read my book Manual for Planetary Leadership for a great deal of this book is an in-depth explanation of just this topic, and how this process has infiltrated all fields and aspects of our Society and Civilization. It is quite fascinating reading if you would like to see how this process carries on in other areas of Earth life as well!

The glory of the Sixth Ray is Devotion. This is embodied in the Master Jesus' commandment to "Love the Lord thy GOD, with all your heart and soul and mind and might, and to Love your neighbor as you Love yourself." The glory of the Sixth Ray is that it brings an enthusiastic unconditional love and Spiritual passion to one's relationship to GOD, the Masters, to family, friends, people, and life itself. It is essential in life to fully embrace the emotional body, and have total Spiritual passion, enthusiasm, and joy. The Sixth Ray brings this total devotion and idealism. The glory of the Sixth Ray is that it makes us strive also for the highest within us, and pursue excellence at all times. The corruption of the Sixth Ray is becoming overly emotional and letting one's emotions run away with you and becoming victimized by them. It is also giving your personal power away to GOD, the Masters, a Guru, and other people. Another corruption and glamour of the Sixth Ray is putting Masters, Spiritual Teachers, and other people on pedestals. Another corruption of the negative ego fear based thought system that distorts the pure Sixth Ray is being to idealistic to the point of being a negative perfectionist. One can become so idealistic that they can become almost dysfunctional or impractical. The other great danger and corruption of the Sixth Ray is lack of Spiritual discernment. These are the main things to watch out for in how the negative ego/fear based thought system can distort the Sixth Ray of Devotion and Spiritual Idealism. The corruption of the Sixth Ray professionally is in the Field of Religion where Ministers of all faiths are taken over by faulty negative ego concepts and beliefs and the true religious doctrine becomes contaminated. We have seen this take place in all the major religions where their doctrine is preaching negative ego based concepts and theology that has no relationship to what GOD, the Masters and Angels really believe. This is why so many people have left their Religion, which is unfortunate, but they had no choice. This is why more people have been killed in the name of GOD than for any other reason I believe. It is also why different religions compete with each other and why most religions but not all of them state that theirs is the only way to GOD, which of course is total illusion. It is also why there are so many false prophets, cults, and religious leaders being caught in scandal, as the negative ego and corruption ultimately becomes exposed.

The glory of the Seventh Ray is its emphasis on freedom and its ability to set up divine structures and systems within self and society to help lead towards even greater freedom within self and within our Society. The glory of the Seventh Ray is also the ability to use Spiritual magic in the form of transmutation and alchemy to transform misqualified energies into the purity and substance of GOD. The corruption of the Seventh Ray can come in many forms. It can come from the negative ego/fear based minds misguided understanding of what true freedom is. Many people think they are free, but, in truth, they are not. As His Holiness the Lord Sai Baba has said, "The mind creates bondage and the mind creates liberation." Many people think they are free, but, in truth, they are being very much run by the negative ego, the emotional body, their mental body, the inner child, lower-self desire, and their subconscious mind. Another aspect of the corruption of the Seventh Ray by the negative ego/separative thought system is a misuse of structure. Either first not having enough, or on the other side of the coin having too much, where a certain amount of spontaneity and free flow can not take place. There is a proper balance to find here. Another corruption and glamour is setting up structures for the wrong purpose and goals which are really of the negative ego and not of the Divine Plan. Another corruption and glamour of the Seventh Ray is the use of magic without Spirituality. This is very common, and is one of the first signs of a cult. Slick fast talking teachers, who have some magic or alchemical abilities, however, their motivation, in truth, is totally governed by the personality, negative ego and lower-self. They are more interested in gaining power, fame, money and having sex with their followers, than truly doing Spiritual magic to be of service. Lightworkers beware, for there are millions of teachers out there who fit into this category. A great many lightworkers are very naïve and Spiritually undiscerning, and are to easily impressed by magic that is motivated by impure motivations. The freedom is not giving free reign to one's negative ego, lower self, inner child, and emotional body. This is not freedom, but being a victim. True freedom stems from total self-mastery of one's energies in service of GOD, unconditional love, and a balanced, integrated ideal. The corruption of the Seventh Ray in a professional sense comes in the form of the misuse of money. Money is, in truth, a Divine substance of GOD that is meant to be used as a means of helping self and others. The corruption of money comes in many ways. It can come in the form of greed and miserliness. It can also come in the form of spending it too freely and wasting it on lower-self, frivolous purposes. The corruption can come in not valuing money, using it for a Spiritual Purpose in life and not saving it in the appropriate balance. It can also come from not giving it away for needy purposes in a balanced appropriate manner when the time is right. Money is the energy we use to make changes in the Physical/Earthly world. One of the reasons the Earthly/Material world doesn't change as fast as it could is that most lightworkers do not have as much money as they would like. This is part of the development of the Seventh Ray. The ability to have prosperity consciousness and not poverty consciousness. To not be afraid of money. To see the making of large amounts of money as part of your Spiritual path. Money is not the root of all evil, as some would suggest. Money in and of itself is neutral. The negative ego /fear based thought system is the root of all evil. It is when the negative ego/lower self/separative mind controls money, that problems occur. It is every Son and Daughters of GOD to have as much money as they can imagine. It is part of their lesson to learn how to make money. The key point here being, the more money you have the more you can serve others. If you do not have money, then you become dependent on others to give you money. There are periods of time, of course, that this is okay and totally appropriate in everyone's life. In the long haul so to speak however, the ideal would be that each person be responsible for themselves and be able to make as much money as they can, for the more you have the more you can give. The great corruption of the Seventh Ray professionally is the enormous number of people in our Society who have money and greedily hold on to it. They do not help others or society, and they also use their money to hurt others and prevent others from gaining. Be aware of this my Beloved Readers, that the law of karma exists, and every "jot and tittle of the law is fulfilled." Those that misuse their money will ultimately lose their money. For the law of karma also extends over past and future lives. Part of the movement into this New Millennium and the Seventh Golden Age is the understanding that our Planet as a whole is now moving into a Seventh Ray Cycle from a previous Sixth Ray Cycle. Part of the energies of this Seventh Ray Cycle is to also now ground our Spirituality on Earth. For too long our

Spirituality has been floating around on the Spiritual, mental, and emotional planes. In this New Millennium and Seventh Golden Age it is now time to create Heaven on Earth. It is now time to fully ground our Ascension in our physical bodies, into, and onto Earth life. It is now time for each person to fully ground their Spiritual mission on the physical Earthly plane. It is now time for lightworkers to become the Masters of money on all levels and to help use and allocate the money in our Government and economy to create the utopian Ascended Master Society that is its destiny build in this Seventh Golden Age. The proper use of the Seventh Ray both personally and collectively holds a great key to the transmutation and transformation that now needs to occur along with all the other Rays as well.

The final glory of the Seven Rays of GOD which form the true Personality of GOD which is extremely important to understand is how these Seven Rays in GOD's Personality work perfectly together in perfect synthesis and integration. In a true full fledged Ascended Master this is also the case for the microcosm is like the Macrocosm.

The true Glory of GOD is seeing how these Seven Rays work together in perfect harmony and balance with self and within Society. In truth, we have yet to see this take place within our society. In my next book, I am going to endeavor to explain how this can take place, and I have been guided to call this "The Divine Plan for the New Millennium and Seventh Golden Age." For our purposes here, suffice it to say that, in truth, there are not that many even on a personal level who have learned to fully develop all Seven Rays and to also integrate and balance them in daily living. This is one of the great signs of a true full-fledged Spiritual Master on Earth. For this is the Personality of GOD. More and more, however, are beginning to realize this ideal. Many in the Spiritual Movement are focusing on the Spiritual or Heavenly Level, and gaining initiations and building their light quotient and light bodies, as well as communicating and working in the Celestial Realms, and this is good. However, my beloved readers, if the Seven Great Rays are not balanced properly on the Psychological Level, true God Realization will not have taken place, no matter what your level of initiation is. True God Realization must be done on the Spiritual, Psychological and Physical/Earthly level. All three levels must be realized, not just the Spiritual Level. If the Seven Great Rays are not developed and balanced within self and the lower aspects, and/or corruption of these Rays are not transcended, then enormous corruption of the Spiritual work people are doing will take place. There are many who will not like to hear this, however, if you are truly a true lover of GOD then listen very closely to what I have to say. If the Psycho-logical Level of God Consciousness is not developed properly, and there is negative ego/fear based distortion and corruption of these Rays, then this will color and affect all Channeling, Spiritual Teaching, Clairvoyant work, your Spiritual Vision, and all your Relationships. For as I have said many times in my writings, the single most important relationship in your life is your relationship to your self. If you are not right with self, this will skew all other relationships including your relationship to GOD, the Masters, and the Angels. This is because your thoughts create your reality. You can not have faulty thinking within self, and within your own personality and psychology and expect this not to affect all the Spiritual Channeling, Teaching and Healing work you are doing. Your relationship to your self, your relationship to your personality, your relationship to your psychology, your relationship to your own subconscious mind affects everything. It is the foundation of your Spiritual House. How can the first floor of one's house be corrupt and the second floor be working fine. The second floor works through the first floor. It is not separate from the first floor. It flows through the first floor. All Channeling, Spiritual Teaching and Spiritual Vision flows through ones subconscious mind, psychology, belief system, interpretations, perceptions, philosophy, and Spiritual Psychology. You cannot separate them. My beloved readers, this is why it is essential to learn to balance these Seven Great Rays within your own personality and psychology. This is a weak spot among a great many lightworkers. These Seven Great Rays of GOD serve as a "Lens." It is also incredibly easy to get stuck in the lens of power, or love, or wisdom, or action, or art, or science, or devotion, or freedom, structure and magic. Even if your Monad and/or Soul is under the influence of a particular Ray as incarnating Sons and Daughters of God are, it is absolutely essential that you learn to see from a Full Spectrum Prism Consciousness through all Seven Rays in a balanced and integrated manner and not through just one or a few. This takes great psychological work and focus on your part. We all know people who are too stuck in power, or are too stuck in addicted love, or too stuck in the teacher know-it-all role, or too stuck in art and can't function in life. We all know people who are too stuck in science and the intellect, or in devotion and idealism to a Guru and are blinded. We all know a people who are too stuck in structure or lack of structure, can't deal with money, misuse magic, and do not know what their Spiritual Freedom is. These are the same great pitfalls and traps of the Spiritual Path. These are not all of them, but some of the main ones. Develop yourself most important in your personal power and surrendering to GOD's Will, Love/Wisdom, Active Intelligence, Harmony and Beauty, Science, Devotion and Idealism, Ceremonial Order and Magic. It is essential we develop our selves in these Seven Great Rays not only psychologically but also in the professional aspects of these Rays. I am not speaking here in the sense of taking on these professions, but being developed in them. Develop your political side, the Spiritual teacher side, your business side, your artistic side, your scientist side, your Spiritual leadership side, and your economic mastery side. Not only develop all these aspects, but also learn to not get stuck in each of their "Lenses." This is easier said than done, for it takes great psychological introspection and vigilance to not allow oneself to fall into these "Lenses." This is especially true because of the fact that each person's Monad and/or Soul is under the influence of one of these Rays. I am not saying here that one should deny how GOD created them and should not fulfill one's Spiritual Mission under that theme, so to speak. However, be balanced and integrated in all Seven Rays while under the influence of that theme.

Most of all, my beloved readers, be aware of the negative ego/fear based/separative/lower-self thought system and how it corrupts and creates glamour, illusion and maya in everything it touches if you allow it into your mind. Only allow yourself to think with your Spiritual/Christ/Buddha mind and not your negative ego/fear-based mind. Think with your Love Mind, my beloved readers, and not your Fear Mind. There are only two ways of thinking in the world and everything stems from Love or from fear. Everything stems from the negative ego thought system or the Spiritual/Christ/Buddha thought system. It is the negative ego/fear-based thought system that creates the distortion and corruption of the Seven Great Rays. Ever be joyously vigilant against the negative ego. This, my beloved readers, is the "Road Map" to achieve true God Consciousness. There is no work more important on your Spiritual Path than learning to properly master, develop, balance and integrate the Seven Great Rays in your psychology and personality, and to not allow the negative ego/fear-based thought system to enter your consciousness and corrupt your proper understanding of these Rays. Also to not get stuck in the "lens" of any one of these Rays, or this will become a negative ego distortion as well. This is the "Great Work" of the Spiritual Path. Continue the work on the Spiritual plane you are doing but do your Psychological and Personality Level homework, for it is equally as important and, in truth, even more important, for the Psychological Level is your Spiritual vision that colors your perception of the Spiritual Level. To be a clear channel for Spirit you must be a clear and balanced psychological channel as well. Once you have mastered these do not forget to also put equal attention to doing your homework on the Physical/Earthly Level as well; for GOD is as much in your physical body and in the Material/Earthly world as he is in the Heavenly realms, mental realm, emotional realm or psychic realm. There are Four

Faces of GOD, Spiritual, Mental, Emotional and Physical. To truly realize GOD, all four must be mastered and equally honored. To not master, honor and sanctify the Material face of GOD is to also disown the Divine Mother, the Earth Mother, and the Goddess energies. For the Goddess energies are also intimately connected to the Material Face of GOD. Our true Spiritual mission is to become our Mighty I Am Presence on Earth in a very grounded and balanced manner. Our true Purpose is to manifest our Spiritual mission on Earth and to get involved with Earth life. Our true Spiritual mission on Earth is to transform our Civilization and Society into an Ascended Master Society and to create Heaven on Earth, not to achieve liberation and leave the Earth as soon as we can. We are all the Light/Love/Power bearers for the New Millennium and Seventh Golden Age. Let us each now take on the "Full Mantle of the Christ/Buddha/God Consciousness" in a balanced and integrated manner and be about the business of fully transforming our selves and our world into the true Glory of GOD!

9

How to Clear the Negative Ego through Balancing the Feminine and Masculine

Another way of approaching the clearing of the negative ego is through the need to balance feminine and masculine energies. Whenever these two complimentary aspects of Self get out of balance, negative ego qualities develop. As with the archetypes, rays, astrological signs, houses, and planets, they each have a negative and positive expression. Before we can understand the negative expression, we first must understand the positive expression of the yin and the yang.

The balance of the yin and yang is the basis of Taoism. When yin and yang are in balance, we live in the "Tao." Imbalance and negative ego could be looked at from this frame of reference as the same thing. The following list shows the positive yin and positive yang.

Feminine and **Masculine**
Loving and Powerful
Open and Closed
Sensitive and Organized
Nurturing and Willful
Unfocused and Focused
Process-Oriented and Goal-Oriented
Listening and Talking
Warm and Concentrating
Flowing and Strong
Feeling and Thinking
Fluid and Rational
Flexible and Disciplined
Pleasing and Work
Right Brain and Left Brain

Every man and every woman needs a balance of both of these energies within themselves. This is called androgyny. When this balance is lacking within ourselves, we usually seek it outside of ourselves in another. Hence, we have the father-daughter relationships and mother-son relationships, or variables on this theme.

One of my favorite examples of living in the Tao, is the idea of surfing a wave. If you go too fast when you are body surfing a wave you will get dumped by the wave. If you go too slow you will miss the wave. The idea is to stay in the Tao. This applies to every aspect of life. There is a time to talk and a time to be silent. There is a time to be assertive and a time to be receptive. There is a time to think and a time to feel. There is a time to be right brain and a time to be left brain.

If you choose to be yin when it is time to be yang, you are out of balance. If you choose to be yang when it is time to be yin, you are out of balance. The key word here is "appropriateness." In every situation and moment of life there is an appropriate response as guided by your own soul and Mighty I Am Presence. If you stay attuned to your Higher Self you will always be guided properly in every situation. When guided by the voice of the negative ego you will be guided inappropriately. Most people don't realize that the yin and yang or masculine and feminine have a negative expression. This manifests when one is "too yin" or "too yang."

Negative Yin
Inferiority complex/Low self-esteem
Hurt too easily/Weak
Prone to rejection /Sadness
Depression/Fearful
Victim/Needy
Dependent/Clinging vine
Too sentimental/Too open
Hypersensitivity/Hedonism
Meditating too much/Too flexible
Too right brain/Lack of self-love

Negative Yang
Anger/Violence
Rigidity/Too intellectual
Workaholic/Too organized
Too much first ray energy/Talks too much
Too closed and shut down/Too left brain
Superiority complex/Critical
Impatient/Attacking
Controlling/Manipulative
Argumentative/Intolerant
Intimidation/Aggressive
Hatred/Demanding
Too harsh

Yin energies without the proper balance of yang energies turn sour. Yang energies without the proper balance of yin energies turn sour. Imbalance of your feminine and masculine energies manifests as negative ego emotions and feelings rather than Christ emotions and feelings. Imbalance equals negative ego that equals lack of Godliness in that moment. One can, in truth, never lose their Godliness for that is beyond what can be lost. One can, however, lose ones realization of their Godliness in any given moment which is us falling into glamour, maya, and illusion like a bad dream.

This issue of balancing of the feminine and masculine obviously relates very much to balancing ones four bodies (physical, emotional, mental and spiritual) and the need to balance ones three minds (conscious, subconscious and superconscious).

This need for balancing the feminine and masculine could be seen in Carl Jung's "Theory of Types" when he said there were four types of people: *Intuitive, Feeling, Thinking and Sensation/Function.*

People tended to lean towards one or two types within themselves. This is not a judgment, however, the ultimate ideal is forever balance.

In astrology and Chinese medicine, they speak of the need to balance the four elements: *Fire, Water, Air, and Earth.*

In nature we see this balance again in the four seasons: winter, spring, summer, and fall.

We see this same need for balance in the left and right brain:

Left Brain/Right Brain
Logical/Imagination
Deductive reasoning/Dreaming
Rational/Intuitive
Verbal/Psychic
Physically observable/Creative
/Inductive thinking
/Asking and listening

One side of the brain is not better than another. One needs both sides to fully realize God, and to clear away negative ego. The keys here are striving for balance, integration and moderation in all things at all times. Another key is to listen to the voice of the Holy Spirit and your own Higher Self at all times and not the voice of the negative ego and lower self. To achieve this you must maintain mastery over your energies and secondly be able to listen to the still small voice within.

The masculine side provides the power to master your energies. The feminine side will provide the ability to listen to the intuitive guidance that is always forthcoming in every situation. This will also allow for the blending of the first ray and the second ray. This is the blending of the power and the love with the wisdom. Power without love is like Nazi Germany. Love without power is to become emotionally dysfunctional.

A woman likes a man who is strong, but sensitive and loving. A centered man wants a woman who is loving and sensitive, but who can be strong and powerful. More and more these two sides of ourselves, which might be considered the ultimate archetypes, are coming together. The key to our society changing is for this merger and integration to first occur within oneself. The ultimate example of this in our universe is the Lord Melchizedek, our Universal Logos!

Masculine and Feminine Balance List
Masculine/Feminine:
Caution/Courage
Sun/Moon
Self-Confidence/Humility
Assertive/Receptive
Left brain/Right brain
Scientific/Musical
Logical/Intuitive
Fire/Water
Heal/Earth

Able to accept everything/To be able to differentiate
Thinking/Feeling
Occultist/Mystic
Psychological/Psychic
Focused/Flowing
Closed/Open
Firm/Loving
Detached/Sensitive
Goal oriented/Process oriented
Work/Play
Talking/Listening
Fixed/Flexible
Air/Water
Fire/Earth
Disciplined/Spontaneous
Organized/Fluid
Prayer/Meditation
Willful/Allowing
Deductive/Inductive
Asking/Listening
Mathematical/Artistic
Active/Passive
Yang/Yin
Inner parent/Inner child
Impersonal/Personal
Apollian/Dionysian
Structure/Freeflow
Acetic/Hedonistic
Patriarch/Matriarch
Heavenly father/Earth mother
Divine mother/Divine father
Linear thought/Imagination

Waking/Dreaming
Horizontal reality/Vertical reality
Form/Formless
Doing/Being
Control/Surrender
Selfish/Selfless
Yogi/Aphrodite
Intuition/Sensation function
Contained/Expressive
Tough/Nurturing
Mother/Father
Serious/Humorous
Priest/Priestess
Adventurer/Homebody
Teacher/Student
Obeying/Ruling
Lightning-like speed/Circumspection
Caution/Courage
To possess nothing/To command everything
To have no ties/Loyalty
Contempt for death/Regard for life

Duality of Cerebral Functions
Left side of body & head/Right side of body & head
Non-dominant/Dominant
Unconscious/Conscious
Spatial relations/Verbally aware
Pictures/Language
Images/Words
Symbolic/Literal
Metaphorical/Definitive
Intuitive/Logical

Synthesize/Analyze
Accepting/Discriminating
Abstract/Concrete
Musical/Mathematical
Artistic/Scientific
Simultaneous/Sequential
Wholistic/Linear

Methods of Obtaining Information
Left Brain–Yang/Right Brain–Yin
Logical/Imagination, Dreaming, Inner Senses
Deductive Thinking/Intuitive, Psychic
Physically Observable/Creative
Rational/Inductive thinking
Verbal/Asking & Listening

Yin and Yang
Positive Yin/Positive Yang
Loving/Personal Power
Compassion/Discipline
Forgiving/Assertive
Joyous/Discernment
Cooperation/Focused
Self-Love/Self-Mastery
Self-Worth/Responsible
Acceptance/Non-attachment
Humility/Patience
Humble/Faith
Gentle/Decisiveness
Peaceful/Organized
Flexible/Perseverance
Sensitive/Giving
Receptive/Logical

Open/Confident
Intuitive/Co-creator
Feeling/Non-judgmental

Negative Yin/Negative Yang
Hurt/Rigid
Depression/Neurotic
Rejected/Anger
Moody/Violence
Defensive/Uptight
Fearful/Attacking
Insecure/Critical
Worry/Superiority
Lazy/Impatient
Low Self-Esteem/Hate
Guilt/Revenge
Victim/Intolerant
Needy/Prideful
Self-Pity/Resentful
Loneliness/Jealousy
Shyness/Selfish
Procrastination/Workaholic

10

Spiritual Tests

One of the most important understandings of the entire Spiritual Path is the understanding that Earth is a Planetary Mystery School, and that every single thing that happens in life is a Spiritual Test. Planet Earth is a Spiritual School to teach Souls to become "Integrated Ascended Masters and/or God Realized Beings". Everything that happens in life is a teaching, lesson, challenge, and opportunity to grow. Most people do not realize, or they forget that each and every moment of our lives, we are being Spiritually Tested. Every thought we think is a Spiritual Test. As Edgar Cayce said, "Thoughts are things." The Course in Miracles states in the lesson book, "There are no neutral thoughts." What this means is that every thought that enters your mind from within or without is of GOD or is of the negative ego. Every thought that you think stems from the Christ/Buddha Consciousness or lower-self consciousness. Every thought you think stems from oneness or separation. Every thought you think stems from Love or fear. All day long, even when we think, we sleep, and dream, thoughts are coming to us from within and without. Every single moment of life is a Spiritual Test to think only GOD Thoughts.

The same is true, my beloved readers, with every feeling and emotion you create. This is a Spiritual test. Your attitude, perception, interpretation, and belief system cause your feelings and emotions. This is an indisputable fact and law of the Universe. We each cause our reality by how we think. If we think with our Melchizedek/Christ/Buddha Mind, we will create only Spiritualized, positive feelings and emotions. If we think with our negative ego/fear based/lower self mind, we will create negative feelings and emotions. Every moment, even when you are by yourself, is a Spiritual Test to see if you can keep your emotional body in a God Consciousness and positive state, at all times.

Every word you speak, every moment of your life is a Spiritual Test. Are your words coming from the negative ego or are they coming from the Heart of GOD? What is the mental motivation of your words? Are they Sourced from the selfish, self-centered negative ego, or were they motivated from true God Consciousness? What is the feeling tone of every word? Is there any attack energy, anger, or criticism, or do they carry the feeling tone of unconditional love and nonjudgementalness. Every moment of your life that you speak is a Spiritual Test.

My beloved readers, every action you take no matter how small or infinitesimal is a Spiritual Test. Is that action coming from and motivated by GOD and God Consciousness, or by negative ego and separative/fear-based consciousness? Is that action adding to your Spiritual Path or decreasing it? Is that action a waste of time or a good and balanced use of your energy?

My beloved readers, every use of your energy, no matter how small and infinitesimal is a Spiritual Test. Is your energy helping self and others, or hurting self and others? Is the use of your energy adding to your Light Body or decreasing it? Are you wasting energy or are you using every particle of your energy for a greater Spiritual purpose, for Love, for balance in a larger perspective and for healing self and others? Every moment of your life is a Spiritual Test to see if your can use your energy to only serve GOD and not to serve the negative ego, fear, the lower-self, lower-self desire, the carnal self, separative thinking, and victim consciousness.

My beloved readers, in every situation of life there is an appropriate response or an inappropriate response. Every moment of life is a Spiritual test to learn to respond appropriately from the way GOD would have you respond. Who gives us the guidance on how to respond? This guidance comes from our Higher Self, our Mighty I Am Presence, the Holy Spirit, and our own Melchizedek/Christ/Buddha ideals that we have taken on consciously and programmed into our subconscious mind. Every moment of life is a Spiritual test to see if we can respond in a balanced manner instead of an imbalanced manner.

Every interaction with another person is a Spiritual Test to see if we can remain in unconditional love, forgiveness, nonjudgementalness, patience, service, oneness, and egolessness at all times. Every interaction with an animal, plant, or mineral is a Spiritual test to stay in harmony with GOD with His three lower kingdoms.

Now, my beloved readers, what happens if we do not always pass these Spiritual Tests every moment? The answer is nothing in the sense that everything is forgiven and everything always remains in unconditional love. Mistakes are positive not negative, and every mistake can be turned into a positive if you gain the golden nugget of wisdom from that mistake. GOD always forgives and it is just necessary for people to forgive themselves. I will add here however, that every moment of life is a Spiritual Test and Spiritual Opportunity to realize GOD or not realize GOD. When you think a negative thought you lose your realization of GOD on the mental plane in that moment. When you allow yourself to feel a negative emotion, you lose your realization of GOD in that moment on the emotional plane. When you behave inappropriately, you lose your realization of GOD in that moment on the physical plane. Now it is important to understand that it is impossible to never make a mistake. It also cannot be emphasized more emphatically that mistakes are positive and part of the learning process. So, the Spiritual Path for everyone is up the mountain five steps, and down four, up three down two, up three down one. I will say, however, the more overall integrated Spiritual Mastery you gain, the fewer mistakes you will make and the quicker will be your Spiritual progress. The nice thing about GOD is that He always welcomes His Sons and Daughters home like the Prodigal Son, no matter what they have done in past lives, or this life, as long as they are willing to change their ways. One does not have to be perfect to evolve. If you truly want to realize GOD however, at the highest level, then you must be unbelievably "joyously vigilant" over what you are causing and creating on every level I have mentioned in this chapter. Every time you allow yourself to slip and give into the negative ego or lower self there is no judgement from GOD, however, you will have lost your opportunity to realize GOD in that moment. You all know how much better it feels to realize GOD every moment on all these levels. You also know how terrible it feels to be out of harmony with GOD and out of harmony with Love. It is also important to understand that the continual positive choices on your part to continually realize GOD on all levels will build your Love quotient, Light quotient, and Power quotient. It will also speed up your Initiation and Ascension Process. It will also cleanse your karma. Every right choice speeds up your Path to total God Realization and is creating and cementing good habits into the subconscious mind. It is also helping the planet and helping your Spiritual Brothers and Sisters, for all minds are one. It also helps your Brothers and Sisters in an outer sense by demonstrating Melchizedek/Christ/Buddha consciousness at all times. If you are truly responding appropriately at all times, then your entire life will be a selfless path of service as well. You will not need to be selfish that often because you are whole and complete within self and are one with GOD in your realization in each and every moment. Hence, every bit of energy on every level of your being can go to loving and serving others. Once God Realization is achieved on a Spiritual, psychological, and physical Earthly level, one's only purpose to be on Earth is to serve. In saying this, one needs to stay balanced and integrated and to enjoy one's life. With this context, one's total joy in life is to serve, because "true pleasure is serving GOD." Never forget your Brothers and Sisters are incarnations of God as well, even if they do not realize it.

True Spiritual Testing does not take place just when things are going well. True Spiritual Testing of an individual takes place when emergencies, crisis, stress, and attacks occur. Anyone can pass Spiritual Tests living in a cave or never leaving your house. The true test of a Spiritual Master is to get involved with Earth life and relationships with people of all kinds. This is where the true testing occurs. Can you stay out of your negative ego and remain in the Christ/Buddha Consciousness when raising children? Can you stay out of your negative ego and in the Christ/Buddha Consciousness in a romantic relationship? Can you stay out of your negative ego and in the Christ/Buddha Consciousness with family members, extended family, parents, and in-laws? Can you stay out of your negative ego and in the Christ/Buddha Consciousness with your boss, business partners, business associates, and/or employees? Can you stay out of your negative ego and in the Christ/Buddha Consciousness with fellow Spiritual Leaders, Spiritual Teachers, Lightworkers, Spiritual competitors for clients or students in your field or profession? Can you stay out of your negative ego and in the Christ/Buddha Consciousness when people attack you, get angry with you, or judge you fairly or unfairly? Can you stay out of your negative ego and in the Christ/Buddha Consciousness if someone slanders you publicly or professionally? Can you stay out of your negative ego and in the Christ/Buddha Consciousness if someone steals a large sum of money from you? Can you stay out of your negative ego and in the Christ/Buddha Consciousness if your spouse or relationship partner doesn't want to make love and/or have sex? Can you stay out of your negative ego and remain in the Christ/Buddha consciousness if your spouse or relationship partner is in a bad mood and emotionally off-centered and is taking it out on you? Can you stay out of your negative ego and in the Christ/Buddha

Consciousness if you or others around you are making tons of mistakes regardless if they are large or small? Can you stay out of your negative ego and in the Christ/Buddha Consciousness watching the news, watching opinionated politicians and/or reporters, or reading the newspaper? Can you remain in the Christ/Buddha Consciousness when physically sick or during extended chronic health lessons? Can you stay in the Christ/Buddha Consciousness when someone you are close to passes on to the Spirit world? Can you remain in the Christ/Buddha Consciousness during a traffic accident or when getting a ticket? Can you remain in the Christ/Buddha Consciousness during a messy divorce or fight with your partner? Can you remain in the Christ/Buddha Consciousness and out of the negative ego when someone is holding a grudge against you? Can you remain in the Christ/Buddha Consciousness and out of your negative ego when everything is taken away in your life like Job in the Bible? Can you retain this Christ/Buddha Consciousness during a natural disaster such as a major earthquake, hurricane, tornadoes, flood, or fire? Can you retain your Christ/Buddha Consciousness and stay out of your negative ego if you lost all your money, had a divorce, your physical health broke down, and you lost your job?

My beloved readers, these are the true Spiritual Tests. Can you live in the "marketplace," be fully involved in Earthly life and relationships of all kinds, and keep your Spiritual Mastery and balance? This is the true test of a full-fledged Ascended Master and God Realized being! It must be understood that 100 percent perfection is not required to pass these tests. Some of these would be extraordinarily difficult. Mistakes are positive and we do not want to practice any kind of negative ego perfectionism that expects us to be perfect at all times and never make mistakes. This is impossible and unrealistic. The main purpose for this exercise is to just be clear as to what the ideal is, and to strive for it. Going through an exercise like this can be a preparation for maintaining the proper attitude and perspective when lessons like these come. This is a blueprint in a sense for the potential Spiritual lessons and tests people on Earth often face. My beloved readers, I highly recommend setting your attitude and perspective now, almost like programming your conscious and subconscious computer, so you will not be knocked off balance when these things do happen, and you are mentally and emotionally prepared to respond from your Christ/Buddha mind to the best of your ability. Again, perfection is not required. You can actually achieve Ascension by balancing only 50 percent of your karma. The key point however, is the more you can learn these lessons, the more you can realize GOD psychologically in that moment. So Earth is a school to practice. There is no such thing as death and we are allowed to come back as many times as we need to learn all these lessons and other ones on the Spiritual Path. My suggestion however, is to take advantage of this incarnation and aim as high as you can on a Spiritual, Psychological, and Physical/Earthly Level to realize GOD on all levels. By doing this we not only help ourselves, but by doing so we are helping others as well.

Now, my beloved readers, there is one more series of "Spiritual Tests" that are the most severe of all, and where most lightworkers and initiates "miss the mark and do not pass." The Spiritual Tests I speak of here are when a person or lightworker moves into a position of Leadership and/or Spiritual Leadership over others. What I am speaking of here is when a person has become a Master of some degree and has become successful in an inner and outer sense. They have lots of clients and students. They may have become very financially successful and may have become very famous. They may hold positions Spiritually or in the world, of great Spiritual Leadership. They may have very large followings. They may be in positions of great worldly and Spiritual power over others. They may give extremely large workshops, seminars, classes, and may be on television, radio, be authors, and in newspapers and magazines. My beloved readers, I think you get the picture. It is now, that the true Spiritual Testing begins. If you or others have made it through the first two lists, now the real Spiritual Testing begins. Does the power the person now has go to their head? How do they treat others? How do they treat those not in their league? How do they treat their employees? How do they treat people who call them on the phone? How do they deal with other Spiritual Leaders? Do they let the fame go to their head? What are their true motivations for doing what they are doing? Do they put GOD before money? Do they put GOD before fame? Do they put GOD before power? Do they have sex with all their students? How do they react when criticized? Do they practice what they preach once they are off the stage and out of the limelight? How do they react if someone tries to take away their position of power, fame, or money? Are they the exact same person they were before they were graced with this power, fame, and wealth? Are they on a path of true Christ/Buddha Consciousness or has self-aggrandizement taken over? Has their channel remained clear or has it been corrupted by negative ego? Have they truly retained their GOD purity and egolessness or have false Gods and symbolic idol worship of negative ego attributes taken over? How do they treat their students or disciples? Is their true motivation to fully empower their students or is it always to retain their position of authority? Do they truly put everything on "The Altar of GOD?" Have they allowed their channel or teachings to become clouded by personal selfish agendas? Do they have Spiritual ambition or negative ego ambition? Is the focus of their work about themselves or about GOD and the Masters? Do they co-create with other Spiritual Teachers and Leaders, or are they islands unto themselves? Are their books, channelings, and teachings focused on telling you how great they are, or really on selfless service? Are their teachings continuing to be balanced on a Spiritual, psychological, and physical Earthly level, or has the negative ego begun to fragment and create lack of balanced integration in the teachings? Do they continue to maintain Mastery over their mind, emotions, behavior, lower self desire, inner child, subconscious mind, sexual energy, and energy in general or have they let down their standard, now that they have achieved their Ascension, Seven Levels of Initiation and have climbed to the top of this particular Planetary Mountain?

My beloved readers, these are the true tests of the Spiritual Path. Most people have a hard time passing the second list in this chapter. Many Spiritual Leaders reach this third level or list before they have mastered the second list. Even those who have mastered the second list, in my Spiritual observation, do not pass the third one. The Bible speaks of the Spiritual Path being "a straight and narrow path." In my Spiritual observation as a Spiritual Leader, Spiritual Teacher, and Spiritual Psychologist, most do not meet this high mark and high calling. The usual cause is that they are more developed in their Spiritual Body than they are in their Psychological Body. Lack of proper mastery and integration of the psychological level will always ultimately corrupt the Spiritual Level. You cannot live on the second floor of a building when the first floor is falling apart or has become corrupted. My beloved readers, in all humbleness and with absolutely no judgement in my heart, I cannot tell you how many Spiritual Leaders, Spiritual Teachers, Spiritual Channels, Spiritual Scientists, and Spiritual Friends that I have seen fall from grace and become corrupted. It is mind-boggling! It is why the inner plane Ascended Masters have asked me to focus so much work on the concept of "Integrated Ascension." Spiritual Leaders, Channels, Spiritual Teachers, and lightworkers are achieving their Ascension and Seven Levels of Initiation, but are not integrated. When the true Spiritual Tests come in lists two and three they are not able to pass them. The most amazing thing is that even though they are falling from grace, corruption of the negative ego is happening on a massive scale, and they are even tumbling down the mountain Spiritually because of this corruption of the negative ego, they do not have the slightest awareness that they have fallen. This is the extraordinary delusionary nature of the mind and the negative ego. They are in a negative hypnosis and realize it not. The main cause of this is not because they are bad people, for there is no such thing. They just have not received the proper psychospiritual training, before moving into such positions of Spiritual Leadership and power. I have said this repeatedly and I will say it again. The world does not need more channels. It needs more trained Spiritual Counselors and Teachers who can train large numbers of people around the world how to master their mind, emotions, body, and behavior, and most of all master the negative ego thought system and replace it with the Christ/Buddha thought system. If this lesson is not learned all Spiritual practices will ultimately become corrupted. This statement is not meant as a judgement but just as a simple statement of truth. The negative ego has infiltrated and contaminated religion. It also is to a great extent infiltrating and contaminating the New Age Movement. Lightworkers must be aware of this and have great Spiritual discernment within self and in regards to others.

In conclusion, be Spiritually discerning as to the Spiritual Leaders, Spiritual Teachers, Channels, Authors, Healers, and Spiritual Scientists you work with. There are good ones out there. Make sure they are meeting the "High Calling and True Mark" of a true Spiritual Master. The lesson is not to be judgmental, but it is to be Spiritually discerning. This Spiritual quality needs to be much more developed in lightworkers.

In final conclusion, my beloved readers, strive for the highest level you can of "Integrated Spiritual Mastery and GOD Purity." It is indeed a rare quality in this world. This chapter is meant to give you the "Divine Blueprint" and roadmap of the Spiritual Tests you will face and need to pass to truly become an "Integrated God Realized Being." Be forewarned that the negative ego thought system is incredibly tricky, slippery, and seductive. It is going to take a 100 percent effort on your part, and you are going to have to claim and cultivate an enormous amount of "Joyous Vigilance and True GOD Purity" to pass all of these Spiritual Tests. Half the battle is having the Blueprint and knowing what the Spiritual Tests are. My Beloved Readers, the rest is up to you. Do not settle for false Gods and idol worship of such paltry gifts such as power, fame, money, and sex. If certain things come to you, so be it, and thank GOD for it, but do not make a false God out of these things. GOD has given you the understanding and abilities to master and learn these lessons. All that is required of you is great Spiritual focus and dedication. This chapter has been written to make you aware of the Spiritual Tests that are present in your life and that may be coming. This chapter has also been written to "Spiritually Challenge" you in this moment, to dedicate your life and every ounce of your energy on every level of your being to become the "Highest and Most Pure Integrated God Realized Being" you can, in service of GOD on all levels, every moment of your life! This, my beloved readers, is the "Noble Calling and Mission we have all Incarnated to Fulfill!"

11

The Spiritual Science of Blind Spots, Mind Locks and Lenses

In my humble opinion, this next chapter is an extremely cutting edge understanding in the field of Transpersonal Psychology, Soul Psychology, and Spiritual Psychology. It is something I have not written about before or seen in any other book I have ever read. It is the Spiritual Science of blind spots, mind locks, and lenses. As you all know we just don't see with out physical eyes, we see with our mind. How can one hundred people see any given event take place and every one will have a different version? How can at a jury trial, twelve people hear the facts yet there can be so much conflict as to whether the person is guilty or not? How can half the population think O.J. Simpson was innocent and the other half believe he is guilty? How can half the population of any given country belong to one political party and the other half to another? How can millions of people become susceptible to cults, when it is so obvious to others how corrupt certain individuals and organizations are?

My beloved readers, the Spiritual Science of blind spots, mind blocks and lenses is a most fascinating psychospiritual science. To begin this discussion let us look at the basic masculine/feminine balance. If a person is too feminine and too overidentified with their emotional body and right brain, then they will automatically develop enormous numbers of blind spots in their masculine side. They will have extremely poor Spiritual discernment. They will likely be very poor in business and mathematical areas. They will likely be very child-like and have blind spots in being more adult and impersonal. They will also have a great many blind spots to the negative ego's thinking because when the emotional body is too in control the negative ego automatically becomes the programmer.

On the other side of the coin, if someone is too masculine and identified with the mind, they will have blind spots to the appreciation of heart energy and feeling energy. They will have blind spots in romantic relationship functioning. They will have blind spots to their own criticalness and judgementalness.

If a person is too Heavenly they will have blind spots as to how to function effectively on the Earthly plane. If a person is too Earthly and too grounded they will have blind spots to proper development of their Spiritual life.

The same thing can happen in relationship to the Seven Rays. If a person is more identified with the First Ray of Power, then they will have blind spots in development of their Second Ray of Love/Wisdom. If a person is highly developed in the arts or Fourth Ray, they often have blind spots in relationship to the Fifth Ray of Spiritual Science. If a person is highly developed in the more "feeling" rays, two, four, and six, which are Love/Wisdom, Harmony, and Devotion, then they often have blind spots in rays one, three, and five. Rays One, Three and Five being Power, Active Intelligence, and Spiritual Science. The same is true in a reverse sense.

The same is true in Carl Jung's theory of types. He suggested there were four types of people: intuitive, thinking, feeling, and sensation function. People are often strong in one or two types, and weak in the other two. If one is intuitive thinking, one tends to have blind spots in their feeling and sensation function. Sensation function being the focus on one's five physical senses. Some people focus on this, others do not think it is important. The same is true of all these types. The ideal of course, is to integrate all four types in a balanced manner. If one is too thinking and logical, they will have blind spots in understanding their own feeling nature and understanding the feeling nature of others. If one is very intuitive, they often have a hard time being grounded and really working practically with the Earth. People who are overidentified with their sensation function often have a hard time accessing their intuition and Higher Spiritual nature.

If you are identified with the collective programming of Earth's history, then you will have a hard time understanding and appreciating the Goddess energy. If you are overidentified with the Goddess, the reverse is true.

The same concept of blind spots relates to astrology. If you have a lot of "water" in your horoscope, you may have blind spots dealing with "air." If you have a lot of "fire," you may have blind spots with "earth" and vice versa.

An unbelievable key principle in understanding the Science of blind spots is that which you cannot see within self you cannot see within others either. If you are not in control of the negative ego within yourself, you will not be able to discern the negative ego in others. If the emotional body within self runs you, you will not be able to see this happening within others. The same is true of the mind and/or Spirit. So from this profound statement and understanding, you can see how important it is to develop one's self Spiritually, psychologically, and in a physical Earthly sense, otherwise you will not be able to see those same undeveloped aspects within others. What most people do is attract to them, those people that have the same imbalances they have. This has a reinforcing affect of their imbalanced psychology and/or philosophy. The only people they get feedback from are people with the same imbalances.

Let us now take this discussion a little bit further, to professions. A Spiritual Psychologist sees a great many things others do not see because of their training. An artist sees a great many things that others do not see in the realm of beauty. A psychic sees many things that others do not see. A channel sees many things that others do not see. A clairvoyant sees many things that others do not see. An energy healer sees and feels many things that others do not see or feel. A gardener sees a great many things that others do not see. A Spiritual scientist sees many things that others do not see. I could go through hundreds of other professions, which would add to this list. The key question now is what does this show us. Because of our training and focus in this life and past lives, we see through that which we have been trained in, and we have blind spots in areas we have not been trained in. This is why it is to our benefit to strive to be as integrated and balanced in all the rays, astrological signs, elements, types, four bodies, numerology, tarot, archetypes, professions, and lenses.

The twelve major archetypes are an example. If we are overidentified with one or more archetypes then we will have blind spots in the other archetypes. This is why it is to our benefit to be integrated in all twelve major archetypes. The same is true of the cards in the tarot deck.

Now let's take this discussion of blind spots even further. To understand GOD Consciousness it must be understood that GOD sees live through a full spectrum prism consciousness. All of the aspects in this chapter GOD see through simultaneously. If we are going to be like GOD, we must do the same in the development of our God Consciousness. This is why I recommend to people to follow a Path of Synthesis and a more eclectic path. This is why I have written a thirty volume "Easy-to-Read Encyclopedia of the Spiritual Path." Every form of psychology, every Spiritual path, every Mystery School, every Guru, every well-known channel and/or Spiritual Teacher, every religion, and every well-known Spiritual text is a different lens of GOD. When we identify with one or study only one, we have blind spots to other forms of worship. GOD sees through all lenses not just one or a few. I have written these books to help my readers to develop a more full spectrum prism consciousness and to help remove blind spots within self, and hence in how they see others and their world.

In speaking before about professions, even you may make money in one profession, this does not mean that you cannot become a Master Spiritual Psychologist, Channel, Healer, Author, Intuitive, Psychic, Gardener, Business Person, Economist, Environmentalist, Spiritual Teacher, Political Expert, Minister, Artist, Spiritual Scientist, Counselor, and on and on. Most of us have had hundreds of past lives with different professions, and training on both the inner and outer plane, so this is not as impossible a task as you might think. I know at different times in my life that I have focused my development in all these areas and more. Wherever I have an undeveloped aspect in any area mentioned in this chapter, I work on developing it and this increases my full spectrum prism consciousness and removes more blind spots.

Which country you are born into and where you live is another lens. GOD sees through the cultures of all countries. If you have only lived and studied one culture, you will have blind spots to other cultures and belief systems. This is why it is a good thing to travel and to study other cultures and even speak other languages.

Another lens and blind spot is the color of our skin or ethnic background. We do not realize how we are programmed into seeing live through our particular skin color and ethnicity. This carries a whole set of belief systems that may or may not be true. If you are white in skin color, try talking to someone living in an African body, really seeing, and experiencing how different their reality is. This is why it is a good thing to expand one's consciousness and ethnicities.

One's socioeconomic upbringing will also create a lens and corresponding blind spots that will limit your full God Consciousness as well. This is why it is also a good idea to break out of this lens and pattern within self, and to communicate and commune with people with different experiences in this regard.

Now, there are many more lenses that we have been programmed to be locked into. I call this phenomena with any of the above mentioned issues or the ones I am about to mention "mind locks." A mind lock is when we get stuck in a certain aspect, lens, or belief system and don't realize it. We are, hence, locked in and only seeing life through a very small number of lenses than all the lenses GOD sees through.

In truth, every belief system is a lens and potential mind lock. Do you identify with being a Republican, Democrat, or Reform Party member? This can be a mind lock and limited lens that blinds you. Your emotions can be a mind lock and your mind can be a mind lock. The negative ego can be a mind lock. Any given subpersonality can be a mind lock. Any given habit can be a mind lock. Any given belief system that you have been given by your parents, teachers, ministers, rabbis, counselors, psychologists, friends, grandparents, workshops, lectures, past life programming, or childhood programming are all singular lens, potential glamour, illusion, maya, blind spots, and potential mind locks.

Now I realize that this chapter can be a little humbling, for how many people in this world have developed themselves in all these areas and hence released themselves from these blind spots, mind locks, and limited lenses of seeing life. Melchizedek, the President of our entire Universe, told me that most people see life through the lens of a fly. He was not being judgmental, he was just contrasting his full spectrum prism consciousness of being responsible for an entire Universe, to that of most people on Earth who see life from such a fragmented, unintegrated, and limited lens perspective. This humbling process, I spoke of at the beginning of this paragraph, is good and is a healthy humbleness and humility, which is one of the steps in achieving true God consciousness. Our negative egos always want to tell us how together and evolved we are. I am amazed in the Spiritual Movement how many people go around claiming to have fully realized GOD. Not only have they not realized GOD in a Cosmic sense, they have not even realized GOD in a planetary sense, a psychological sense, or a physical/earthly sense in becoming an integrated Planetary Ascended Master. Ninety-nine percent of the time it is their negative ego talking and more glamour, illusion, and maya. Even most of the inner plane Ascended Masters that we are familiar with have only realized GOD two inches up a ten inch ruler in the true infinite nature of GOD. Hence, with no judgement intended, you see how comical and delusionary these claims are.

My beloved readers, even being Spiritual can be a mind lock and can enormously limit your perception if you are not properly integrating the psychological and physical/earthly level. Many on the Spiritual path are overidentified with the Celestial Realms and are not doing their psychological and physical/earthly homework. This is a blind spot and mind lock as well as a limited lens, through which one is seeing and experiencing life within self, and in others.

It is interesting to me how a great many people each have a favorite book in my Ascension Book Series and they are all different. This is because of the different lenses people are coming from. For example, some people approach my work from a psychological lens. Some people approach my work from a Spiritual or Ascension lens. Others still, approach it from a more grounded physical/earthly lens.

In conclusion, my beloved readers, the key to removing blind spots, mind locks, and limited lenses, is to follow a Spiritual path in life, that I call "Integrated Ascension," and/or becoming an "Integrated Melchizedek/ Christ/Buddha." This focus on integration, balance, and synthesis in all things will allow you to see from a more full spectrum God prism consciousness, and hence remove the blind spots, mind locks, and limited lens seeing that will come from not doing so. It is an approach of being a well-rounded individual. It is an approach of being a Renaissance Man or

Woman. It is an approach of being whole and complete within self and within the true nature of GOD.

The last thing I wish to say to conclude this chapter is, that the vision I have laid out here to remove blind spots, mind locks, and limited lens seeing is a big one. The number one most important thing to do to keep your priorities straight and to make this process work, is to master your mind, feelings and emotions, subconscious mind, inner child, lower self desire and to most of all learn to transcend negative ego/fear based/separative thinking, and learn instead to think from your Melchizedek/Christ/Buddha mind. This is essential for even if you develop yourself in all the areas I have mentioned in this chapter, the negative ego will corrupt the entire process and keep you blinded for it will have you use all that you have gained for the wrong purpose. You will be as blind as ever and not realize it, for this is the delusionary and hypnotic nature of the mind. To avoid this blind spot, mind lock, and extreme limited lens, be joyously vigilant against the negative ego at all times. Never forget that every moment of your life in your every thought, word, and deed, you will be continually Spiritually tested as to if you choose GOD or negative ego in that moment. My Beloved Readers, work on this lesson first, and then fill in the rest in the process of your life, and then you will be on the right track. What I have shared in this chapter and the perspective I have put it in, is the "God Formula" for most quickly and efficiently removing your blind spots, mind locks, limited lens seeing, and achieving God consciousness and a full spectrum prism consciousness, in the specific vein this chapter is focused upon!

12

How to Deal with Attacking and Critical Energy from Others

Since most people on Earth have not been properly trained in how to master their mind and emotions and transcend negative ego thinking and replace it with Christ/Buddha/Spiritual thinking, everyone on Earth will have to deal with being attacked and criticized at times. One might think that great Spiritual Leaders might not have to deal with this like Jesus or Sai Baba; however, they probably had to deal with it even more than most because the more famous you are the more negative egotistical people try to bring such people down. So, the first question we must ask ourselves is why do people attack and criticize others? The answer is simple, it is because they have not been trained how to master and control their own mind, emotions, and negative ego programming. Another answer to this question is that they are run by fear. Fearful people attack. Another reason this happens is that people are out of control. This causes them to get angry in a vain attempt to get back in control, however, this is illusion for their angry response is showing they are still out of control. Another reason people attack and criticize is because they have a lack of self-love and a lack of self-worth. They attack and criticize to try to move to the topside of the negative ego instead of the bottom side of the negative ego. What they don't understand is that they are still trapped in the negative ego. For as the Bible says, "After pride cometh the fall." The only way to escape this roller coaster ride of the negative ego from self-inflation to self-deflation is to transcend the whole system and to see there is another way of thinking, not based on fear and attack or low self-esteem and self-aggrandizement, that does not play this game. Most people on Earth are trapped in this negative ego roller coaster and do not know how to get out of it. One cannot escape it until one embraces Spiritual Psychology.

Another reason people attack and criticize is that they are too run by their emotional body. When you allow your feelings and emotions to run your life, the negative ego becomes the programmer of your feelings and emotions. Another reason why people attack and criticize is that they are jealous. This is, of course, the negative ego again. This type of person again, suffers from low self-esteem and is constantly competing and comparing themselves with others to try to feel good about themselves. They are trapped in that negative ego complex of being better than others are or worse than others. These are really two sides of the same coin. This is also called living in hell, which is what negative ego thinking creates. There is a way of thinking called the Christ/Buddha/Spiritual Consciousness that will transcend this way of thinking, and bring you unconditional love, unconditional self-love, unconditional self-worth, unchanging happiness, and inner peace at all times without having to ever attack, judge, hurt others, compare, compete, and be better than or worse than others. This is why Sai Baba has said, "God equals man minus ego." To realize GOD and achieve unconditional love and inner peace one has to transcend negative ego/fear-based/separative/self-centered thinking. Now that we understand why people attack and judge, let us now examine how to deal with it when someone does this in person, over the phone, or in a letter.

The first thing I would say to do when you are attacked, judged or someone lash's out at you in anger is to remain in your personal power, unconditional self-love and self-worth. Remain in your protective bubble of protection and let their negative energy slide off your bubble like water off a ducks back. Another way of saying this is to let their negative energy bounce off your bubble like a rubber pillow. In doing so your are not letting it implant in your subconscious mind. You are not letting them be the computer programmer of your feelings and emotions. You are remaining a cause of your feelings and emotions and not an effect. You are also keeping your attunement to GOD and your own Mighty I Am Presence. You are also hence responding, instead of reacting. So, the first key lesson is to remain completely silent and say nothing. There is great power in silence. I am not talking about negative ego power, but true Spiritual Power. It takes two to have a war or ego battle and you are not engaging in on. By doing this you have passed the first series of Spiritual Tests that GOD and life have presented you.

Now you must understand that the negative ego in you is going to want to lash back and put them in their place. Do not listen to the negative ego. The negative ego will tell you that this person has put you in a lower position of power. Do not listen to this for this is illusion. For as children say, "Sticks and stones can break your bones but names can never hurt me." You can only be put in a lowered position if you are a victim and let them cause your feelings and emotions instead of you causing your feelings and emotions. The key is to say nothing. This will surprise your attacker and throw them for a loop because they are ready for a fight and you are remaining as still as a Buddha. Do not let you emotional body become engaged. You want to remain totally detached, calm, rational, and objective.

It is never a good idea to communicate with someone when they or you are too emotionally charged, or are caught in their or your negative ego. Contrary to popular opinion and even the advice of some coun-selors and psychologists on a personality level, it is better not to com-municate at those times. Let they other person speak and do not say a word. Let the other person talk themselves out and do not respond until they are completely done. Listen closely to the points they make even if they are communicating in a nasty irresponsible manner. If you do choose to communication do so in a very calm, rational, uncondition-ally loving manner. Do not catch the psychological disease of the other person. Remain in your Christ/Buddha Consciousness. Do not give in to the negative ego, or any anger, attack, or judgmental energy. Respond, do not react. Go through each point and share your Spiritual observations and Spiritual discernments on each point. Remember above all else that this is a Spiritual Test. By how you respond you will be choosing GOD or negative ego yourself. You are being given a chance to pass a great Spiritual Test. Look how the Master Jesus responded when attacked and crucified. You are being given a chance to set a better example. By responding in this manner, the other person is going to be thrown completely off guard. Ninety-nine out of 100 times other peo-ple would respond emotionally and from their negative ego and your are not. On some level, they know they have done wrong. If you really want to gain the Spiritual upper hand, thank them for their feedback. Then apologize if there is any area where there might have been a grain of truth in what they were saying. Their negative ego will be completely flabbergasted at your calm, rational Christed response. In a calm, loving manner you can also tell them that it would have been your preference that they would have shared their thoughts and feeling in a more calm, rational loving manner. If you disagree on some points frame it as you both have a difference of perception and that you should both agree to disagree without breaching unconditional. Frame the disagreement as a difference of looking at the situation with different lens and that that you are both right from the lens you both looked at. When the other person soon realizes that you are remaining defenseless, and harmless and are not responding back with angry and negative ego, their defenses will come down as well for they are already beginning to feel great guilt for how they reacted. Use good Spiritual discernment and say what is appropriate and no when to talk and when to be silent. Do not hand the person a loaf of bread if the are only ready to eat crumbs. Where necessary practice humility which is turning the other cheek. For, in truth, their attacks and judgements have no effect on you. If you are able to do this, you have passed a great Spiritual Test. You have "loved your enemy", as the Master Jesus taught. If the other person is at all reasonable they will be greatly touched by your selfless, Christed response and they will respond in kind and even apologize. Some people however are extremely run by the negative ego and will not. This is not important if the other person learns their lessons; all that matters is that you learn your lessons. For remember if they do not learn their lesson they will have to reincarnate to learn their lesson with someone else but not you for you have learned your lesson. You will have practiced unconditional love and forgiveness. You will be freed karmically from the lesson and will have maintained God Realization in a most difficult Spiritual Test. Very few can do it. Mostly because they have not been trained in Spiritual psychology and how to do it or what even the ideal is. My beloved Readers you must respond in this manner if your want to fully become an Integrated Ascended Master, and God Realized Being in the highest sense of the term. What does it do for you that you are a t a high level of initiation and light quotient if you cannot control your own negative ego and emotional body. You are in this world to set a better example. Do not lower yourself to their level. This is why the best approach is to remain silent until you get your center and balance back when first attacked.

Now I must say, however, sometimes when attacked, and judged the best thing is to say nothing. Or to say something like thank you for the feedback and I am going to take sometime to think about what you have said and I will get back to you when I do this. Some people are so disturbed that saying nothing is the best response. You are not a victim and you are not going to let them program your emotions so what does it matter. Your silence is an incredibly powerful response. When you take your space and think about what happened, I suggest that you get a pen and paper. Write down the key points they stated in a list format and see if any of them have any truth. Get totally clear within self as to what is truth and what is illusion. Later you can go back and respond more intelligently after thinking the whole process through. Sometimes an even better way to deal with the situation is to not do it in person, but to do it by letter. Then you can write everything down on paper and say exactly what you want to say and you are assured of remembering everything, you are assured of saying it in a Christ/Buddha like manner, and you are assured of not being interrupted. When writing such a letter, use the same Christed principles and qualities I mentioned earlier.

Now there are other times you will be attacked in a letter or by e-mail from people you do not even know. This happens more often once you get a little more in the public eye. There are an enormous number of very strange, eccentric, negative ego run, lost souls out there who are filled with low self-esteem, jealousy, competing energy and judgmental energy. They live to attack and judge to try and maintain the feeble self-image and self-concept. They unconsciously believe that by attacking they will at least stay on the upper side of the negative ego. I would say there are about five or ten percent of lightworkers fall into this category. They are extremely disturbed people who are completely run by the negative ego and do not even know what the negative ego is. No matter what workshop they go to they will find fault and criticize. It would not matter in the slightest if you made a mistake or not, they will manufacture them out of the delusion of their owning negative ego thinking. If the entire Cosmic and Spiritual Hierarchy manifested on Earth in physical bodies to do a workshop they would find fault. They same thing happens in the world and not just with lightworkers. Anyone who is on top will be mercilessly attacked by others to bring them down. It happens to any presidential candidate by the media. It happens to movie starts and famous musicians. Negative ego people instead of being happy for another persons success and realizing everyone is God, will attack and criticize to try and make themselves feel good. What a sorrowful existence. Anyone who does workshops, has a Website, writes books, gives lectures or seminars, or is in the public eye will run into this. Judging and attacking is the only way they know how to make themselves feel good. It is because they are caught in the negative ego complex and roller coaster and this is the only way they know how to not feel bad about themselves and feel worse than others. I bring this up so you do not take such attacks and tirades personally. This is why we must not look to others for our approval, self-worth, and self love, but should give it to ourselves and allow ourselves to receive it from GOD and the Masters. This is nothing more than a lesson in forgiveness, unconditional love, and nonjudgementalness. In truth one should feel sorry for such people, and have compassion for them. They are truly living in a hell of negative ego thinking and have not been trained how to escape it. In these types of situations, it is better to remain silent and not respond. These types of people are not open to learning anything and it is better to not waste your time and energy trying. The most powerful response you can make is silence. One of the real keys to dealing with peoples attacks and judgements in life is to develop the highest level of clarity, integrity and flawless character you possible can. The reason I say this is, that if you do are unbelievably clear and flawless in everything you do, then when people do attack or judge you, you will stand on solid ground, and you will know that you have always done the right thing, and pursued excellence and the highest Spiritual ideals in everything you have done. Then when you are attacked or judged you can look back at your actions and know without a doubt that you are clear and in integrity and that the other persons attacks are coming from their own insecurity, jealousy, low self esteem and competition. When you are clear within yourself that everything you do is in integrity and coming from your soul and Spirit, then other peoples attacks and criticism will not be able to have any place to plant within you and will not be able to cause any self doubt.

It is important to be able to receive constructive criticism in life, and it is even important to learn from people's feedback even if they express it from their negative ego. Do not however let disturbed negative egotistical people who are manufacturing things to attack you about have any affect on you. Stand solid in your truth and let their negativity slide off your Golden Bubble of Light like "water off a ducks back."

In conclusion, what I would like to say about this issue of how to deal with people's attacks and judgementalness is that, "an attack is really a call for love." There are only two emotions in life, and these are Love and fear. People attack and judgement because they live in fear. See through the negative ego veil they are manifesting, and give them the unconditional love they are truly asking for. Their meaningless attacks and criticism have no affect on you unless you let them. Stay above the fray. Remain in a transcendent state of consciousness. Take the High Road and not the low road. Remain in your Higher Consciousness. Maintain your Spiritual and Psychological immune system and do not catch their psychological disease. Do not lower yourself to their level. Let them think they have won, for in truth by responding appropriately, as GOD would have you respond, who has truly won. You who have remained in a state of God Realization, or the other person who think they won but has truly won nothing more than their negative ego and lost an opportunity to realize GOD. My beloved Readers do you see the delusion of the negative ego thought system. When I say you won it is not winning in an egotistical sense, it is winning in a Spiritual sense. Never forget your choice is always do you want to be right or do you want love? Do you want Love and peace or conflict, attack and fear? In essence do you want GOD or do you want negative ego? Do you want to pass your Spiritual Test and Realize GOD in that moment, or do you want the momentary illusionary satisfaction of attacking back and getting the upper hand on their negative ego with your negative ego? Do you want to learn your Spiritual Lesson now or do you want to have to reincarnate again and learn this lifetime next lifetime and maybe have them as your mother, father, sister, or brother? The choice is yours may friend. Your Salvation is up to you. God has already given you everything. They key question is will you give Salvation to yourself by choosing to respond from your God Consciousness and not your negative ego consciousness. Each moment of your life choose GOD and not the negative ego and the Biblical words of the Master Jesus will be fulfilled. "Be ye faithful unto death and I will give thee a Crown of Life!"

13

Turning Lemons into Lemonade: A Millennium Perspective

One of the absolute Spiritual keys to effective self-mastery and Self-Realization is the ability to turn lemons into lemonade. It must be understood that life will never always go according to our preferences. This is why the concept of having preferences rather than attachments is so important. If one is attached to having things go the way they want this person is going to have an enormous amount suffering in their life. When we have only super strong preferences, we are happy no matter what happens. We still want our preferences met but our happiness is not based on achieving them.

There is another "Noble Truth," however, which I am going to humorously add to Buddha's Four Noble Truths on the nature of truth and suffering if he doesn't mind. I now humorously add "The importance of turning Lemons into Lemonade." My beloved readers, let me now explain my meaning to begin to lay the foundation for this understanding besides the concept of preference, which is essential we must also understand that from GOD's perspective everything that happens is positive and should be looked at as a gift. The proper attitude to everything in life is "Not my will but Thine, thank you for the lesson!" No matter what happens in life no matter how horrific the example, this is the proper attitude. As His Holiness the Lord Sai Baba has said, "Welcome adversity." From GOD's perspective, there are no accidents in the universe and everything happens for a reason. The reason is always to Spiritually teach a lesson that needs to be learned. Now sometimes the "negative" things that happen are caused from personal karma. Sometimes they are caused by planetary or group karma. Sometimes they are caused by passed life karma. The truth is it doesn't matter why it happened or where it came from, for if it happened, you can be assured that you needed that lesson for some reason and the proper attitude is to welcome it, accept it and look at it as a gift. From GOD's perspective, everything that happens in life is a Spiritual test. In every situation in life, we can respond from God consciousness or negative ego consciousness. We can respond from our lower self or our Higher Self. We can respond from unconditional love or from fear. We can respond from separation or from oneness. We can respond from our Melchizedek/Christ/Buddha consciousness or from personality level consciousness that is not connected to the Soul and Spirit. So, Earth is a school to practice demonstrating GOD or to practice demonstrating being a Melchizedek, the Christ and/or the Buddha. The terms or names we use do not matter for they are interchangeable.

Now the truth of the matter is life is constantly throwing us lemons. The key principle here is will you turn it into lemonade or will you keep tasting the bitter taste of the lemon. Your attitude and perspective govern all this. As His Holiness, the Lord Sai Baba has said, "Your mind creates bondage or your mind creates liberation." So, no matter what happens in life and no matter how catastrophic the occurrence, it is each person's responsibility to turn that experience into lemonade. We constantly see examples of people doing this. They do this as a means to heal one self and to create meaning. Victor Frankl in the concentration camps of Nazi Germany created a whole new form of therapy called Logo Therapy. The woman whose son was killed by a drunk driver creates an organization to prevent this from happening, so others do not have to suffer. The person with aids gives up everything and dedicates her life to travelling the world to raise consciousness about aids. The story of Job tells how a man loses everything, and I mean everything but ultimately turns it into a Spiritual test of his "Righteousness" in believing in GOD. Job's statement in the Bible is one of my favorite quotes where he says, "Naked I come from my mothers womb, and naked shall I leave. The Lord giveth, and the Lord taketh away, blessed be the name of the Lord."

In my own mind I have called this the Job initiation, and I have reminded myself of this on many occasions when I have been asked to give up certain things. No matter what happens in life the key is to "Focus on what you can do instead of what you can't do!"

If you lose your voice and can't speak any more, then become a writer. If you can't walk, then join the Olympics in a wheel chair event. Look at the inspiration Christopher Reeves has brought to himself and the world after becoming paralyzed. If you have an illness and can no longer go outside then dedicate your life to developing your inner life. If you are losing your sight and can no longer read than listen to tapes. If you have digestive problems and can't eat without discomfort, then learn to live on light. No matter how much is taken away and no matter how many things you cannot do, there is always something you can do. Focus yourself and your consciousness on that which you can do! Your own Mighty I Am Presence and the Holy Spirit can always help you to find meaning, another purpose, and another direction to follow no matter what happens. A person who has an optimistic positive attitude will ultimately remain so no matter what happens in their life. A person with a negative, pessimistic attitude will find a way to feel unhappy even if outwardly things are going well. The world is nothing more than a projection screen for our attitudes and interpretations. GOD would have us be 100% positive and optimistic no matter what happens in life, no matter how morbid the example. What ever happens in life is there to teach us certain Christed/Buddha qualities. The Master Jesus knew this for that is why he said on the cross "Forgive them Father, for they know not what they do." The Master Jesus saw this situation as a Spiritual test and lesson in forgiveness, and demonstrated this understanding in a most extreme situation.

No matter what the situation of life, make lemonade out of the lemon you have been handed. If you lose a large some of money and someone rips you off, you are being given the wonderful opportunity to not only practice forgiveness, but to not be attached to money. Whatever the situation of life, you are being given the wonderful opportunity to transcend negative ego thinking and feeling and to practice Christ/Buddha thinking and feeling.

Let's say you make a big mistake and the whole world finds out about it like President Clinton did. That can be transformed into lemonade by practicing true humbleness and humility. If you have to go to jail, look at it as a Spiritual retreat. Malcolm X, while in jail, educated himself. If one has to go to jail use it as a time to totally focus on your Spiritual life and getting yourself psychologically and physically strong. Whatever goes wrong in your life no matter how extreme, use that situation and become an expert in it. Dedicate your life to helping others, so they never have to go through what you just went through. There is no situation of life where GOD, your own Mighty I Am Presence, the Holy Spirit, the inner plane Ascended Masters and your own positive creative Spiritual consciousness cannot turn lemons into lemonade! We have all heard the expression that "This was a blessing in disguise." This understanding stems from what I am writing about in this chapter. The truth is everything, and I mean everything that has ever happened in this world, is happening or ever will happen, is a blessing in disguise. If it happened, it means our Soul needed that lesson. There is no such thing as good luck or bad luck in this world; this is total illusion. Luck does not exist in GOD's reality. The concept of luck is an illusionary fabrication of the negative ego thought system. Everything in GOD's Universe operates out of laws on a Spiritual, mental, emotional, etheric and physical level, and if something happened then there is a cause. This is the immutable law of karma, or cause and effect. We cannot always control what comes into our life on an outer level, however, we can 100% control our attitude, interpretation, and perspective of what happens to us. I remember Elizabeth Kubler Ross said that it was the atrocities of Nazi Germany that inspired her to dedicate her life to being a better person. It is not what happens to you, it is how you use what happens to you.

My beloved readers, in the ultimate sense there is no such thing as death for anyone, there is just translation from dimension to dimension, and the wearing of different bodies. So, in truth, as *A Course in Miracles* states: all perception is a dream. The purpose of Earth life is that it is an earthly school to practice living and demonstrating GOD's dream rather than the negative ego's dream. It is to live the loving happy dream rather than the fearful, attacking, angry dream of the negative ego. If there is no such thing as death, then what is the worst that can happen? Is losing all material thing that important? My beloved readers, it all comes back to Lord Buddha's Four Noble Truths dealing with attachment. If you are attached to people and things, you will surely suffer. If everything in life is a super strong preference and you go after your preferences with all your heart and soul and mind and might, many of them will manifest. Those that don't, or go exactly the opposite will not affect your happiness because they are preferences, which means you will be happy either way. Happiness and inner peace hence, becomes a state of mind rather than anything outside of self. I like Paramahansa Yogananda's saying, "God is my stocks and bonds and financial security." So, the key is to look at everything that happens in life no matter what it is as a Spiritual test. So no matter how bad the lemons are that you are given, you can thank GOD and bless this experience, for it has given you the opportunity to transcend your negative ego and practice Melchizedek/Christ/Buddha Consciousness. Even if everything is taken away on every level, then my beloved readers, all that is left is GOD, and you can say: "Naked I come from my mothers womb, and naked shall I leave. The Lord giveth and the Lord taketh away. Blessed be the name of the Lord!"

You can bathe in passing the Job initiation and retaining your happiness and inner peace even though everything has been taken away. It is then you can rise again like the Phoenix, and give birth to a new creation, by focussing on what you can do instead of what you can't do. You find double meaning by then becoming an expert in the lemons you have been handed, and you dedicate your life and your Spiritual Path, to helping other people not to experience the lemons that you had to go through. By selflessly giving in this manner you have practiced Spiritual and psychological alchemy and turned a negative experience into psychological and Spiritual Gold! You have healed your self, and helped to heal the suffering of others, through the wisdom you have gained, and your own positive, optimistic, creative Spiritual attitude. So let it be written.

14

Seeing Life through the Eyes of Love

The title of this chapter sounds a little like a cliché; however, I tell you my friends, it holds an enormous "Divine Truth" within it. Everyone is searching for Love. Everyone wants Love. An enormous number of people are searching for romantic love. Almost all people need more self love, but do not realize it. People are always trying to find more love in friendships as well as family, and with their children or parents. All Spiritually minded people are always trying to generate love and devotion to GOD, and the Masters, as well as wanting to receive it as well. Love, in truth, makes the world go around. The entire infinite Universe is just a "Play of Love of GOD"!

Why then are so many people lacking in love? Most people on Earth are lacking in self-love. Fifty percent of all marriages end in divorce. Those who are married are not necessarily experiencing a very high level of love in their marriage or relationship. Most people have difficulties often in experiencing love parents, children and certain extended family members. Many people do not feel the love for GOD or the Love from GOD they would like to feel. Most people on this planet do not live in a state of Unconditional Love for everyone and everything. If "Love makes the world go round," how come so many people are not experiencing it to their full potential?

The answer to this question is they do not see life through the "Eyes of Love." What does this really mean? Love has nothing to do with physical looks, and nothing to do with how much money you have, and has nothing to do with your material possessions ands anything outside of yourself. It also has nothing to with being in or out of a family, marriage or relationship. There are plenty of people who have all these things and are surrounded by tons of friends and people but do not really have love.

There is only one way to have love within yourself, in all your relationships, and even with GOD and the Masters, and that is to see life through your Melchizedek/Christ/Buddha/Spiritual Consciousness and Mind. This is because our thoughts create our reality and our thoughts create our feelings and emotions. If we do not learn to think with our Melchizedek/Christ/Buddha Consciousness and Mind then we cannot maintain Love.

God Consciousness is Love Consciousness. A person who has trained themselves to think with their God Mind, hence creates only God feelings and emotions and God actions. No matter what happens in life all they see is Love. The stranger on the street is not a stranger, but is seen as an incarnation of GOD. When people attack a person in this state of consciousness they see it as a call for love, because they realize that person is fearful. When a person sees through the "Eyes of God or Love," they are "Love finders" not fault finders!

The Eyes of Love are so filled with self-love and love for and from GOD, they want love from others but do not need it. It is a preference not an attachment. They look at every situation of life as an opportunity to practice demonstrating Love. When a criminal steals something from them, they look at that as an opportunity given to them to forgive. When someone criticizes them, they look at that as an opportunity to transcend duality and remain unaffected by undo praise or criticism. When you see life through the "Eyes of Love," all attacks and criticisms slide off your Golden bubble of protection like water off a duck's back!

Those who see life through the "Eyes of Love," see every situation of life as a Spiritual Test to practice Love and Oneness. The more the extreme the lesson and Spiritual Test, the more the need for Love. The entire purpose of life is seen every moment to see if they can remain in unconditional love at all times.

When you see life through the "Eyes of Love," all one wants to do is selflessly and egolessly give and serve others, for one feels so filled with self love and love for and from GOD and the Masters. When negative things happen, those with "Eyes of Love," do not look at them as negative buts as lessons and happening for a reason. The reason being, to give and receive more love. The "Eyes of Love," main purpose for living is to be an Incarnation of Love on Earth, but also understands that this cannot be done with out Owning ones personal power fully and having great wisdom. In other words to see through the "Eyes of Love," one must balance ones three fold flame, and the Seven Rays of GOD.

To see through the Eyes of Love, one recognizes the need for total Self-Mastery over one's mind, feelings, emotions, physical body and energies.

The number on Spiritual practice of one that sees through the "Eyes of Love" is to always interpret life and all situations from the Melchizedek/Christ/Buddha mind and not the negative ego/fear-based/separative/lower-self mind. So to experience a reality of only Love in ones life one must always be vigilant to not allow Godless and loveless thoughts into ones mind. The "Eyes of Love," hence is a "State of Consciousness," that is so God and Love Centered, that no matter what happens in life the person chooses Love and not fear, criticism, attack or anger. So as you can see and as you all know, "Seeing through the "Eyes of Love," is no cliché. It is the highest Spiritual Practice a person can aspire to. So what that you gain the whole world, and even a great many Spiritual Initiations, but do not know how to remain in Love. Love is

GOD and GOD is love. The opposite of Love is fear, these are the only two emotions, and all others stem from these. To truly see through the "Eyes of Love," one must transcend fear and fear-based thinking. One who sees through the "Eyes of Love," also practices remaining in "Oneness Consciousness" as well. For Oneness is the first cousin of Love. They go together. For separation is not a part of GOD's reality. Every thought is hence examined by the Master of the "Eyes of Love," to see if it will create Unconditional Love and Oneness or fear, conditional love and separation from self, others, and life. The Master of the "Eyes of Love" experiences only Love in their life because they only think "Love Thoughts." Love Thoughts only create Love feelings and emotions. Love thoughts, feelings and emotions, create a love-filled physical body, which is much healthier and more energized. This all creates Love energy in ones aura and energy fields. This attracts and magnetizes more love to you, which creates more opportunities to love even more.

The Master of the "Eyes of Love" is also extremely optimistic and never pessimistic. This State of consciousness and Vision will see Love and positivity in every situation no matter what example is given. This is the case because this is how GOD sees life and we are made in His image and likeness. The Spiritual path in truth is very simple. If you want to be with GOD in Heaven, then act like GOD on Earth! GOD is the perfect balance of the Three-Fold Flame Love, Wisdom and Power and the Seven Rays and is integrated and balanced in all things. The essence of this is Unconditional Love.

The great lesson we learn here is that to truly become a Master of seeing life through the "Eyes of Love" takes great Mastery, focus, concentration, and commitment. It also takes great introspection, joyous vigilance, psychological and Spiritual work, for it is easy to slip back into the "eyes of fear, separation, anger, attachment, criticalness, materialism, power hungry, fame hungry, greed, upset, unhappiness, depression, grudges, negativity, faulty thinking, misinterpretation, lower self thinking, and negative ego thinking. This can occur also in the twinkling of an eye if you do not closely monitor your thoughts, feelings and energies at all times.

So the achievement of the Mastery of the "Eyes of Love," is one of the greatest achievements any person can achieve on Earth, however it takes enormous dedication and commitment to "Know thyself," and keep absolute mastery over ones attention, attunement and focus at all times. It takes enormous psychological work on self and self honesty to discern ones true motives, and what is truly of GOD and Loving and what is not, for many are tricked and seduced by the negative ego and fear-based thinking and think they are unconditionally loving and are not.

So my beloved readers, strive at all times to achieve this most noble ideal, and remember those who are the Masters of the "Eyes of Love," also know how to forgive and love themselves when they are unloving, and also have the power and wisdom to learn from their mistakes and redouble their efforts each time a mistake occurs. Those with the "Eyes of Love" do not expect never to make a mistake, but they do seek to "Love the Lord thy GOD, with all their heart and soul and mind and might, and to Love their neighbor as they Love themselves"!

15

The Solution to Every Problem and Challenge on a Personal and Collective Level in the World Today

The chapter I am about to write may be the single most important chapter I have ever written in my entire life. This is a very bold statement in that I have written now over 25 volumes in my Easy to Read Encyclopedia of the Spiritual Path. Yet, this chapter may be the single most important chapter of all my books. What is it that could be the solution to every personal and collective problem and challenge in the world today?

The answer to this question is the transcendence of negative ego thinking, and the reestablishment of Christ/Buddha/Spiritual thinking. Every negative thought, negative feeling, negative behavior, health problem, or negative thing that happens in the world has its cause because of the negative ego in a past life or this life. There is no such thing as luck, and everything that happens in life has a reason and a cause. Every inner and outer problem in our society has its cause in the negative ego. It is almost comical to watch the news, and these often "know it all" political commentators, and even politicians at times, speak of the cure to all the different societal and social problems. They speak about all these wonderful outer solutions, however not one of them ever speaks to the true cause. The solutions they give are often very good, however, they are like band aids that treat the symptoms, but not the cause. The same is true of Western medicine, which for the most part treats the symptom and not the cause. The same is true of Traditional Psychology. In truth, it is true of every aspect of our society. Having more police officers solves crime. Does this really solve the problem? I am not saying it isn't a good idea, but is not the solution to the problem.

If a person has cancer in the leg, and you cut off the leg, this may be a good idea from an emergency medical point of view, however it does not solve the issue of what caused the cancer in the first place. The doctor may also give a person a drug to block the symptoms of any given illness, but this does not answer the question as to what caused the illness in the first place.

Our thoughts cause our reality and the Worlds problems and challenges are caused by the collective thinking of mankind from past times and in our present time. For the rest of this chapter, I would like to focus on a great many outer problems in this World, and share with you and show you how transcending negative ego thinking and establishing Christ/Buddha/Spiritual thinking is the panacea and cure all to all the World's problems. I would also like to share with you how "band aid" thinking maybe very useful at times, but will not ultimately solve these problems and challenges.

Let us begin with the issue of child abuse or spousal abuse. If people were not run by the negative ego they would never attack, hurt, or be violent to anyone including themselves. The first principle of Christ/Buddha Consciousness is to give up your attack thoughts and anger, and replace them with unconditional love. Until People are trained to be right with self and right with GOD, all the Earthly laws in the world are not going to solve this problem. People will not be abusive when they learn how to master their mind and emotions, and transcend negative ego thinking and replace it with Christ/Buddha thinking and feeling.

Now lets look at the problems with gangs. Gangs are a manifestation of groups of people who are run by the negative ego. If these adolescents or people were not run by the negative ego, they would be forming Spiritual groups.

Now lets look at politics. Why do we have gridlock in Government, and why does politics have such a bad name? The politicians are run by the negative ego to a very large extent. They have brilliant minds, but the minds are subservient to the negative ego. They are more interested in power, greed, fame, holding their office, and being good Republicans or Democrats. Partisan politics is another name for negative ego. This is the reason for all the attack ads. If Buddha and Lord Maitreya wanted to be Planetary Logos, would they attack each other? Politics is corrupt because we have negative ego politics and not Spiritual politics. Politics is a noble profession if demonstrated from Christ/Buddha principles.

Now lets look at the media. The media panders to glamour, the lower self, greed, self-interest, ratings, and a "gotcha mentality." They will do anything to get good ratings. The regular media is beginning to look like Tabloid Journalism. Would the Christ Consciousness be interested in glamour? Would the Christ Consciousness look for dirt on people's lives just for ratings or self-glory? Would the Christ Consciousness attack and try to "play gotcha" to just build up one's ego or professional status? Would the Christ Consciousness print or put out scandalous stories that destroy peoples reputations and lives without making 100% sure they are true? Even if they were true, would they always do it anyway? Would the Christ Consciousness print or put our gossip? Would the Christ Consciousness allow personal agendas to contaminate their stories? Would the Christ Consciousness have so much violence and lower-self sexuality on television? All of this, of course, stems from people in the media being run by the negative ego within themselves, and being more interested in making a buck, power, and fame, than being in Spiritual integrity.

There is also one other aspect that must be addressed, however. If the public were not so run by the negative ego, and lower self, they would not pay for, or put up with this. If people would not support such products, then it would also not be worth these companies bottom line to do it. Consumers have a part to play as well. I will say however, the public is a little bit of a "captive audience" since this negative ego consciousness pervades all forms of newspapers, magazines, television, radio, and movies.

Now lets look at sports. If people were into the Christ/Buddha consciousness and not into the negative ego consciousness, would boxing or wrestling be a part of Earth life? In hockey, fighting is actually encouraged. How about bullfighting and sticking those swords into the bulls. Even the violence in football is a little questionable, when players play from their negative ego and not from the Christ/Buddha Consciousness and sportsmanship.

Would there be homeless people if the consciousness of our society and people were not run by the negative ego. If people were of the Christ Consciousness we would be our brothers keepers.

If the world were run the Christ Consciousness and not the negative ego consciousness, would there be racism? Do you have any idea what an absurd concept this is to the Christ/Buddha Consciousness. From the Christ/Buddha Consciousness all people regardless of skin color are incarnations of GOD.

Would scientists allow animal abuse, and allow themselves to abuse animals for there own selfish interest, if they were not run by the negative ego? Would a Christed scientist do this in the way worldly scientists do this?

Would businessmen and women be so competitive and cutthroat in business? Would such things as hostile takeovers exist if people were not run by the negative ego? How would Christed businessmen and women act? Wouldn't they be more loving, cooperative, and oneness oriented.

Would people be leaving traditional religion in droves if it were not so filled with negative ego doctrine, and if the Ministers and Spiritual Leaders were not filled with self-righteous, negative ego theory and faulty concepts.

Would our educational system be completely devoid of Spirituality, morals and ethical training, and hold such a separation of Church and State if the Ascended Masters ran our Society? This is because negative ego people run our educational system, and negative ego people run our religions, so they must be kept separate from each other. If they both weren't so egotistical in there thinking, it would be possible to integrate education and Spirituality, without shoving it down peoples throats in a self-righteous, opinionated and dogmatic manner as fundamentalist religious groups often do. There would also not be the competition between religions, and the self-righteous opinion among most religions that their religion is the best and all others are wrong and are run by the devil.

Would lawyers have such a bad name, if so many of them were not run by the negative ego. Being a lawyer is a noble profession, as are all professions. It is the issue of whether negative ego thinking or Christ/Buddha thinking guides a profession.

Would we abuse the Earth Mother and pollute her in the ways mankind has, if people were not run by the negative ego and more concerned with greed and worshipping science, then sanctifying the Four Faces of GOD? Would we use so many pesticides and chemicals in our farming if people in this industry were not so run by the negative ego? The Christ Consciousness would naturally gravitate towards natural and organic forms of farming, and calling in the etheric nature spirits, devas, fairies, and elementals.

Would there be so much junk food, sugar, preservatives, dead food, manufactured food, irradiated food, and chemically sprayed food, if the industry was not so run by the negative ego, and if people weren't so interested in buying it.

Would our prisons be based on punishment instead of redemption and Spiritual education, if the prison systems were not run by the negative ego rather than the Christ consciousness? Would the prisons be so over crowded, and would prisoners not have to serve their jail time? This all comes from negative ego thinking and total mismanagement. Why are so may people in jail in the first place? They have not been taught how to control their negative ego. Does prison teach them this? It should? So should our school system.

Would we care for the elderly so poorly if our society was not run by the negative ego? Would a Christed society not honor and revere the elderly. Would there be so many mentally ill people in institutions if they had been trained properly how to master the mind, emotions and negative ego by parents, school teachers, counselors, ministers, and rabbis. The problem is most of them have never even heard of the difference between negative ego thinking and Spiritual thinking. This is even a foreign concept to Psychologists, Marriage Counselors, Social Workers, and Psychiatrists. Do you realize that in Colleges and Universities, this understanding is not even taught anywhere. I know this for a fact for I have a Masters and Ph.D. in Psychology. My beloved readers, in many ways this world is still living in the Dark Ages.

This issue also applies to the Health Care System. In a Christed Society would we ever allow people not to get proper health care just because they did not have money. The reason that HMO's don't often work is because of the greedy bureaucrats, who are more interested in making money then giving people the proper health care they deserve and need.

My beloved readers, would there be wars between countries if the leaders of these countries were not run by their negative egos. Could you see El Morya, Saint Germain, Sananda, Serapis Bey, Kuthumi, and Paul the

Venetian having a war between their inner plane Ashrams for power and control? Do you see how absurd this is from a Christed perspective?

This issue also pervades the production of worldly energy. Do you really think that alternative nonpolluting sources of energy would not have been invented and put into use if it were not for the "Power Elite," and the greedy electric, power, and oil companies. Our new inventions are either destroyed, or bought up by these industries and buried, so they can make their greedy profit.

Do you think the truth about Extraterrestrials would be hidden from the people of the world for so long, if negative ego run politicians and corrupt leaders were not run by the negative ego? Do you think the Spiritual Leaders of this World in the form of the inner plane Ascended Masters want this information hidden and denied by the corrupted government officials that are in charge of this area of control. If we had Christed Leaders who were of the Christ/Buddha Consciousness this would not happen.

Do you think we would allow Nuclear Testing on the Earth Mother or in space if our leaders were of the Christ Consciousness?

Would adolescents and our young people be taking so many drugs if their lives were not so run by the negative ego and lower self? In a Christed school system kids would be taught Spirituality, meditation, the purpose of life, Spiritual psychology, how to be happy, and how to achieve inner peace. Do you think they would need to take recreational drugs if they truly understood life from the eyes of the Christ and Buddha?

Would there be so much pornography and preoccupation with sex and physical beauty if people were not run by the negative ego, which by definition is overidentified with matter. People are preoccupied with sex because they are devoid of the Christ/Buddha Consciousness, which is the one thing that is infinitely more appealing when truly understood. The negative ego by definition is the lower self and leads to a low life. The Christ/Buddha Consciousness is guided by the Higher Self and leads to a

Higher Life. This would also stop sexual harassment, for it is the negative ego that does not know the proper boundaries in this regard.

Would people get involved in so many cults, if their own vision were not so obscured by the negative ego. Would there be so many cult leaders, false prophets, negative ego-run gurus, and Spiritual teachers if these people were not run by the negative ego?

Would gay people, or any other people for that matter, be discriminated against? Would any type of prejudice exist?

Would there be so many divorces if people were not so run by the negative ego, and not so wrong with self, and hence not right with GOD. People often blame their partners, but, in truth, if both parties were not often run by the negative ego and allowing it to program their mind and emotions, divorce would often not have to occur. This is not always the case, but is sometimes the case.

Would there be so much crime if people were not run by the negative ego. If all these people were trained in the Christ Consciousness and Buddha Consciousness, do you think they would commit crimes? It is not punishment that will stop crime or prison, it is Spiritual education.

Do you think people would choose a profession of prostitution or people would go to a prostitute if they were not run by the lower self and negative ego? Would a person of the Christ/Buddha Consciousness be interested in such a thing?

Once one moves out of the negative ego consciousness and into the Christ/Buddha Consciousness one naturally gravitates towards only eating good food, thinking good thoughts, being interested only in positive Spiritual feelings and emotions, and being only interested in things of the Higher Self and not the lower self. Once this happens, one is not even tempted, or interested in these other things. Would one really want to go to a scary movie, or eat foods that are filled with chemicals and preservatives? Would one really like to go to a violent movie or focus one's energies in low life endeavors? Once this shift is made all this stuff drops away and one cannot even imagine how one was ever involved in such thinking, or behaviors. Once you make the shift, it has no appeal!

I do not bring up these things to criticize or judge. I bring up these things because one cannot solve a problem until one knows what the problem is. What I am showing you here is every worldly problem has its cause in negative ego thinking. Every solution has its cause in Christ/Buddha thinking. All the band aid solutions can be helpful, but if your really want to get to the root cause and remove all problems once and for all then there must be a "polar axis shift on the Earth." The polar axis shift I am speaking of here is not of the axis shift of the Earth. It is a polar axis shift of people's minds, from negative ego to Christ/Buddha/Spiritual thinking. When this occurs, all the world's problems will disappear. To do this lightworkers are going to first have to learn these lessons within self. The second step is to share this with friends, family, and students, and bring this understanding into your profession and given field of study. If every person will do this within their puzzle piece and service mission within the Divine Plan, the world will begin to change and transform at a much quicker rate, which will transform the Earthly institutions of our World and Civilization. Bringing light into this World is not enough. It is also essential to change the psychological consciousness and thinking of the world's people. It is now time to get to the root cause of all these problems and challenges of people and our civilization, and to stop trying to solve them with band aid or symptomatic solutions. It is for this reason and purpose this chapter has been written!

16

The Negative Ego and the Dangers of Lower Psychism

Another danger or glamour of the spiritual path is the issue of lower psychism. Many people are greatly intrigued by psychic powers. It must be understood that being psychic has absolutely nothing to do with being spiritual. This is hard for some Lightworkers to realize. Being psychic has nothing do with spiritual development. It has to do with the development of the abilities of the subconscious mind not the superconscious mind.

It is hard to believe, but I remember one well known psychic I went to twenty years ago, who didn't even believe in God, yet had all these great psychic abilities. Often those who have psychic gifts are very run by the subconscious mind because of their use of its gifts. This becomes a great blessing and great curse simultaneously. Very often to release themselves from this chronic victimization of the subconscious mind and astral body they actually have to let go of these abilities to learn to spiritualize their whole program.

There are a lot of Lightworkers I meet who would love to have these psychic abilities but they don't realize they are much more developed spiritually than the people they are admiring. Lower psychism is one of the many great traps of the spiritual path. Most Lightworkers don't realize that such spiritual senses as spiritual discernment, comprehension, healing, divine vision, intuition, idealism, beatitude, active service, realization, perfection, and all knowledge are much more advanced.

Lower psychism is an astral level ability. To stay stuck there as a psychic rather than become a spiritual teacher, is to stay stuck in the astral plane, which, in truth, doesn't even exist for a realized ascended master. Lightworkers should be much more concerned with developing the senses of the Higher Mind, the buddhic senses, atmic senses, monadic senses and logoic senses, than being enamored with the idea of being astrally psychic.

There is nothing wrong with being astrally psychic. It is just that this ability must be integrated into an understanding of total Self-realization to be used appropriately. Being psychic in this way has nothing to do with one's ability to achieve ascension and to complete the seven levels of initiation. A person who is psychically developed and psychologically and spiritually unclear is going to have completely inaccurate and contaminated information anyway.

I personally know a great many people who are incredibly psychically developed and who are also some of the most disturbed people I have ever met this lifetime. Do not get caught in the side road of fascination with this aspect of life for it will detour you from your true mission. I do not mean to denigrate people who are psychic for this is a wonderful ability, as long as it is used only in service of the purposes of the soul and monad in an integrated way and not as a glamour and trap of the negative ego keeping you stuck in the fascination of lower psychic development.

Djwhal Khul said part of the trap is becoming enamored with the psychic world and then inflated by the negative ego in its perception of importance so that it loses perspective and acts as a damaging system, often attracting astral entities and becoming a twilight master, so to speak.

On the other side of the coin, you have the person with the brilliant mind who is not necessarily classically psychic but because of this psychological brilliance can function as a type of magician, and again twilight master. Hitler was this type of person. I see this in a great many of the leading people in the field of psychology, who have not come into full merger with their soul. They are masters at the psychological level but not on a spiritual level. They are using their lower mental senses and higher mental senses in a similarly abusive manner as the psychics are. These two cases could be called the lower expression of the mystic, and the lower expression of the occultist.

I have seen this lower expression of the occultist in people involved in NLP, psychology, hypnosis, and on the TV infomercials teaching various forms of success and mind training. These are people that are brilliant, but because the soul and monad have not fully merged they are serving two masters, both the negative ego and the Spirit.

This is usually completely unconscious. In both these examples of the lower mystic and the lower occultist, the Dark Brotherhood taps in and uses them usually without their awareness. The true culprit is always the negative ego. Psychics often are under great psychic attack in many of these cases from astral entities and from negative Extraterrestrials and they can't figure out why. They don't realize they are stuck in lower psychism, and don't understand what true mastery of the subconscious mind, emotional body, and desire body really is. The lower expression of the occultist is caught up in the "power", of being able to manipulate and control power. Because soul merge and soul infusion has not taken place, the "motives" are suspect.

Very often, Djwhal Khul said, there is a war going on between their lower self and Higher Self. This is a war between the individual's desire to connect with the Higher Self and be purely an instrument of Higher Consciousness and the desire to be clever in their manipulation, control, receiving attention and importance in the ruling and destiny of people, and over-identified with being the one who knows.

We have all heard the expression "a little knowledge is a dangerous thing." Here are people having astral and mental senses, abilities, and gifts but spiritually are like children in terms of their maturity. Because the negative ego is in control in both instances, it clogs and contaminates the channel and attracts astral and mental entities at best, to be one's inner guides. Often times these entities claim to be of the higher dimensions and ascended nature, when they are as confused or negatively manipulative as the people who are attracting them. People can only channel at the level of their clarity. In some cases there is an actual conscious pact made with the Dark Brotherhood. This is more common than people realize.

We have all seen movies where the person sells their soul to the devil. In this case, it is selling their soul to the Dark Brotherhood, and as a Dark Brotherhood disciple for power, fame, money, and glory on a personality level. Most of the time this is taking place unconsciously.

Most people don't realize that the mental senses have a whole range of powers, as do the psychic senses. The Ascended Master is most importantly developed in the buddhic senses, atmic senses, monadic senses, and logoic senses. Each plane of consciousness contains what might be called super-senses. The danger here as can be seen on the following chart is people get stuck and fascinated with the powers of these lower senses. This is like people living on the inner plane who think the higher astral plane of higher mental worlds are the most advanced in the universe and are very happy to stay there indefinitely. You can see this in the psychic type magazines you can buy in the metaphysical type bookstore that are filled with all this lower psychic stuff of people putting hexes on, and other dark stuff that is a blatant negative manipulation of others. This is living in a psychic world not a spiritual world.

In truth, the field of psychology is the same thing. It is a world of personality level exploration pretty much completely devoid of soul and spirituality. Enormous numbers of people become trapped in this world for long periods; usually by going to counselors and psychologists who are trapped in this world themselves. They are not bad people, just unconscious people who are locked in a third and fourth dimensional state of consciousness.

In the ideal state of affairs, one develops all senses on all levels which are used then by the Higher Self and Mighty 1 Am Presence for the purpose of spiritual growth and service of humanity. This issue of becoming caught up in the astral senses and astral world and in the lower mental senses and the lower mental world is an area of study that most people on this planet are not as aware of as to their dangers and glamours as they need to be. The writing of this chapter has been to bring this area of discussion into "Greater Light"!

The Senses and the Supersenses

ATMIC PLANE:
Atmic Senses:
All knowledge
Perfection
Realization
Active service
Beatitude

BUDDHIC PLANE:
Buddhic Senses:
Idealism
Intuition
Divine Vision
Healing
Comprehension

CAUSAL PLANE:
Higher Mental Senses:
Spiritual Telepathy
Response to group vibration
Spiritual Discernment

CONCRETE MENTAL PLANE:
Lower Mental Senses:
Discrimination
Higher Clairvoyance
Planetary Psychometry
Higher Clairaudience

ASTRAL EMOTIONAL PLANE:
Astral Senses:
Emotional Idealism
Imagination
Clairvoyance
Psychometry
Clairaudience

PHYSICAL ETHERIC PLANE:
Physical Senses:
Smell
Taste
Sight
Touch, feeling
Hearing

17

How to Clear the Negative Ego through the Ascension Buddy System

This next tool for clearing the negative ego may be one of the most important of all. We have all heard the saying that it is hard to see the forest through the trees. It is always much easier to see the faults in others then it is to see the faults in ourselves. No one person is an island unto themselves.

The premiere principle of the New Age is "group consciousness." A sure-fire sign when a lightworker and high level initiate is in trouble is when they isolate themselves from other lightworkers and the entire spiritual community at large. It is much easier to live in a cave by yourself than it is to live in the marketplace and work in fellowship with other lightworkers. Given these facts I cannot recommend more highly that if possible you develop an ascension buddy system with your close spiritual friends. This is a pact that you make with each other to work together on your path of ascension as a team.

This may involve meditating together, possibly serving together or working together. It will involve sharing, talking, studying, and gathering information together. Helping one another as much as you possibly can, almost like you have tied your spiritual progression together as a team. The gains of one in this pact will help the other and vice versa. Did not Jesus say, "Where two or more are gathered in my name"? This pact will accelerate both of your evolutions, and does not have to be limited to just two people. It could be three or a whole group of people working together for this purpose. Use your intuition.

The ascension buddy system taken to its highest level actually becomes a group etheric body and a three-fold organism in one larger body with each person maintaining their individual and group identity simultaneously. This step can only be taken when it is spiritually appropriate and when the ascension buddy system has been firmly established for an extended period of time.

The next question is how does the ascension buddy system help to clear the negative ego? The key word here is "feedback"! It is hard for all of us to see our own stuff. It is much easier to see the faults in others than it is to see the faults in ourselves. The concept here is to have either ascension buddies or even just close friends who know you and spiritual in their orientation sit you down and tell you when you are out of line. This process has been invaluable for me.

No matter how clear any of us on this planet think we are, we all "trip out" at times. We all have our "blind spots" and our "character flaws". We all have negative ego. There is not a single person on this planet, even the Avatars who are completely clear of this. Sanat Kumara and Vywamus said even they still have small remnants of negative ego to clear. If they do, you better believe we do.

Since it is hard to see our own stuff, the ascension buddy system and good spiritual friends can be a lifesaver in this regard. So in your ascension buddy system make a pact to give each other feedback when you get mentally, and emotionally out of line within Self or in regards to other people.

The purpose of the ascension buddy system has a psychological component as well as spiritual component. This pact you make will give each other permission to give each other feedback in a strong but loving way without "ego-sensitivity" (defensiveness) from either party.

We need people to give us a swift loving kick in the butt sometimes, to give us a wake-up call. This is nothing to be defensive about but rather something to be grateful for. Sit down with your ascension buddies or your spiritual friends and make this pact and agreement to do this for each other.

We have inner feedback functions that help us with this such as dreams, feelings, intuitions, ideas, pain and suffering, synchronicity, and just life. However, without people to help also, the pitfalls of glamour, maya and illusion are still too easy to fall into no matter how diligent you are. We all are interdependent on one another and this is a good thing not a bad thing. The forming of an ascension buddy system will also be a wonderful exercise in expanding one's consciousness and going beyond the self-centered nature of the negative ego on all levels.

The spiritual path as we evolve is constantly moving us in the direction of greater and greater identification with the group and moving farther and farther away from self the higher you go. This will be a wonderful exercise in beginning this process now. See if you can really get out of all competition, and self interest, and really put your ascension buddies welfare as equal to your own, to the point that their suffering is your suffering and their gain is your gain and vice versa.

The first step is to be God in your self. The second step is to be able to be God in a relationship or a group. This is why it has also always been stated that the true test of your spiritual development is to be involved in a romantic relationship or marriage. For as we all know this will test one to the nth degree. It is possible for your ascension buddy to be your partner or spouse. There may be others who join with you.

What is nice about the ascension buddy system is that it is not romantic except in the aforementioned situation. It is a group consciousness based upon friendship, similarity of spiritual goals and purpose, and sometimes professional and service interests. This is a wonderful testing-ground to develop your character. We need feedback from our friends to tell us when we are out of balance. The nature of the beast is that we don't realize it and the negative ego doesn't want to admit it.

I also want to add here that this doesn't always have to be done out loud. This can be done telepathically, through prayer, affirmations or visualization. At times it may be done by example, a letter, a note, a gift, a spiritual treatment or a gentle touch. It is, however, the ideal if the lines of communication are open on a verbal level and all ego sensitivity can be transcended. Ego sensitivity brings out the tendency to get defensive, fall into rejection or hurt unnecessarily because a character flaw of lack of personal power, and lack of self love, self worth, overall psychological weakness, and fragility.

The process of clearing the negative ego is a combination of self-recognition, self-awareness, self inquiry, and being open and courageous enough to allow oneself to receive feedback from ascension buddies, spiritual friends and life itself. Very often God or life is giving us feedback through people we barely know but the ego is too defended and closed to hear God speaking to you through these people and life's lessons.

There is one other point that must be considered here. In choosing your ascension buddies and spiritual friends, choose well-rounded and balanced people. I bring up this point because I have seen a few Lightworkers who have spiritual friends and ascension buddies who all share the exact same set of blind spots. In the case, I am thinking they are all over-identified with the emotional body. In this case, they are all supporting each other's imbalance. I do not mean this as a judgment, just a point of consideration.

This can also happen in the reverse where a particular group of people bonded together may be too mental, too heavenly, or too materialistic. It can take form in any direction of imbalance in the four-body system. The danger here is that the entire group supports each other's projection and neurosis. The ascension buddy system in essence is creating a support system that holds up a mirror in love. It cannot be said any clearer or eloquently than this last statement. It is essential to give this feedback in a loving not critical and non-judgmental way. It is also important to have good discernment as to when it is good to give feedback and when it is better to remain silent.

I have seen some groups who are like naive children who feel a need to be what I might call being "obsessively honest." We must be adult and mature about this process and not become obsessive about giving feedback either. In some cases, things are best left unsaid or dealt with inwardly. The God-realized being does what is "appropriate" in any given situation, for the best result of all concerned.

There may be even a third stage to this process that might be called "spiritual community," in a larger context. A great many lightworkers may have not only have an ascension buddy system and certain key spiritual friends but also a larger spiritual community of involvement.

There is also a feedback that comes from these rings of "spiritual community" that is important to be open to. This may come from students, fellow lightworkers, and fellow spiritual leadership people in the field. This reminds me a little bit of the four jewels in the Buddhist teachings, where they speak of the Buddha, the doctrine, the guru, and the spiritual community. The four jewels I speak of here for clearing the negative ego are self-recognition, ascension buddy system, spiritual friends, and spiritual community.

If our negative ego is in the way God will speak to us through one of these vehicles, you can count on that. The problem here is that many lightworkers because of the negative ego are in a state of "denial" and non-openness to feedback. The ideal is to have a strong sense of Self and to be open. There are cases where this can work in reverse and the lightworker is too open to feedback because of lack of self worth, lack of self love and a lack of this strong sense of self I speak of. A balance is needed here. In truth, the entire universe is just one massive communication network. It is essential to keep all these lines of communication open within self and to life while still remaining powerful, centered and the master of your Self and life!!!

Another key to this process of clearing the negative ego for Lightworkers is to know in their ascension buddy system, among their friends, and in their spiritual community that it is "safe" to recognize the control the negative ego has and one will not be put down, or judged, or criticized. That there will be support, forgiveness, and unconditional love. The denial occurs because people don't feel safe. The true purpose of the ascension buddy system, good friends, and a spiritual community is to create this atmosphere and safety that most of us have not had in our upbringing or in society at large.

Another key to the ascension buddy system is to utilize and take advantage of the spiritual gifts and abilities your ascension buddies have to help each other. In any given ascension buddy system or spiritual community for that matter, one person may channel, another may be an excellent spiritual counselor, another clairvoyant, another more telepathic, another, a healer, another well studied and an occultist, another a psychic, and on and on and on. Do not be afraid to ask for help and to offer your help.

This is, in truth, the beauty of the ascension buddy system to have all these different abilities combined together in one group consciousness. One type of ability is not better than another. All abilities are needed to have the most advanced type of service module and group consciousness brain, so to speak. Take advantage of the different abilities of the people in your spiritual community and give yours freely. We are in this world to help one another. Each person is a different sunbeam of God, so each person brings their own unique, special and divine perspective, and Christ qualities. The underlying theme of the ascension buddy system is to support one another to become self-responsible. The sharing of spiritual gifts, be they mystic or occult in nature, will ultimately move each person in the group in this direction.

18

How to Clear Specific Diseases from the Perspective of the Masters

The idea for this chapter came to me one day while driving my car. The idea was to look through the DSM-III diagnostic handbook and list some of the common psychological and/or physical diseases and run them by the Masters in our meditations and get a short little synopsis as to their cause and cure from their perspective rather than the field of traditional psychology, which to say the least is quite limited in perspective. I was really looking for short concise answers as to mental, emotional, physical or karmic causation. A person could write a book about each one of these diseases. Please don't take this as the be all end all final statement. However, what is shared here can give one a handle and golden key to Self-mastery and healing in these areas. I began with asking about multiple personalities, which has always been something I have been curious about.

Multiple Personalities

Multiple personalities could be entities, from a trauma caused hole in the auric field. It could also be separated subpersonalities that have fragmented out of fear. Or both. It could also be past life aspects that come through fragmented, unintegrated and unhealed. For example, a murder in a past life may bring up a trauma for that individual, and cause them to fragment or split off, into a personality that is constantly replaying the murder. This may draw in an entity, implants, parasites (negative elementals) which impinge upon the whole organism. This split can occur on a dual level or be multiple (three or more). This means a whole group of injurious parts have now fragmented off, as portrayed in such movies as *Sybil* and *The Three Faces of Eve*; all breaking threads of connection and all competing for the dominance of the personality or organism.

To heal, the person must create a stationary flow of the soul (Higher Self) to the personality, which functions as a witness or observer for the integration and balance of all parts, in the same way that we need to balance and integrate all our archetypes, rays, and astrological aspects. In our case these parts have not split off or fragmented as in the case of a multiple personality. We are also hence not dealing with astral entities, implants, or parasites in this same kind of split-off manner.

The healing of a multiple personality comes in the removal of implants, parasites, astral entities, core fear, and the integration then of these personalities or archetypes into an integrated whole. The removal of the core fear, implants, parasites and astral entities along with proper philosophical understanding of the need for integration and the conscious mind being the unified director, will make healing a lot easier.

People who have had this dysfunction can become quite integrated and functional, with the help of a qualified therapist. It is usually very severe trauma, like extreme child abuse, that has triggered this whole process. However, just because a person has had extreme child abuse doesn't automatically mean that they will become a multiple personality. In truth, this is quite rare.

Definitions of Common Negative Emotions

This next section was channeled by an old spiritual teacher of mine who has since passed on to the spiritual world, Paul Solomon. Paul was and still is a wonderful spiritual teacher, and many called him the next Edgar Cayce. The following are definitions of some of the attitudes and belief systems that cause some of the well-known negative emotions. I think some of them are quite amazing, and extremely accurate.

Anger: loss of control over others and attempt to regain it. (Corollaries of anger: frustration, irritation, aggravation, indignation, impatience, annoyance, etc.)

Fear: entertaining a fantasy of a danger that has not occurred.

Hate: misplaced expression of love/protection of myself because of how much a person's opinion of me means to me when I don't feel safe with that person.

Worry and Anxiety: incapacitating the self to keep from (or avoid) preparing for a situation.

Guilt: indulging in concern over a past situation in order to avoid taking action now.

Hurt: denial of responsibility for one's own feelings. Feeling another is not doing what I want he/she to do.

Confusion: laziness of mind to keep from dealing with a situation or making a decision.

Self-pity: indulging in helplessness as a luxury (substitute for self-love).

Grief: loss of control over a source of attention or love.

Resentment: anger and hurt.

Jealousy: misidentification and feeling of inadequacy and insecurity to a known or unknown competitor, or fear of loss.

Self-righteousness, Indignation, Contempt, Disdain: feeling superior in order to feel like a good person.

Boredom: not taking responsibility for your own happiness or own entertainment.

Loneliness: placing responsibility for your happiness on someone else.

Rejection: unsuccessful attempt to gain approval.

Shyness: waiting for someone else to tell me I'm okay.

Homesickness: loss of source of attention and source of self-identity.

Embarrassment: feeling that another will think I am a nincompoop.

Regret: feeling inferior because I feel I've performed inadequately.

The following information came through in a Sunday morning meditation. This information comes from the combined intelligence of Djwhal Khul, Lord Maitreya, and Melchizedek with Djwhal Khul seeming to take the leadership role for this particular chapter.

Migraine Headaches

"Migraine headaches are unintegrated material coming up through the psyche where the person has not acknowledged their soul connection, is therefore unable to assimilate the pattern of behavior, and feels a pressure from this blocked flow of energy. Karmic themes from this lifetime and other lifetimes come into play here, having to do with pressures around the brain, temples, neck and shoulders. The proper integration of the soul allows one to not have to take on a burden they cannot carry or to avoid their own karma." Djwhal also said that there could be chemical or environmental causes. There can also be karmic causes from past lives.

Migraine headaches are always, however, connected with psychic pressure. He said that there could also be a pressure in the head that is created with the influx of high frequency spiritual energies. The high frequency energies cause the brain fluids to be detoxed of lower frequencies, imperfections, and impediments, which causes an expansion of the energy field within the brain, and an increase in the convolutions of the brain. This can cause sometimes quite a strong pressure, especially in the third eye and temples. Certain areas in the brain are often congealed or closed, especially around the sinus areas. The new energy field has to gradually penetrate the old field.

Djwhal Khul said this could be a process that is uncomfortable for some. It is a natural evolutionary process and not to be considered a separation from the soul, as was described in the aforementioned section. One can ask for energetic adjustment in the field around the head from the Arcturians, Masters, or inner plane Healing Masters to help in this regard.

Arthritis

Djwhal said it was "a withdrawing of the life energy psychically and spiritually. A withdrawing of love. An inability to channel out love and warmth." This causes a concentration and build-up in the joint area of a deposit of psychic material. When there is an outflow of love and acceptance there is not a rigidity.

Asthma

Djwhal said, "It is often a reaction to circumstances at birth or early childhood which have to do with suffocation. This can be psychic suffocation in which there is no freedom for the individual to exist. There may be a basic intolerance in the mother in being able to sustain motherhood. There is an unconscious attempt to stifle the child, to reduce the energies of the child, to control the child. The child hence has a reaction of feeling like it is being smothered. This can also be a reaction from actually being smothered or drowned in a past life. An inability to get the breath.

"Not enough life force is provided between the fetal environment and the early childhood. This creates an aura of sickness and/or of breath or energy. Asthma can be cured not only by physical methods, but also by doing a type of regression. One goes back to re-experience one's birth, asking to re-experience the relationship with the world through the relationship of the Spiritual Mother as opposed to suffocating by a personal earthly mother. Forgiveness is part of the process here also."

This also reminds me of one of the Edgar Cayce readings where a child had asthma and it was caused by a past life deep-seated guilt. Here the condition was caused by a lack of self-forgiveness for a past life mistake.

AIDS

Djwhal said here that all the viruses such as AIDS and others of similar genre are caused because of the imbalance that is occurring at the third dimensional level at this time. As the new energies are coming for evolution, there is a resultant struggle between the old and new. This might be termed the Christ and Antichrist energies. This also might be termed energies of love and hate or control. This struggle causes lower astral fourth dimensional entities to feed on this etheric conflict.

All disease begins in the invisible dimensions first, be it etheric, astral, or mental bodies. Along with the astral entities are negative elementals that feed upon this etheric struggle also. There is also much fear-based programming around viruses. This mass collective consciousness fear-based programming has a very negative effect on humanity's immune system. Viruses begin first as astral, etheric, or even mental viruses and then move into the physical.

The idea is to keep these other bodies clear and the physical will become invulnerable to disease. Diet and environment are important in the sense of keeping physical toxins out of the system. If the four-body system is kept fundamentally clear viruses or bacteria cannot grow. The fact is there are viruses and bacteria everywhere and this is nothing we need to be afraid of. Viruses and bacteria has no possibility of manifesting in a person whose four-body system is balanced and who is soul and monadically infused.

From the perspective of the Masters AIDS can also function as a catalyst for some to help them leave the planet when they need to be placed elsewhere, physical existence not being the "be all an end all" goal of existence. As I mentioned in my other books, Hanna Kroeger has found a cure for AIDS with her herbs. Other more New Age doctors are having great results using energetic medicine and homepathics to build the overall immune system.

HIV and AIDS is not a guaranteed death certificate. Some of the symptoms many people experience has more to do with their beliefs about AIDS than the actual disease. Other symptoms have more to do with all the drugs they are being given, which is having a damaging effect on their immune system. AIDS like everything in life is not bad. It is a lesson no different then all lessons in life and must be used as a teacher and catalyst for spiritual growth.

Catatonic

In this case, Djwhal Khul said that a person has created a wedge, or dark gray shelf between themselves and their God-Self, out of fear. The need here is to be completely unconscious of life, and to respond out of the most feeble life form. A person who is catatonic is barely conscious. Almost to the point of being brain dead. They have literally created a palpable substance of separation. To reach someone who is catatonic takes extreme patience, and unconditional love to break through that wedge. It is much like working with a person who has become possessed. It takes a person of great faith to ignite the Three-Fold Flame of Love, Wisdom, and Power within an individual such as this, to help them accept themselves and their life.

The catatonic person is so afraid they are not even able to function. This could also be caused by a previous life thread coming up in the consciousness or from extreme abuse or experience in this lifetime. Djwhal said this may also happen when a person has been annihilated in a past life in a war, for example, the etheric body is in extremely bad shape, yet the person chooses to reincarnate immediately with no healing in between lifetimes.

It is very important for lightworkers to understand how damaged and tainted an etheric body can become. This is a very serious situation, for prior to ascension the physical body works off the etheric blueprint. If the etheric body is damaged there is very little possibility of true healing. We have all had very traumatic past lives. This is why it is a good idea for everyone to call in the inner plane Healing Masters and the Etheric Healing Team and the Angels specializing in the etheric body to completely repair the etheric body to make it correspond with the true monadic blueprint.

This is another classic example of the shortcomings of traditional psychology and Western medicine that doesn't deal with this aspect. The catatonic is almost in the twilight zone. They are not physically dead and yet not psychologically alive. They are in No Man's Land. The catatonic is not that different from a person who is having a life threatening illness and lapses into a coma. Djwhal Khul said in this case it is best for the healer in charge to call forth and help the person connect with their Angels.

I saw an interesting TV show recently in which a very young body lapsed into a coma after being hit by a car. No matter what the doctors or family did the boy would not come out of it until they started to talk about his pet dog. The love the boy had for his dog began to cause a response. They were eventually able to bring his dog to the hospital and a full recovery occurred. The love for and from an animal, especially for children, can be an enormous healing influence.

Narcolepsy

A narcoleptic is someone who is constantly falling asleep. Djwhal Khul said that it is difficult for this person to stay firmly connected to third dimensional reality. This is a type of defense mechanism of an unconscious nature to escape the lessons of the third dimension. Djwhal said that the narcoleptic is often escaping to the fourth dimension in a type of dream state reality. Another possibility is someone who trances out very easily as in a case of someone who is very suggestible to hypnotic suggestion and is a classic somnambulist. This would be a deficiency in the psychic boundaries and ability to protect themselves psychically from suggestion. Another possibility is that the person is being exposed to certain environmental toxins and is having an allergic reaction to these toxins and is going unconscious again as a defense mechanism.

So, we see here with the narcoleptic and, in truth, all forms of psychological or physical disease that there are mental, emotional, physical, environmental, and past life karmic reasons that can be a potential cause. There is not always just one quick pat answer or sole reason.

The narcoleptic actually has the potential to become a good meditator and have access to multi-dimensionality if this process can move to a psychic experience that is controlled rather than uncontrolled. The simplest answer here as to the cause of narcolepsy is the "unconscious avoidance response." Some people, when they don't want to do or go someplace, just get sick. The ideal here is to make the tough decisions in life and consistently use all your energies once a decision is made.

Insomnia

In the case of an insomniac, we have the opposite situation. Instead of falling asleep at inappropriate times as in the narcoleptic, here the person can't fall asleep at appropriate times. Djwhal said this is often connected to an inability to let go, a fear of resting, or a fear of surrendering. It can also be connected to a haunting memory in the conscious or subconscious. This memory could be from this life or a past life. It can also be a fear of being powerless in their life. This can also be caused by a type of neurosis where they have so much pressure and responsibility in their life they feel they cannot afford to take time off to sleep. Fear is obviously connected here as with probably every single one of the symptoms mentioned in this chapter. It could be a fear or fight or flight, where the person feels they must be on the alert, possibly from a past life trauma that the person is not even aware of consciously.

Endocrine Diseases

This has to do with the major glands: pineal, pituitary, thyroid, thymus, adrenals, kidneys, and gonads. These diseases usually manifest as the glands being underactive or overactive. This is connected usually with one of the seven chakras being over or under active in function. This has a direct affect on the functioning of each gland. This over or under activity in the chakras can stem from an imbalanced philosophy, or psychoepistemology. It can develop from an imbalance in the functioning of the three minds or four bodies. It develops from a person's unconscious over-identification with one or more of their chakras, which is extremely common.

The reverse of this is, of course, an under-identification with one of the chakras. An emotional person might, for example, over-identify with the solar plexus and heart and not use the third eye. This would tax the organs and glands connected with the solar plexus and cause an underdevelopment in the pituitary.

Hives

Animosities, grudges, or unkind thoughts are usually the psychological cause.

Polio

In one past life reading of Edgar Cayce's, a man had polio that was caused by jeering and mocking others in a past life. In a similar situation, a child had infantile paralysis that was caused by a past life of using drugs and hypnosis to hurt others.

Constipation

Constipation can have a physical or dietary causation, but can also have a psychological component. The constipated person is often very fearful, and hence uptight, constricted, and too controlled in their psychology. The person with chronic diarrhea is just the reverse. Their psychology instead of being too yang is too yin. We have all heard the expression of having diarrhea of the mouth. Without self-control, discernment, and appropriate response present, our thoughts create our physical bodies. We are what we eat as well as what we think!

Manic Depressive

Manic-depressive behavior occurs when a person allows themselves to be run by the emotional body, negative ego, and subconscious mind in a victim psychology. The ideal here is to have personal power and self-mastery over the three-fold personality (physical, emotional, mental). When the emotional body and subconscious mind run the conscious mind, the negative ego becomes the programmer of your emotional reality and you are on an emotional roller coaster. The ideal is to develop self-mastery and see that your thoughts cause your reality and to develop evenmindedness, equanimity, unchanging joy, and inner peace at all times regardless of what is going on outside of self.

Panic Attacks

Panic attacks, in its simplest understanding, are caused by the negative ego being in control. The essence of the negative ego is fear. The person who has panic attacks is constantly being victimized by the negative ego with this fear at inappropriate times or challenging times. There is a battle for the control of the personality going on. Personal power in service of love must take command here for this to be resolved. It does not matter if the fear is from a past life or this life.

Obsessive Compulsive

A person who is obsessive/compulsive is being run by a subpersonality in the subconscious mind that requires order and structure. The opposite of this would be the person who is, for a lack of a better word, a "slob." The slob lives a life of complete non-order and lack of cleanliness. Again too yang or too yin. The key here is to not be a victim of one's mind. In the obsessive/compulsive person, the mind is running the person instead of the person running the mind. The lesson here is for the conscious mind to not necessarily get rid of this part but rather to make choices as to when to listen to it.

As soon as free choice comes into play, the disturbed quality of this part becomes diffused. What we see here from this lesson, and all the symptoms described in this chapter, is that they all stem from "imbalances in the psyche." By this I mean either being too yin or too yang. Too heavenly or too earthly. Not balanced in the four-body system. Not balanced in the three minds. Not balanced in one's relationship of the inner parent to the inner child. Imbalanced in the understanding of the need to transcend and die to the negative ego and to only think with one's Christ Mind. Being a victim instead of a Master. Not recognizing that one's thoughts are causing their reality.

These basic and simple principles when not held as an ideal, manifest as symptoms or psychological or physical disease. These symptoms, pathologies, psychological and psychic diseases are not bad, they are just lessons. They are actually gifts if looked at properly, teaching you obedience to God's laws. They are signposts that an adjustment needs to be made in your philosophy, or psychoepistemology. They are teachers showing a need for greater balance within these principles. It is these symptoms that are the suffering and fire of life that are relentlessly pushing everyone to ascension and God-realization.

Senility

When an elderly person becomes senile, they are in a sense returning to a child-like state. This can be caused by both physical and psychological factors. A child is basically just run by the subconscious mind. As one moves into adulthood the conscious mind takes charge and takes control. In senility due to the breakdown of the physical vehicle, due to old age, illness, environmental poisoning and/or psychological reasons such as giving up, or loss of personal power and self-mastery, the person again becomes run by the subconscious mind. It is a return to a state of being victimized by the subconscious mind, emotional, mental, and physical vehicles. This can stem from an improper philosophy, and often a lack of meaning and purpose.

Melancholia

Melancholia is an extreme state of prolonged sadness and depression. There is always a victimization by the emotional body occurring here. An inability to let go of anger in one's life. Extreme attachment is always involved here. As Buddha said, "All suffering is caused by attachment." Victim consciousness, lack of purpose, and self-pity is very prevalent.

Possession

Where obsession is being victimized by a subpersonality, possession is being victimized by an astral entity. It is always the person's psychology and philosophy that allows this to occur and attracts this in. Victim consciousness is operating here. There is no judgment in this and it is extremely common. It is important to clear the unwanted entity out as soon as possible. Use the matrix removal program in combination with going to Djwhal Khul's inner plane ashram and have the Masters remove them.

The only entities you want hanging around you are Christed and Ascended Beings of the fifth dimension or higher. When a person is run by the negative ego they tend to attract these lower astral entities. Almost all drug addicts and alcoholics attract them. The lesson here is to move from victim to Master, from effect to cause, and you will never be bothered again. We all have to deal occasionally with lower astral or dark force entities hanging around at times. Possession is a more extreme case of this.

Agoraphobia

Agoraphobia is when the negative ego, being fear, is projected onto the idea of it being dangerous to leave one's house. As with all phobias, it is all within one's own mind. Your thoughts create your reality. Fear can be projected onto everything or love can be projected onto everything or everyone. There are only two ways of thinking. This fear can be built in this life or a past life. It can be helpful here to do a regression and see where it came from. This is done in a hypnosis type situation, and often can clear it up right away by just partially or completely experiencing the situation which catalyzed. I use the word catalyze here for the true cause was always your thinking, not any outside situation.

Fear projection or phobias will always be created and manifest until full personal power and self-mastery is claimed and full command of the negative ego, subconscious mind, mental body, emotional body, physical body, and inner child are claimed. The fear and phobia is God's way of forcing you to either become dysfunctional or a God-realized Master. As *A Course In Miracles* says, "There are no neutral thoughts." All thoughts are of the negative ego or are of the Christ Mind. One is being forced to learn to think with their Christ Mind and to extend only love and never attack fear consciousness. The world is nothing more than a mirror of your own thinking. The idea here is to learn to stop "projecting fear" and to learn to only extend love!

Anemia

In the Edgar Cayce readings, a man in this lifetime had anemia and it was caused from a past life where he killed someone.

Leukemia

In another Edgar Cayce reading, a man had leukemia this lifetime and this came from a past life where he had knifed or shed someone else's blood with lower-self motivation. In this lifetime, he was now shedding his own blood. As Edgar Cayce said, "Every jot and tittle of the law is fulfilled." These last two are not the only causes but certainly are a great motivation to not create karma in this lifetime.

Liver Problems

Liver problems are often connected to too much negative anger, and/or over-planning or over-thinking. On a physical level, drugs of any and all kinds are deposited in the liver.

Pancreas Problems

This can stem from a number of reasons. One is a lack of sweetness or joy in life. On the other side of the coin, it can also be caused by too much focus on the sweetness or pleasures of life. One other interesting correlation of the pancreas is connected also to the use of the will. Too much use of one's will or not enough use of the will can adversely effect the pancreas. As with the liver it is connected to the proper integration of the third chakra in balance with the other chakras. On a physical level too much sugar, starch and even oil in one's diet can cause pancreas problems.

Heart Problems

This is obvious: inability to give love to self or others. The other side of the coin is an inability to receive love from self, others or God.

Homosexuality

I am listing this here, but, in truth, this is not an imbalance at all from the perspective of the Spiritual Hierarchy. It is a normal part of God's Creation for a certain percentage of the population, and any attempt to change this and look for a psychological, spiritual or karmic cause is faulty thinking.

Sociopath

This is a very interesting psychopathology. A sociopath is someone who has no "conscience." They are completely run by the negative ego, and they will say and do anything with no consideration of others. They are often pathological liars. Their word means nothing. They are clearly disconnected from their Higher Self and oversoul. It also stems from a lack of education of the difference between negative ego thinking and Christ Thinking.

What is scary is that I know a number of people who are clearly on a spiritual path and have New Age type businesses that I would call sociopaths. It is mind boggling to me that they can believe in New Age stuff, and even in the Masters, yet be so incredibly run by the negative ego. The sociopath usually also has enormous amounts of anger and is almost trying to punish the world. This can be karmic with the etheric body being extremely damaged in a past life and then quickly incarnating again before healing has taken place on the astral plane. Usually a lot of implants and psychic parasites are found.

Crib Deaths

Crib deaths have to do with the phenomena of a soul incarnating into a physical body at the time of birth and at the last second changing its mind. This can be a spontaneous occurrence or on occasion calculated for some karmic reason for the incarnating soul and for the parents. A physical body cannot live without a living soul to inhabit it.

Fear, Anxiety, and Paranoia

These are all derivatives of negative ego, which can be most easily defined as fear-based thinking. There are only two emotions, fear and love. All other emotions stem from these two. Perfect love casts out fear. There is fear-based thinking and love-based thinking. Fear is projected attack. If you believe in attacking others you will always live in fear. Edgar Cayce said, "Why worry when you can pray?" I would add why worry when you can pray, do affirmations, visualizations and own your personal power. Being loving at all times to self and others will remove fear. Giving up attack thoughts will remove fear. Praying, affirmations, and personal power will remove fear. Denial of the negative ego and the embracing of the Christ Consciousness erases fear. Paranoia is fear taken to a more extreme and exaggerated condition. Fear here is being projected onto everything and everyone.

The world and people are nothing more than a mirror and projection screen for your own thinking. The single most important lesson of life is to learn to project onto this screen and mirror only Christ thoughts and not negative ego thoughts. There are about 1% of our thoughts that might be considered reality-based fears that can serve as a protective function for the physical vehicle. Ninety-nine percent of our fears, however, are illusionary and stem from faulty thinking.

Alcoholism or Drug Addiction

This is always an escape. It is using a drug to escape emotional and psychological problems. What the person really needs is a spiritual teacher to help educate them about the purpose of life and how to heal themselves through the kinds of things I speak of in my books. What exacerbates this problem is what starts always because of psychological and emotional dysfunction also moves into a physical addiction. This is why the person must often get physically detoxed before true psychological healing can really take place. Alcoholism and drug addiction attract astral entities, negative elementals and extraterrestrial implants, which also need to be cleared for a full recovery. Proper integration of all three minds needs to be achieved, owning one's full power in God, personal power, and the power of the subconscious mind.

Narcissistic Personality Disorder

This is another character disorder I have often seen among lightworkers. Narcissism is an extreme case of self-centeredness. It seems also to be connected with being run by the inner child. A person who is narcissistic filters everything through a lens of "How does this affect me?" It is an over-preoccupation with the concerns of self. True God-realization is really just the opposite. It is to Self-actualize self so very little time needs to be focused upon self and one's life can be dedicated to the helping of others who are less fortunate then you.

I have seen a great many very high level initiates having very high levels of this type of character disorder which never ceases to amaze me given their initiation level. It just continues to point out the great discrepancy that can occur between one's spiritual development and psychological development. The narcissistic person processes everything in life as to how does this affect me, and never asks the question how does this affect others. It is similar to how a five-year-old child behaves. The physical body has grown and become an adult but the mental and emotional consciousness is still stuck in this self-centered and often very self-indulgent stage.

Alzheimer's Disease and Amnesia

Alzheimers disease is the person's losing over time their memory and cognitive faculties. There has been some interesting studies done that one potential cause of this may be aluminum poisoning. Americans use aluminum foil and aluminum pots and pans all the time. I remember I used to cook fish in aluminum foil two or three times a week and one time I went to my homeopathic doctor who did bioenergetic testing and he said I had aluminum poisoning without my telling him this fact.

With many diseases, we must keep the physical toxicity factors in mind. There can also be obvious psychological and spiritual diseases involved. A person with amnesia may just not want to remember as a type of defense mechanism. This could be a past life lesson or some kind of trauma to the brain. It is a fascinating phenomena how most people who have been sexually abused as children have no memory of it. It is usually in adulthood that these memories began to arise again. This is a healthy defense mechanism of the human psyche that helps people to cope.

Sleep Walking

Djwhal Khul said that in the case of sleep walking the astral body and the physical body merge together and the person sleepwalking is actually walking around in their astral body. Because of this merger, the physical body is carried along for the ride. Usually the astral body leaves at night and travels on its own plane of existence.

I will never forget the story of one of my clients about twelve years ago who was a young adolescent and who was doing a lot of acting out. He came in for a session one day and told me a story of how he was planning to steal his parent's car one night and go visit his girlfriend. He was planning this out all night; however, at the last minute he changed his mind before bed and decided not to do it. The only problem is that all his planning had programmed his subconscious mind. While sleep walking later that night he stole his parent's keys and opened the garage door and actually pushed the car out into the street without starting the ignition. He was afraid that starting the ignition would wake his parents up. He then pushed the car about two blocks down the street, got in it to start it up, and "woke up." The person is actually doing this on the astral plane and doesn't realize that they are bringing their physical body along for the ride.

Epilepsy

Djwhal said that epilepsy is a short circuit within the body and within the nervous system, that creates a short circuit within the brain pattern. It can often be connected to an overload of psychic and spiritual energies. What can happen here is that there can be a discrepancy between the readiness of the four-body system to receive these energies. As a person becomes more soul and monadically attuned and infused and the etheric body more aligned with the Divine pattern and strengthened, it is possible for a healing to take place. Vywamus is a good Master to call on for the healing and repair of the electrical system along with the Lord of Arcturus and the Arcturians.

There also are certain karmic causes of epilepsy. In two different Edgar Cayce readings, over-indulging in sexuality in a past life, and misusing psychic powers for an evil purpose in past lives caused epilepsy.

Dyslexia

Dyslexia has to do with certain electrical wiring in the nervous system and etheric body being crossed. This condition is where people displace letters and numbers. I have personally noticed that these people are often very gifted individuals. Djwhal said that one possible cause was that in a past life the person was more right brained and in this lifetime they were using the other brain more. On a subconscious level, they have not let go of the previous programming which at times overrides the existing program. It is connected with a third dimensional blockage. The right brain tends to block the use of the left side of the brain at times.

This may also explain my personal observation that these people are often very gifted, because of this right brain development in past lives. The dyslexic often is connected to a whole other level of intelligence. Unfortunately in our society they are severely punished for not fitting into the classic left brain norm. The Masters said dyslexia is connected to the right brain being more predominate, with the left brain being more difficult to access.

The reverse of this of course would be the person who is more left brain predominate and has a difficult time accessing the right brain. This is less noticed in our society, and this person is considered normal and is your classic scientist who is Godless and is totally disconnected to the soul and Higher Mind. Here we would have the worship of the intellect and no connection to intuition, imagination, and psychic senses.

The dyslexic doesn't operate the way they are expected to in school. They do operate how they are expected to operate in spiritual school. Now the ideal, of course, not that one side of the brain is better than another, is that they both must be integrated and balanced to their mutual full potential. Another way of saying this is the difficulty of left handed people to function in a right handed world. Stress can also play a part as to the severity and occurrence of dyslexia. The Masters added here stress due to competitiveness and comparing.

Miscarriages

The Masters said that this is usually a lesson for the person who had the miscarriage. The cause can be physical, psychological, karmic, or energetic. The incoming new baby doesn't incarnate until right around the time of birth so that is why the lesson is more for the mother and husband then the new soul. As with crib deaths, there is sometimes an antipathy or allergic reaction between the mother and soul on an emotional level that could be one cause.

There are obviously medical reasons why this can happen. In one case I heard about at a lecture, a woman and her family had an electrical fence around their house. She had over eleven miscarriages. As soon as they got rid of the electrical fence she was able to carry a baby to full term. A possible karmic reason would be a mother who had abandoned her child in a past life and now the child was abandoning her for spiritual growth reasons.

Very clearly, a miscarriage is a catalyst for spiritual growth if it will be used by the consciousness for this purpose. Many people in the third dimensional world pin the whole purpose in life on family and kids and not on God and their spiritual path. A person like this might be a prime candidate for a miscarriage because of the attachment and over-identification with having a child. The basic law of life is that that which one is attached to is ultimately taken away. One must learn to be involved in life but not attached. One must learn to have strong preferences but not addictions.

Schizophrenia

The image I got when asking about this was a lightening bolt splitting the person and the consciousness. This split can be caused from a past life or present life trauma. It can be connected to an imbalance of the feminine and masculine sides. It can be a loading down of negative alien implants more on one side of the brain then another. This can also be similar with negative elementals.

The circuits are eroded due to these factors. This creates havoc in the nervous system, which leads to the nervous or psychotic breakdowns. This is in part due to gaps and holes in the circuitry of the etheric and nervous system field, thus leading to a very aberrant pattern. In the case of the schizophrenic, you have erosion of the psychic walls. In the case of the multiple personality, you have the build up of the psychic walls.

Depression

Depression is a loss of personal power and in essence a subconscious and even conscious giving up and disconnection from the spiritual warrior archetype. The Masters said that depression could also be connected to a lack of understanding of the normal cycles of life and death within a given lifetime. Each initiation is a kind of death and rebirth process which people on the emotional level are often confused by. For example, at the fourth initiation the person disconnects from their Higher Self, who has been their teacher for eternity, only to be connected to a high level teacher which is the Spirit or monad. This is often disconcerting to the mental and emotional vehicles if not understood.

Some depressions are also brought in from other lifetimes, which stemmed from decisions that were made in these past lives that were not correct. This created a deep-seated guilt that became so heavy it led to a depression of the whole system. This can be seen as dark cloudy areas within the aura, where a lot of pain has built up from past lives or this life. This can also be seen as red areas in the aura, where there is irritation, and pressure because the person knows they have to do something to rectify some karmic lesson from their past.

This is often connected to the manic depressive roller coaster ride that stems from over-identification with the emotional body, subconscious mind, and negative ego, not yet having learned to cause their emotions through the science of attitudinal healing. The person in a depression may try a visualization of using a red ladder, which cultivates the first ray of power to climb out of the soup, so to speak. Often there is an etheric wound connected to the depression as well as a negative imprint (a sword in the heart for example).

Again, implants and elementals and astral entities can be involved here. Again, we say how limited traditional psychology is missing as much as three-quarters of the pie in terms of what is often really going on. There is the saying that depression is anger turned inwards. Anger and depression always go together. Anyone who is chronically angry will also be chronically depressed during more receptive periods. The person who is depressed does not need negative anger but rather positive anger or personal power and spiritual warrior energy to pull themselves out of the pit. Anger and depression are two sides of the negative ego coin. Their true antidote is personal power and love.

The harder the blows of life, the stronger and more powerful you must become. Here we have the importance of the spiritual warrior archetype and the positive use of the destruction archetype. Cayce called it positive anger. It is the cultivation of first ray energy at times of crisis to not allow life to beat one down. Surrender is a Christ quality as long as it is combined with personal power and love simultaneously. The person who is manic-depressive must learn evenmindedness, equanimity, and unchanging inner peace and joy regardless of outside circumstance. The person who is prone to depression finds happiness outside of self inserted of in their "state of mind"!

Depression most definitely could be anger turned inward, or a negative anger turned outward. Anger should not be blocked but rather channeled as a source of power towards love and Christ ideals. The etheric wounds I spoke of earlier, such as a sword or other object still embedded in the etheric body, must be removed for it is creating an added pressure to the system. Eventually hospitals will have teams of people who can work medically, nutritionally, psychologically, psychically, spiritually, etherically, mentally, and emotionally so a complete clearing and healing can occur.

In some ways it is amazing that people ever heal in hospitals; adding to this the fact that there is so much negative energy embedded in the walls and only the physical level is addressed. Even that level is not very effective given the rejection of such things as homeopathics, herbs, acupuncture, nutrition, radionics and so on. The drugs used poison the liver and body and create other problems, so really it is just for emergency functions that they have any real value. I personally never would go to a medical doctor except in this kind of situation.

Ronald Beasely, the great spiritual master from England who is no longer in embodiment, used to say that hospitals should be burned down every five years because of the build up of negative energy. It is hard for a person to heal in that kind of atmosphere. The level of healing they are working on is literally just a sliver of the whole pie. Can you imagine how great it will be in the future when a person goes to a hospital and has a medical doctor, spiritual counselor, psychic healer, nutritionist, massage therapist, wholistic practitioner, acupuncturist, hypnotherapist, radionics specialist, naturopath or homeopathist, social worker, family counselor, channel, astrologer, clairvoyant, and healer all consulting together and working together as a team for a complete healing?

Psychotic

A person who is psychotic is completely run by the subconscious mind and negative ego. There is no conscious control. There are always gaping holes in the aura, and usually they are possessed. This can manifest into a suicidal or homicidal form. The psychotic is filled with negative elementals and alien implants. The psychotic truly needs to be hospitalized to become stabilized for the long process of healing and recovery to occur. The psychotic's field may actually be black.

The Neurotic

The neurotic is not as bad off as the schizophrenic or psychotic. The neurotic is much more common, and their auric fields tend to be gray rather than black. The neurotic is still functional in the world where the psychotic and schizophrenic are clearly not. In the neurotic the circuits are often weak, mixed, confused, gray or cloudy, and often filled with etheric mucous. The neurotic often has different kinds of obsessive or compulsive behaviors that are all a product of allowing the subconscious mind to control the conscious mind too much. Not enough mastery has been achieved over the mental, emotional, physical bodies, and negative ego.

This is also connected to improper inner parenting skills in regard to the inner child. The neurotic has not snapped, had a nervous breakdown, or had a split in their personality. It is still in the realm of minor dysfunction not major dysfunction. Sometimes this can be connected to being unprepared for rising of the kundalini. This happens often among lightworkers where the spiritual bodies are more advanced then the psychological bodies. The energies rise and the Light comes in with greater intensity and the psychological self is not equipped to channel this energy properly through the mental and emotional vehicles. It thus may manifest as fear, negative emotions, uncontrolled sexuality, and lower self-desire.

This is why it is very important to refine and develop all three levels equally (physical, psychological, and spiritual). The rising of the kundalini can, in truth, manifest in all the symptomologies listed in this chapter if the person is not balanced in their overall understanding.

Contagious Diseases

One of the great illusions of Western medicine is the concept of contagious disease. There is no such thing. There are only people with low resistance. This applies on the physical as well as the psychological level. The concept of contagious diseases was invented by a person with victim consciousness. We each are God and the cause not the effect of anything outside of ourselves. This applies to the negativity of others as well as the bacteria or virus infections of others. There is no disease that is contagious if you are in balance and, hence, have a strong immune system. Disease cannot grow in a healthy body environment. Even in regards to AIDS, not all people who are exposed to AIDS get it.

Cancer

Cancer basically has to do with a disintegration of certain cells in the body. This whole book is really dealing with the need for balance and integration of one's psychoepistemology, archetypes, rays, feminine and masculine energies, and so on. When a person is not spiritually psychologically, and physically balanced and integrated this manifests within the cells because of the Hermetic Law, as within so without, as above so below. Prolonged lack of integration and balance spiritually and psychologically will ultimately manifest physically. Now there are many reasons for cancer. Some forms can result from physical toxins such as prolonged exposure to pesticides, or radiation. Some forms of cancer can come from energetic poisoning like electrical power lines or prolonged use of cellular phones, or police officers using those radar guns. Other times it can come from the emotional body and prolonged running on negative emotions that eventually debilitate certain cellular structure.

It can result from the mental body and prolonged negative thinking. It can come from the spiritual body in the sense of prolonged lack of integration and fusion with the soul and Spirit. Living in a bad marriage or in a job you dislike can take a toll on the body. Improper nutrition, or prolonged use of alcohol or drugs. Anyone of these things or a mixture of these can be the cause. Sometimes cancer is a past life karmic lesson. The Masters said that sometimes the cancer is the body's reaction to prolonged affect from alien implants, and negative elementals. Tumors are often formed around these areas. This again is an example of the shortcomings of Western medicine who may cut out the cancer, but since the implants and elementals are still there it just grows back again.

The Masters basically said that all disease has to do with negative elementals or aberrant thoughtforms. Disease is the physical manifestation of negative ego thinking. Perfect health is the manifestation on the physical level of Christ thinking. The negative thoughts of the negative ego grow in the mental body, which creates a negative feeling in the emotional body, which builds negative energy in the etheric body, which eventually manifests into the physical structure.

This is really the "law of manifestation," working in the wrong direction. As sons and daughters of God, we can't help but to manifest every moment of our lives. The question is not whether we can manifest, but rather what are we manifesting. It is just as easy to manifest health as sickness; it is just a matter of choice. As *A Course In Miracles* says, "Sickness is a defense against the truth." The truth is that each one of us is the Christ, Buddha, the Eternal Self and perfection is our divine birthright if we will just claim it.

Cancer can also be genetically predisposed. One way to remedy this is to ask the Masters to clear your entire genetic line, and to know that you do not have to be a victim of family genetics either. This is a choice also which most people aren't aware they have. One of the best cancer preventatives is to ask the Arcturians to clear all cancers in the entire body from the etheric, mental, emotional, and physical fields.

Another cancer preventative from Edgar Cayce is to eat six almonds a day. Apparently, almonds have some ingredient in them that repels cancer. Hanna Kroeger, the renowned herbalist, says that a fungus causes cancer and that she has herbal remedies that will clear this up in a matter of weeks. The main thing is to work on all levels in a holistic and synergistic approach

19

The Psychological Causes of Disease
by Djwhal Khul

To begin this chapter I thought the best way to start would be to quote Djwhal Khul's first law of healing as stated in the Alice Bailey book *Esoteric Healing*: "All disease is the result of inhibited soul life, and that is true of all forms in all kingdoms. The art of the healer consists in releasing the soul, so that its life can flow through the aggregate of organisms which constitute any particular form."

All initiates of the Great White Brotherhood are healers. Not all initiates may work on healing the physical body, however all initiates are transmitters of spiritual energy. The four bodies that need healing are the physical, etheric, astral, and mental.

Djwhal Khul says that 90% of the causes of physical disease occurs within the etheric and astral body. This is because most people in the world are still emotionally polarized or identified. In a million years hence, when the human attention is more focused collectively in the mind, then the cause of disease will have to be sought in the mind realm.

The first work of any group of healers is to establish themselves in love and to work towards group unity and understanding. The two qualities of any true healer are "magnetism and radiation". The healer must be magnetic to his own soul, to those he would help, and to the energies needed to stimulate a transformation within the client. The healer must then understand how to radiate soul energy, which will stimulate into activity the soul of the one to be healed. The radiation of the mind of the healer will illumine the mind and will of the patient. The healthy radiation of the astral and etheric body of the healer will work in a likewise fashion upon the patient.

All disease is caused by a lack of harmony. Disease results as a lack of alignment between soul and form, and/or subjective and objective reality. Lack of harmony, which we call disease, affects all four kingdoms of nature. The outer environmental causes of disease are four-fold, according to Djwhal. They are accidents, infections, disease due to malnutrition, and heredity.

The psychological causes of disease are also four-fold. These are:

1. Those coming from the emotional and feeling nature.
2. Those that have their origin in the etheric body.
3. Those based on wrong thought.
4. Those complaints unique to disciples and initiates.

Much of the failure of the healing methods people use come from the following reasons:

1. Inability to locate what body the trouble is stemming from.
2. Knowing where the patient stands upon the ladder of evolution.
3. Inability to differentiate whether the disease is from inner personal conditions, inherited tendencies, or group karma of some kind.
4. Inability on the healer's part to know if the problem should be dealt with allopathically, homeopathically, through right inner psychological adjustment, through soul power, or through occult methods invoking the help of a Master.

Djwhal says that healing is brought about basically through three ways.
1. Through methods of traditional medicine and/or surgery.
2. Through the use of psychology.
3. Through the activity of the soul.

It is the astral body for the majority of mankind that is the outstanding cause of ill health. The reason is that it has such a potent affect on the person's etheric body, which is the energy body and battery for the physical body.

Basically we are speaking here of uncontrolled and ill-regulated emotions such as fear, worry, irritation, anger, criticism, hatred, superiority and inferiority complex, and so on. It is the corollary of the astral body, which is lower-self desire, which leads people to over-eat and drink. Poor diet, hence, has its cause in the astral body. Other diseases caused by the desire body are the sexual diseases and over-indulgence in sexuality, which has a weakening effect on the etheric and physical vehicles.

The true healer needs to be trained not only in healing, but also in psychology, medical matters, and esoteric knowledge. Your average medical doctor has absolutely no understanding of the etheric body or the chakras, let alone the soul. The esoteric healer needs to be more aware of the physical earth plane knowledge that the doctor has.

Disease is most definitely a purification process when looked at esoterically. Traditional doctors must understand that disease may be a gradual and slow process of the soul withdrawing from the body to free it for other service. The overwhelming desire to keep the physical body alive, by most traditional medical doctors, is not always appropriate.

The astral body is the cause of most disease because it is the body the bulk of humanity is centering their consciousness in. It is also the most developed of the bodies being the latest to develop in collective mankind. It reached its high point of development in Atlantean days. This is also augmented by the energy coming from the animal kingdom, which is entirely astral in its point of attainment. Although we are in the

Aryan root race, the mass of humanity has not achieved a mental polarization and identification yet.

The Three Major Diseases

The three major groups of diseases, according to Djwhal Khul, are tuberculosis, the sexually transmitted diseases (venereal, syphilis, AIDS), and cancer. Two other diseases which Djwhal says affects those who are a little above average are heart diseases and nervous diseases. These five groups, and there are various subdivisions, are responsible for most of the illness of humanity. The three most important aspects of diagnosis are the psychological, the work of the endocrinologist, and the physician.

Mankind also inherits disease from four basic sources:
1. From his own past in this life or past lives.
2. From the general racial heritage of humanity.
3. From the condition of planetary life.
4. From parental inherited tendencies.

It is when the upper chakras above the diaphragm are awakened that a long series of lives with heart and nervous system lessons occur. These have been called diseases of the mystics.

The sexually transmitted diseases, except for AIDS (man-made chemical warfare experiment gone awry), are remnants from over-indulgence in Lemurian times when man was totally polarized in the physical vehicle.

Cancer is from the Atlantean root race and is astrally and emotionally connected. Cancer is a disease of inhibition just as syphilitic diseases are over-expression, and overuse.

Tuberculosis is a disease of the Aryan race, although began in later Atlantean times. Tuberculosis is caused by the shift of polarization from the emotional body to the mental body, or from Atlantean consciousness to the Aryan consciousness. It is a disease of depletion of the emotional body.

Cancer came from the shift of life force from the physical polarization to the emotional polarization, or from the Lemurian consciousness to the Atlantean consciousness. As the race develops tighter emotional control, Djwhal says, cancer will begin to disappear.

Many of the problems of humanity are caused by the burial of sick, diseased bodies in the soil instead of cremating them. Djwhal has prophesied that in the New Age burial for bodies will be outlawed, and cremation will become the norm.

Diseases of Worry and Irritation

Diseases of worry and irritation have the following effects on people:
1. The lower the vitality of the person, the more susceptible they are to disease.
2. The connection is poor in certain directions or aspects of the equipment.
3. The connection between the etheric and physical body is so loose that the soul has very little control over its vehicle.
4. The fourth reason is the opposite of the third. The etheric body is too closely knit with the personality and physical vehicle.

The third cause of disease in the etheric body is the overstimulation of the chakras. This, of course, has a very deleterious affect on the glands, which effects the blood stream and all the organs.

Causes of Disease Arising Out of the Mental Body

The first cause of disease from the mental body is from "wrong mental attitudes." The second cause is mental fanaticism and dominance of thought forms. The third cause is frustrated idealism.

Diseases of Disciples

Most of these diseases arise from the transferring of the solar plexus energy into the heart. This transfer causes stomach, liver and respiratory problems. Djwhal says that all diseases and physical difficulties are caused by one of the following three conditions:

1. A developed soul contact which produces a vitalization of all the chakras. This necessarily produces stress and strain on the physical body.
2. The attempt of the personality to negate soul control. The stress on the physical body here is obvious.
3. A shift in the life force from personality to soul control, or from lower self to higher self, which causes re-adjustment problems within the physical vehicle.

Medicine in The Next Century

Medicine in the next century will focus on five basic premises:
1. Preventive medicine.
2. Sound sanitation.
3. The supply of right chemical properties to the physical body
4. An emphasis on understanding the laws of vitality, vitamins and minerals, and sunshine.
5. The use of the mind in healing will be regarded above all else.

The Four Groups of Healers

In the future there will need to be much more synthesis and integration between the following four groups of healers. These four, as described by Djwhal Khul in the Alice Bailey book *Esoteric Healing*, are:
1. Physicians and surgeons
2. Psychologists, neurologists, and psychiatrists
3. Mental healers, new thought workers, unity thinkers and Christian Science practitioners
4. Trained disciples and initiates who work with the souls of men

Liberation and Freedom

The ideals of liberation and freedom are integral to achieving perfect health for an individual and humanity as a whole. Djwhal says that there have been four great symbolic happenings in the past 2000 years that have epitomized the theme of liberation. These are:

1. The life of Christ, Himself.
2. The signing of the Magna Carta.
3. The emancipation of the slaves.
4. The liberation of humanity by the United Nations.

Karma and Health

Djwhal has delineated nine types of karma. These are:

1. Elementary group karma of the primitive man.
2. Individual karma of the self-conscious developing man.
3. Karma related to the life of discipleship.
4. Hierarchical karma.
5. Karma of retribution.
6. Karma of reward.
7. National karma.
8. Racial karma.
9. Educational karma.

Karma is not an inevitable and inescapable happening. It can be off-set, where disease is concerned, by four lines of activity. These are:

1. Determining the nature of the cause and the area of consciousness where it originated.
2. Developing those qualities which are the polar opposite of the effective cause.
3. Practicing "harmlessness."
4. Mental acceptance, wise action along medical lines, the assistance of a healer or healing group, clear soul inspired visualization as to the outcome.

This could mean perfect health and the preparation for service on the inner plane.

How to Ascertain Location of Congestion

Traditional medical testing is extremely limited, expensive, and doesn't deal with the subtle bodies or psychological level, so it is not really useful in finding the location of congestion. The three methods Djwhal has recommended, which will be much more in practice in the future, are:

1. Clairvoyance
2. Clear knowing, which is a soul faculty.
3. Occult transference or occult empathy, where the healer registers the patient's difficulty in their own body.

Causes of certain types of diseases, arthritis and diabetes, have their origin in the astral body. Diabetes is the result of wrong inner desires, according to Djwhal. This can originate in this life or a past life. Syphilis and arthritis are caused by over-indulgence in "physical desire." Diseases such as measles, scarlet fever, smallpox, and cholera have their cause in the emotional body.

Fever is an indication of trouble and is a way of purifying and eliminating impurities. It is an indicator, not a disease in itself. This is why, if possible, it is best to let the fever have its way for a time. It has a definite therapeutic value as long as it is not too high temperature wise, nor lasts too long. Over-emotionalism is that astral correspondence to a fever. Over-mentalizing is the mental plane correspondence to a fever.

Germs

Where there is an inherent weakness in the physical body, there is a corresponding weakness in life force in that area of the etheric body. This congestion or area of arrested development leaves an opening for germs to grow. Where the vitality is strong and the soul and life force is flowing, germs cannot grow. I repeat, there is no such thing as contagious disease. There are only people with low resistance.

Humanity is one, and all people, whether they have Eastern or Western bodies, are prone to the same diseases and symptoms.

Mental Disease

The major causes of mental disease, according to Djwhal, are:
1. Disease of the brain
2. Disorders of the solar plexus
3. Astral domination
4. Premature clairvoyance and clairaudience
5. Obsession
6. Absence of mind
7. Soulessness

The Future Schools of Healing

The following list of the future schools of healing is from the Alice Bailey book *Esoteric Healing*:
1. Psychological adjustments and healing
2. Magnetic healing
3. Allopathic healing
4. Homeopathic healing
5. Surgical healing in its modern forms
6. Electro-therapeutics
7. Water therapy
8. Healing by color and sound and radiation.
9. Preventative medicine
10. Osteopathy and chiropractic
11. Scientific neurology and psychiatry
12. The cure of obsessions and mental diseases
13. The care of the eyes and ears
14. Voice culture
15. Mental and faith healing
16. Soul alignment and contact

The Rays and Disease

The syphilitic diseases are due to a misuse of the third ray energy. Tuberculosis is a result of the misuse of the second ray energy. Cancer is a misuse of the first ray energy.

The Basic Requirements of Healing

Djwhal Khul has enumerated ten basic prerequisites for healing. They are as follows:

1. The recognition of the great law of cause and effect.
2. Correct diagnosis of the disease by a competent doctor and spiritual clairvoyant.
3. A belief in the law of immediate karma. This means knowing whether it is one's destiny to be healed or make one's transition to the spiritual plane.
4. A recognition that healing of the physical body might be detrimental from the desire of the soul. In other words, the soul might want the physical body to die.
5. The active cooperation of the healer and the patient.
6. A complete acceptance by the patient of the dictates of the soul.
7. An effort on the part of the healer and patient to express harmlessness.
8. An effort by the patient to hold a spiritual attitude instead of a negative egotistical attitude.
9. The deliberate elimination of qualities, thoughts, and desires that might be hindering the inflow of spiritual force.
10. The capacity of the healer and patient to integrate into the soul group.

It is of the highest importance for people and/or patients to remember that continuance of life in the physical body is not the highest possible goal.

Djwhal Khul, in the Alice Bailey book called *Esoteric Healing*, has listed fifteen qualities required by a healer. Do remember that all disciples on the path are healers, for all disciples channel spiritual energy.

15 Qualities Required by a Healer

1. The power to contact and work as a soul. "The art of the healer consists in releasing the soul."
2. The power to command the spiritual will.
3. The power to establish telepathic rapport. This has to do with the healer knowing the inner thoughts and desires of the patient intuitively.
4. He must have exact knowledge. This quality has to do with understanding the knowledge of how to contact and invoke the soul and receive impressions. This is the exact science of knowledge the healer must have.
5. The power to reverse, reorient, and exalt the consciousness of the patient. The healer must become proficient as to "lifting the downward focused eyes unto the soul."
6. The power to direct soul energy to the necessary area.
7. The power to express magnetic purity and the needed radiance.
8. Power to control the activity of the mechanism of the head. This has to do with linking the minor chakra centers in the head.
9. Power of the chakras.
10. Power to utilize both exoteric and esoteric methods of healing.
11. Power to work magnetically. This means to be able to magnetically draw the power of the soul and spirit through oneself as a channel for the healing of the patient.
12. Power to work with radiation. This is the power to not only receive soul energy, but to send it.
13. Power to practice at all times complete harmlessness.
14. Power to control the will and work through love.

15. Power to eventually wield the law of life. This ability comes when ones merger with the spiritual triad (spiritual will, intuition, Higher Mind) is achieved. The spiritual triad merges with the three-fold personality. Third Initiation is soul fusion. This would be monadic fusion, at fifth and sixth initiations.

The Healer and His Attunement

The healer in the New Age will have the ability to make the following contacts with great ease:
1. With his own soul.
2. With the soul of his patient.
3. With the particular type of energy in the soul or personality ray of the patient.
4. With his own chakra that is needed in any given healing for transmitting spiritual energy.
5. With the chakra in the patient's etheric body which controls the area where the disease is located.

A person's disease is subject to three influences:
1. A person's past ancient errors.
2. A person's inheritance.
3. His sharing with all natural forms, which the Lord of Life imposes on his body.

The Healer and His Ability To Diagnose

There are four aspects to a healer's ability to diagnose a proper treatment for his patient. These are:
1. The healer must train himself to know whether a patient is mentally or emotionally based.
2. He must be able to ascertain the psychological basis of the problem.
3. This will then lead to his ability to find the location of the disease.
4. This will allow him to know the area affected, and the chakra in the etheric body that controls that area.

When a patient is a mental type, the approach must be through a higher center, in the crown chakra. The healer must learn the following eight principles in relationship to himself:

1. Rapid alignment between the soul, mind, crown chakra, and physical brain.
2. The use of the mind, illumined by the soul, in psychological diagnosis.
3. Methods for establishing a sympathetic rapport with the patient.
4. Methods of protecting himself during the transfer of energy brought about by this rapport.
5. The establishing of a right relationship with the patient.
6. Physical diagnosis, and the locating of the area to which relief must come, via the controlling of the chakra.
7. The art of cooperation with the patient's soul so the etheric body focuses all its inflowing energies in order to bring relief to the diseased area.
8. The technique of withdrawing his/her healing power when the patient is stabilized.

The Third Eye and The Perfected Man

In the perfected person the following relationships can be found, as described by Djwhal Khul in the Alice Bailey book *Esoteric Healing*:

1. The eye of the soul–The agent of the spiritual triad–Will
2. The third eye–Agent of the soul–Love
3. The right eye–The distributor of Buddhic energy
4. The left eye–Conveyor of pure manasic (mind) energy.
5. The ajna center–Focusing and directing point for all these energies.

In the disciple who is beginning to function as a soul, it is interesting to see the differences.

1. Third eye–Distributor of soul energy.
2. The right eye–Agent for astral energy.

3. The left eye–Agent for lower mental energy.
4. The ajna center–Focusing point of these three energies.

The Laws and Rules of Healing

In this part I am just directly quoting with no explanation, the nine laws, and six rules of healing according to Djwhal Khul as transcribed by Alice Bailey in her book called *Esoteric Healing*. Some of the laws are a little esoteric and hard to understand at points, however some of the truths are so profound that I thought it would be worth the reader's time to place them in this chapter. For a greater explanation of these laws, for those who want to learn more, do read Alice Bailey's book.

LAW I
All disease is the result of inhibited soul life. This is true of all forms in all kingdoms. The art of the healer consists in releasing the soul so that its life can flow through the aggregate of organisms, which constitute any particular form.

LAW II
Disease is the product of and subject to three influences:

First, a man's past, wherein he pays the price of ancient error (reincarnational history);

Second, his inheritance, wherein he shares with all mankind those tainted streams of energy which are of group origin (racial-cultural history);

Third, he shares with all the natural forms that which the Lord of Life imposes on His body. These three influences are called the "Ancient Law of Evil Sharing." This must give place some day to that new "Law of Ancient Dominating Good"which lies behind all that God has made. This law must be brought into activity by the spiritual will of man.

Rule One

Let the healer train himself to know the inner stage of thought or of desire of the one who seeks his help. He can thereby know the source from whence the trouble comes. Let him relate the cause and the effect and know the exact point through relief must come.

LAW III

Disease is an effect of the basic centralization of a man's life energy. From the plane whereon those energies are focused proceed those determining conditions which produce ill health. These therefore work out as disease or as freedom from disease.

LAW IV

Disease, both physical and psychological, has its roots in the good, the beautiful and the true. It is but a distorted reflection of Divine possibilities. The thwarted soul, seeking full expression of some divine characteristic or inner spiritual reality, produces within the substance of its sheaths, a point of friction. Upon this point, the eyes of the personality are focused and this leads to disease. The art of the healer is concerned with the lifting of the downward focused eyes into the soul, the Healer within the form. The spiritual or third eye then directs the healing force and all is well.

Rule Two

The healer must achieve magnetic purity, through purity of life. He must attain that dispelling radiance which shows itself in every man when he has linked the centers in the head. When this magnetic field is established, the radiation then goes forth.

LAW V

There is naught but energy, for God is Life. Two energies meet in man, but another five are present (seven rays-seven chakras). For each is to be found a central point of contact. The conflict of these energies with forces and of forces twixt themselves, produce the bodily ills of men. The conflict of the first and second (the soul and personality) persists for ages until the mountaintop is reached–the first great mountaintop. The fight between the forces produces all disease, all ills and bodily pain which seek release in death. The two, the five and thus the seven, plus that which they produce, possess the secret. This is the Fifth Law of Healing within the world of form.

Rule Three
Let the healer concentrate the needed energy within the needed center. Let the center correspond to the center which has need. Let the two synchronize and together augment force. Thus shall the waiting form be balanced in its works. Thus shall the two and the one, under right direction, heal.

LAW VI
When life or energy flows unimpeded and through right direction to its precipitation (the related gland), then the form responds and ill health disappears.

Rule Four
A careful diagnosis of disease, based on the ascertained outer symptoms, will be simplified to this extent–that once the organ involved is known and thus isolated, the center in the etheric body which is in closest relation to it will be subjected to methods of occult healing though the ordinary, ameliorative, medical or surgical methods and will not be withheld.

LAW VII
Disease and death are the results of two active forces. One is the will of the soul, which says to its instrument, "I draw the essence back." the other is the magnetic power of the planetary life, which says to the life within the atomic structure, "The hour of reabsorption has arrived. Return to me." Thus, under cyclic law, do all forms act.

Rule Five

The healer must seek to link his soul, his heart, his brain, and his hands. Thus can his presence feed the soul life of the patient. *This is the work of radiation.* The hands are not needed; the soul displays its power. The patient's soul responds through the response of his aura to the radiation of the healer's aura, flooded with soul energy.

LAW VIII

Perfection calls imperfection to the surface. Good drives evil from the form of man in time and space. The method used by the Perfect One and that employed by Good, is harmlessness. This is not lack of negativity but perfect poise, a completed point of view and Divine understanding.

Rule Six

The healer or the healing group must keep the will in leash. It is not will that must be used, but love.

LAW IX

Harken, O Disciple, to the call which comes from the Son to the Mother (soul to body), and then obey. The Word goes forth that form has served its purpose. The principle of mind then organizes itself and then repeats that Word. The waiting form responds and drops away. The soul stands free.

Respond, O Rising One, to the call which comes within the sphere of obligation: recognize the call emerging for Ashram or the Council Chambers (heart center or head center) where waits the Lord of Life Himself. The Sound goes forth. Both soul and form together must renounce the principle of life and thus permit the Monad to stand free. The soul responds. The form then shatters the connection. Life is now liberated, owning the quality of conscious knowledge and the fruit of all experience. These are the gifts of soul and form combined. This last law is the enunciation of a new law which is substituted for the law of

Death, and which has reference only to those upon the latter stages of the Path of Discipleship and the stages upon the Path of Initiation."

Summation

One more time I wish to acknowledge that the information for this chapter was garnished from the Alice Bailey book *Esoteric Healing* which I highly recommend for those who would like to take even a deeper look at this subject. We all owe a great debt to Alice Bailey for the wonderful telepathic information she was able to bring forth from Djwhal Khul on this subject!

20

A Battleplan as to How to Deal with Chronic Health Problems

This particular chapter is an extremely important chapter in this book. I would venture to guess that 50% of all lightworkers suffer from some kind of chronic health lesson. In a person's entire lifetime on Earth, probably 99% of all people will have chronic health lessons at some point. Every person on planet Earth, except maybe the descent of an Avatar such as Sai Baba and Lord Maitreya, has some weakness in the four-body system. I have never met a single person in my entire life that doesn't, including myself.

Some people have a weakness in their physical vehicle in some area. Some have a weakness in their emotional vehicle. Some in the mental vehicle. Others in their spiritual vehicle. And others have a weakness in their bank account. If this weren't the case, you probably would not be incarnated on this planet.

Part of the reason for the physical health problems is also a spiritual one. Spiritual evolution is moving so quickly that certain health problems are unavoidable and are just a byproduct of growing spiritually so, in truth maybe consider it a good sign. Other reasons for health problems are all the environmental pollution, pesticides, car exhaust, water pollution, metals poisoning, and the like. Another reason is that this is a very tough school and keeping the mental body, emotional body, physical body, and spiritual body all balanced all the time is no easy task.

Add to that the enormous amount of psychic negativity we all have to deal with living on this planet and which we see on television and the mass media. Then add to this all the past life karma that we are processing that can debilitate the body when wanting to move fast on the spiritual path. Add to this the genetic weaknesses we come in with from past lives and our genetic heritage. Add to this still the fact that we must process the karma from our twelve soul extensions from our oversoul and then must process the 144 soul extensions from our monad in terms of integrating and cleansing their karma. Then we have to deal with the collective consciousness karma.

We all live in a gray cloud of astral debris that surrounds this planet. The same is true of the etheric body, mental body, and physical body of this planet. On the physical level, this is called smog, pollution, gigantic holes in the ozone layer, and depletion of rain forests. The food we buy from the market is dead and processed. The meat is filled with chemicals. The chickens have cancer and salmonella bacteria. Our food is being nuked by radiation and the FDA has approved this. There is a fast food restaurant on every corner. People eat way too much sugar. The produce is not energized because the nature spirits do not inhabit the farms because of the use of pesticides and man's inability to work with nature. Even the produce contains only 10% of the energy it should.

People then don't clear, pray, and energize their food before they eat it with some kind of soma board, energy plate, or formal prayer procedure. Although it may look healthy, 90% of the time it will have a negative spin on it if you tested it with a pendulum. That is because of pesticides, the people who have touched it in the market, or because of the red radar that is pumped through it at the grocery counter. Added to this is the fact that most people don't have good habits of food combining and overeating, or just laziness in regards to diet. In addition is the enormous amount of stress we are all under in our modern day society, with workaholic tendencies. We also have to deal with alien implants and dark force attack at times.

The effects of occasional negative thinking, worrying, family responsibilities, money pressures, negative imprints, lack of self love, and relationship problems, are more factors. All these things cause a weakening of the immune system over time. Then we have accidents of innumerable kinds that take a toll on the body, and other traumas such as divorces, deaths in the family and lost jobs. We have damage to the etheric body from past lives that has not been repaired which causes people to be working off an imperfect blueprint. Imbalanced psychoepistemologies, which are pretty much universal with everybody, also take a toll on the physical body.

We also have to fight off all the negative suggestions that get into the subconscious mind, such as in winter time the television ads that say flu season is here. One has to remain constantly vigilant to not let the subconscious mind be programmed by all these negative suggestions of people, friends, coworkers, family members and mass media. People are getting sick all the time around us with colds, flu, bacteria infections, and viruses.

It is true that there is no such thing as a contagious disease only low resistance, however the problem is most people have a lowered immune system from all the above mentioned factors. If you live in a big city you can add the sound pollution which takes a toll much more then you realize. Take for example car alarms. If sound can heal, what does a car alarm do? Most spiritual people are very sensitive, much more than the average person, and it can be very difficult living in a world such as this.

A lot of lightworkers not used to doing such things as having to make money and be the spiritual warrior they have to be to just make it.

People with kids have an even greater burden. Then we have modern day plagues such as AIDS and Epstein Bar. The problem is our environment doesn't really support us because so much of it is based on third dimensional not fifth dimensional consciousness. Given all these factors it is amazing and miraculous that our physical bodies hold us up as well as they do.

Another thing to factor in here is the higher one evolves the quicker your karma returns and the more sensitive you become. Where as a child or adolescent you could eat a bag of cookies and ice cream and feel fine. Now one cookie may foul you up or make you not feel right. Also the older one gets the more careful one must be. In our busy society most people don't exercise enough, get enough sunshine and fresh air, and don't eat as well as they should. I could go on and on and on.

You should congratulate your physical body and body elemental for holding up as well as it has. God forbid you do get sick and you have to stay in a hospital. With all the terrible energy, terrible food, and narrow-minded physicians it is amazing people ever recover.

Another factor here is that the higher one evolves in the initiation process the more planetary karma they begin processing through their system. This is part of the responsibility of becoming an Ascended Master and cannot be completely avoided. People in the healing professions often take on karma of their students and patients, not only during sessions, but often at night while they sleep. So much goes on at night on the inner plane that people don't recognize.

The most important thing is to not look at disease or ill health as a bad thing, for it is not. It is just a teaching lesson, challenge, and opportunity to grow. Earlier in my life, I almost died from a very serious case of hepatitis. In the long run, as I look back I would never be in the place I am now if I hadn't gotten so ill. Illness teaches us obedience to God's Laws. This experience completely changed my life forever.

One of the most difficult lessons in this world is dealing with chronic health lessons. I personally have great compassion for people who deal with this for I have dealt with it myself. It is hard for people who have never dealt with chronic health lessons to understand. As I said earlier their lessons may be on emotional, mental, spiritual or financial levels which can be as great a hardship and sometimes even worse.

Lesson 1
The first most important lesson is that health problems are not bad. They are good, for they are teaching you something you need to learn. Djwhal Khul says disease is a purification process. If looked at properly it will help you to become stronger. If looked at properly it will accelerate your spiritual growth.

Lesson 2
When dealing with chronic health problems first look at it as a blessing in disguise and a teacher, secondly and most importantly do not give your power to your physical body. This is the great error of faulty thinking that most people make. They see their personal power as being connected to their physical vitality and wakefulness. When they get tired and run down they connect their personal power to this. A most important thing in life is to maintain your personal power at all times regardless of what your physical, astral, mental, or spiritual bodies are doing. As the Bhagavad-Gita says, "Remain in evenmindedness whether you have profit or loss, victory or defeat, sickness or health."

God-consciousness remains the same regardless of the state of health or lack there of. I cannot emphasize the importance of this more. If you do not do this every time your body goes out, your emotional and mental bodies will take a dive bomb with it.

Lesson 3
Just because you don't have perfect health doesn't mean you can't have a life. Many people have cancer and live very full and effective lives.

Many people have arthritis or chronic pain and still live full and active lives. Don't be a perfectionist. If you wait to have perfect health to live, you just may never live. Mother Teresa has serious heart problems and look at all she does. I have had digestive sensitivity most of my adult life. I have not let it stop me. I call this the Saint Francis Initiation. Saint Francis (Kuthumi in a past life) had enormous health lessons yet continued to serve. This concept and understanding has been, in the past, very meaningful to me. I recognized through this that I was being tested by God. If you have health lessons, be like Saint Francis and proudly and with great dignity live your life.

I remember a story Yogananda told of his great disciple Sri Gyanaata who had 20 years of chronic health problems. When she finally died and he gave his eulogy for her God spoke to Yogananda and told him He was especially proud of Sri Gyanaata for she served him for the last twenty years with poor health.

Lesson 4

The next lesson for those with chronic health lessons of some kind is the Job initiation. I think you all know the story of Job, how he was tested by God and the devil to test his righteousness in the Lord. The story of Job is the story of each person on this planet who has at some point had everything stripped away. There is not a soul in incarnation that, in one of their lives, if not most of them, has not gone through this initiation. Actually, it is part of passing the fourth initiation, which is the renunciation initiation and the lesson of letting go of attachments. When the Job initiation hits, everything is lost. Health goes, often the marriage goes, the job goes, inner peace goes, and so on down the line in any combination. This is a spiritual test.

Every person can serve God when things are going well. How many people keep the faith and righteousness in the Lord when everything goes wrong? This is the true test. Money, fame, fortune, relationship health, and power are idol worshipping if put before God. After suffering greatly Job finally realized this and said, "Naked I come from my mother's womb, and naked shall I go, The Lord giveth and the Lord taketh away, blessed be the name of the Lord."

If your health, relationship, fame, money, job, even life were taken away, could you make this statement? See the things that happen in life, even chronic illness, as spiritual tests given to you by God to test your faith. This will advance you spiritually like no other spiritual practice you can practice. Remember to achieve ascension you do not have to have perfect health. I myself have had very serious chronic health problems for over twelve years in regards to my liver and pancreas. Yet in this time I have been able to achieve and complete my ascension and have been given a major position in the spiritual government. Never in a trillion years would I have ever dreamed this would be offered to me. But I have used my health lessons to forge me like cosmic fire into developing super-human mental, emotional and spiritual abilities to compensate for the digestive weakness.

Lesson 5

Focus on what you can do instead of what you can't do. Using myself as an example again, when I got so sick from hepatitis there were a great many things for a very long time I was not able to do. Instead of feeling sorry for myself and being depressed about my loss, I tried to turn a lemon into lemonade. I gave up my spiritual counseling practice, took a sabbatical, and focused on my spiritual growth.

Enormous growth occurred during this period of spiritual study and meditation. My chronic health lessons, although improved, still existed so I decided to write instead of focusing so much on individual counseling. You are now looking at a man who has written eleven books and has become a world famous author. I never planned to write books, I did it because physically it was not good for me to have an individual counseling practice.

The other adjustment I made was to only do larger groups to conserve my energy. My health lessons forced me to leave my individual counseling and instead do larger group work, which was a blessing in disguise. After a while this started taking a toll on me also, so now I do groups for 1000 people maybe twice a year. I would never have done this in a million years on my own. I can thank my health lessons for this.

My health lessons have taught me tremendous self-discipline and self-mastery for if I got off my diet I would have instant karma. The health lessons have taught me to have absolute steel like strength and willpower on mental, emotional, and spiritual levels. I had to learn this or I would have physically died. I have allowed my physical health lessons to teach me to become very strong mentally, emotionally and spiritually.

On an earthly level a third dimensional person might look at my process the last ten years and say I didn't do very well physically. From a spiritual perspective I was making quantum leaps, which the Masters ultimately noticed to the point of offering me the job to take over Djwhal Khul's ashram and becoming the high priest spokesperson for the planet; ascension movement, and world famous through my books and Wesak workshops.

I know for a fact that 99% of the world who went through what I went through physically would have been long dead or had a nervous breakdown. Because of the spiritual training that I had before this lesson, I was able over time to turn this into an asset rather than a deficit. My health is much better and stronger now that I have completed my ascension, but there are certain weaknesses that remain. I have learned to make adjustments and not feel sorry for myself or judge this. This brings me to the next key lesson in dealing with chronic health lessons.

Lesson 6
The next lesson is a super key and one in which many fall by the wayside. With anything that happens in life, including health lessons, you can either be angry, depressed, or move into acceptance. This is usually

a process for most people and was for myself. Anger and depression do nothing ultimately and the sooner you can move to acceptance the better. The crazy thing about my life is that I have moved literally about ten million times farther getting so ill physically than I would have if I had never gotten sick. I know this for an absolute fact.

This lesson is connected with what the Masters call the "blessing system." Whatever happens in life no matter how negative, bless it. The negative ego will tell you to curse it. The Holy Spirit will tell you to bless it and look at it as a stepping stone to soul growth. Sai Baba says that whatever happens in life the idea is to "welcome adversity." Paul Solomon said that whatever happens in life say, "Not my will but thine, thank you for the lesson." We each have our cross to bear. Mine has been a physical weakness in my digestive system, other people have a million and one other physical health lessons. Still others have their weak spot in the emotional or psychological body. Others are weakest in spiritual development. Ill health does not cause depression or anger, it is your "attitude" that does.

Lesson 7

The next lesson has to do with the development of the spiritual warrior and the first ray archetype and energies. People who have chronic physical health lessons must be more mentally and emotionally powerful than the average person. When one of your bodies is weaker than another, then one's personal power and fighting spirit must be developed to awesome proportions to be able to pull you up and keep up that persevering spirit.

I call this lesson the "Arjuna Initiation." Arjuna was the disciple of Krishna (Buddha was Arjuna in a past life and the Lord Maitreya was Krishna). The battle was about to begin and Arjuna fell into a depression losing his fighting spirit. This is what happens to many with chronic health lessons. Krishna then gave Arjuna a passionate speech about the nature of reality. At one point Krishna says "Get up and give up your manliness and get up and fight. This self-pity is unbecoming of the great soul that you are." Arjuna did get up and fight and became Krishna's greatest disciple. Krishna said fight for me with love in your heart and you will incur no sin.

Yogananda said, "Life is a battlefield." Christianity speaks of life in the time of the battle of Armageddon. Contrary to popular opinion life is a battle. It is a battle between the lower self and Higher Self, between illusion and Truth. Between fear and love. Between the negative ego and the Christ Consciousness, Between the Great White Brotherhood and Ascended Masters, and the Dark Brotherhood.

The purpose of life is to win this war. So what that you gain the whole world but lose your own soul. The battle is to master Self. Health lessons will not stop you from achieving your graduation from the wheel of rebirth. I know this for a fact for I am a living example. The Masters have great compassion. They are concerned more with attitude and things of the spirit!

Lesson 8

The lesson dealing with chronic health lessons I call the "*Reader's Digest* Initiation." I don't know if you have ever read the *Reader's Digest*, but they have these great stories about people who have overcome unbelievable obstacles. The stories are quite inspiring. I always wanted to be like one of those people and make my life an inspiration to myself, others and God. This chapter is really my "*Reader's Digest* story."

Whatever lessons your are dealing with be it health problems, a divorce, a death, money problems, relationship problems, etc., make up your mind to pass the Reader's Digest Initiation which I have just invented. Make your life a living testimony of the triumph of the human spirit. We hear these types of stories all the time, such as a man with no legs walking across the United States, or that Chinese student who stood in front of the tanks during the Tien Amin Square massacre armed with nothing more than his school books.

My life is a living testimony of the triumph of the human spirit and the power of the will under unbelievable adversity. I do not say this to be egotistical. I personally am more proud of what I have overcome to get to where l am, than anything else. I do not want to bore you with the details of my life, but rather to just give you the intuition and feeling and sense of what I am talking about. We are all great souls, and destined great things. Make your life a living testimony of the power of your spirit and your will. Let nothing stop you from achieving your spiritual and material goals.

Lesson 9

This next lesson for people dealing with chronic health problems is to always remember that health lessons are temporary in the sense that once you physically die you will have a perfect body again. This is a temporary situation that may be able to be healed in this lifetime or maybe not. This does not matter. It is okay to have a preference for this to be so, but not an attachment. Happiness is a state of mind, not a state of physical health. Do everything you can to heal yourself on all levels but until you achieve this goal remain happy anyway.

Lesson 10

I call this next lesson the "Hanna Kroeger Initiation." Hanna Kroeger, if you have not heard of her, is a 90-year-old lady who is one of the finest herbalists on the planet. She does all her work with a pendulum, which allows her to energetically test everything. If you have not read her books, I highly recommend them. She has cures for AIDS, cancer, and every ailment known to man. She is a genius and totally of the Christ. One of her handbooks that is meant to be used in conjunction with a pendulum, tests the seven kinds of illness that can manifest in the body. It is quite comprehensive and literally any physical health problem you have will fall under one of these seven levels which then has thousands of subsidiary divisions.

After ten years of purifying myself through every known remedy known to man and eating a perfect diet for seven straight years, I am in quite excellent health. I never get sick, and the only health lessons I have left are a little weakness in the third chakra area and a little sensitivity in one lobe of my liver that can be irritated by being a workaholic (which I am), or improper diet (which I never indulge in). Other than this, I consider myself in literally perfect health.

I found this pendulum handbook for diagnosis of one's health quite interesting. With a friend of mine, we both went through the whole procedure with our pendulums. It took about an hour. What was fascinating to me after ten years of digestive sensitivity from the hepatitis was that I came up absolutely perfectly clear on every level and was as clean as a whistle in terms of parasites, pesticides, metals, bacteria viruses, and literally everything, except for one thing.

In one small subheading what came up was that I was completely physically clear, and that any remaining health lessons or weakness "was for the glory of God." This was actually in her book. I was amazed that she actually even had this in her book. Now this story occurred about four years ago and my health has actually improved greatly because of the completion of my ascension and the light quotient and advanced light technologies I am always using. However I found this little statement to be quite meaningful and a confirmation of everything I believed in and had been working towards my whole life. I think this little section may apply to many Lightworkers who may be reading this book. For this reason, I am officially calling it the "Hanna Kroeger Initiation." Whatever lessons you are dealing with dedicate them to the glory of God. So what that there are many things you may not be able do. The purpose of life is to achieve your ascension and liberation and to serve. Even if you are bedridden, these things can be achieved

Lesson 11

The next lesson is a super key to dealing with chronic health lessons. This is to call in the inner plane Healing Masters constantly. This will be like a meditation. You will feel the presence of the Masters with you and this will bring great comfort spiritually, emotionally, mentally, and physically. The healing team is literally a Godsend and has rescued me before lectures and other major social events thousands of times when I have been feeling physically or emotionally off-balance.

The second part of this lesson is to call in the Lord of Arcturus and the Arcturians constantly if you have physical health problems. The Arcturians are the number one reason why my physical body has returned to its present state of health. I realize that this is a big statement, but it is true. I literally run their energies constantly.

I call for a 100% light quotient increase and then request that they heal and strengthen my pancreas and liver and whatever else needs healing. Literally, instantly I get relief. I have tried every being in the universe in regards to my health and by far the Arcturians are "the cat's meow." I ask to be connected to their computers and to be "put on line." I constantly call on them to balance all my meridians after working or writing all day.

I am in love with the Arcturians. The reason that they are so effective is that they are using their advanced technologies and computers to do their work. They have said that there is no illness in the universe they have ever come across that they could not help with. Plus, the spiritual benefits are enormous.

The third aspect to this lesson would be to constantly go into Djwhal Khul's ashram and call in the matrix removal program as discussed in the chapter on alien implants, elementals and astral entities. The matrix removal program will keep you clear and should be done every day if needed. It feels wonderful!

Also, call on the Prana Wind clearing device from the Arcturians to keep your meridians, veins, and arteries clear which will keep your energy flowing properly. I am sharing with you here all the tricks I have come up with.

Lesson 12

Sit in the ascension seats I have listed in my *Beyond Ascension* book and *The Complete Ascension Manual* book as much as possible. The ascension seats and all the light invocations will have an enormous effect on the physical and etheric bodies. What I am suggesting is to be running the higher frequency energies all day and all night long. Ask before bed for the Arcturians to run the energies all night long. They have really helped me to resurrect my physical and etheric bodies which had taken quite a beating this lifetime. Their technology is incredible. Ask them to work with you on a full-time basis.

Lesson 13

Eat to live instead of live to eat. Good diet is important at all times, but if you have chronic health lessons, it is even more important. If you eat a good diet, disease will literally not be able to grow. Be very disciplined in this regard and cut out sugar if you can, or as much as possible, as of course all drugs. Get as much fresh air, exercise, and sunshine as you can. The sunshine will energize the etheric body. Go for ascension walks every day if you can either calling in light quotient building or one of the various ascension seats.

Realizing your tremendous connection to the Ascended Masters will lessen your feeling of missing things that health lessons might limit you from doing. All the things I am mentioning here should also be done by people who don't have chronic health lessons, as they are the ultimate in preventative medicine.

Lesson 14

Make sure to call in the etheric healing team to repair your etheric body completely and ask for the anchoring of your perfect monadic blueprint body, which can be done prior to your ascension.

Lesson 15

Seek balance and moderation in all things. As the Buddha said, the middle road is the path to Self-realization.

Lesson 16

In extreme cases of ill health, focus on salvaging the incarnation and making as much spiritual growth as possible. During the time I was the sickest and actually had hepatitis I was not trying to make a life, I was trying to just salvage my life. The hepatitis corresponded with my Job initiation, so I took this attitude which gave me a lot of comfort. I salvaged my life through focusing on spiritual studies and meditation and what at first was salvaging my life soon became probably far more advancement then most people ever make in good health.

If ever I would fall back in my health, I would call back this attitude which would make me feel better. This may sound strange to some, who have not had chronic health lessons, however each of these tools and principles are like little tricks to keep the emotional body and mental body on an even keel even though the physical body might be in pain or having problems. The real problem comes not when the physical body has problems, but when the emotional body takes a dive bomb also.

Physical health problems are actually not that bad if you have inner peace. This chapter contains some of the mental programming and positive self-talk you can give yourself to keep yourself in an enthusiastic and inspired state of consciousness.

It is important to understand that most illness can be healed especially with the advanced technologies I speak of in my books. There are some lessons that may not be destined to heal and that is okay. Whatever your lessons make your life an inspiration, an example for others, self and God. I can't help now but think of Christopher Reeve, who played Superman in the movies, and had the horseback riding accident and broke his neck. If you ever think that you have problems, think of something like this and you should count your blessings.

Yet, I gather even Christopher Reeve has a wonderful fighting spirit that he has cultivated. Whatever lessons we have in life, no matter what they may be, are happening for a reason. It is not an accident or fluke of nature. Everything in God's universe works in divine order. Whatever lessons you have are perfect and need to be there or they wouldn't be there. Use whatever your lessons are on any level for spiritual growth, and to demonstrate Godliness. It is my hope and prayer that some of the ideas and tools I have presented here in times of physical, emotional, mental, or spiritual testing will be found to be useful!

Lesson 17
Go and see a good homeopathic doctor that specializes in using bioenergetic types of testing using vega type of medical technology to help cleanse all residual toxins from the body such as metals, chemicals, parasites, mercury fillings, radiation, bacteria, viruses, vaccines, fungus, environmental toxins, to name a few. Without homeopathics or herbs, these toxins deplete the immune system.

Lesson 18
Try and learn how to use a pendulum if you can. Some people have a knack for it more than others. It would be of enormous benefit If you could learn how to use one, testing all the foods you eat as well as supplements. If not, then see a good nutritionist and if possible one who is psychic in their abilities, or uses a pendulum, and does not give advice from just an intellectual point of view. Also, drink lots of fresh pure water

Lesson 19
Throughout the day, call in light quotient building from Metatron, the Arcturians, Melchizedek, and other Masters of your choice. This

along with the ascension seats and Arcturian technology, inner plane Healing Masters and Djwhal's ashram will greatly energize your etheric and physical vehicle. I have never met anyone who after following this prescription did not feel a great increase in physical health after following this program. The higher you go in initiations that greater the stabilization of light quotient and the greater the realization of the mayavarupa body, so never give up hope. Physical immortality and complete resurrection of the physical vehicle is the light at the end of the tunnel if you stay unceasingly on the mark and on target.

Lesson 20

Call forth three times a day for a planetary and cosmic axiatonal alignment. This particular ascension technique is especially good for physical health for it balances all the meridians and aligns them with Spirit. This is something every person should do as a preventive health practice and it will also serve to accelerate your spiritual growth.

Lesson 21

"Sickness is a defense against the truth." This is a quote from *A Course In Miracles*. The truth is, we all are the Christ. The Christ, being perfect, can only have perfect health and all else is illusion. The negative ego is in reality illusion so all sickness in the ultimate reality is an illusion. No matter what your physical health lessons are many times a day affirm you are in perfect radiant health. Paramahansa Yogananda said that even if you are 99 years old and on your deathbed, you should be affirming only perfect health. Affirm this, visualize this, and pray for this. Try not to talk about health problems with friends.

The subconscious mind will manifest into your physical body whatever image or thought you program into it good or bad. Ignore appearances and keep your mind on the Mighty I Am Presence and the perfected state at all times. In truth, all that exists is perfection. Convince your subconscious mind of this regardless of the appearance of your physical body. Eventually the physical body can't help but respond in kind. Be the computer programmer of your computer. Be God every moment of your life in every thought, word and deed. Think only positive thoughts. Spiritualize your emotions. Be vigilant over your mental, emotional, physical, and etheric diet. Pray to God and the Masters constantly, do not let go of the Angel of Healing until it blesses you like Jacob of old.

If you practice all the things mentioned in this book and in this chapter, then there is no way in this universe you are not going to get better. Be loving at all times, and dedicate your life to service in whatever form is appropriate at this particular phase of your life. Let go of all self-pity, and thank God for all your blessings and all your lessons!

Lesson 22

Remain grounded, especially if you have chronic health lessons. Bring heaven to Earth. Some lightworkers are hovering above their physical bodies and are not really in them, which makes it hard for the physical body to heal. Just as the feminine and masculine sides must be balanced, the heaven and earthly sides must also be balanced and integrated. Ascension is infusing the soul and monad into the physical body on Earth, not living in the spiritual world and celestial realms which a lot of lightworkers do.

There is nothing wrong with meditating there but the idea is then to come back and get grounded. Live in all parts of your body including hands, arms, feet, and legs. It is helpful to keep a grounding cord connected to the center of the Earth. Run energies from the Earth up through your feet as well as heavenly energies downwards. Ask that your personal kundalini be connected to the planetary kundalini. Spend time in nature and with trees.

Spend more time being instead of doing when going through a healing crisis. Be sure to sleep as much as the physical body needs. This may change at different ages and stages of your life. Find your perfect body rhythms. Mine for example is to sleep about five hours and take an hour nap in the late afternoon. This is the most energizing lifestyle for me, however each person is different. If you do have chronic health lessons, pray every night before bed for healing from all the Masters. Request that a healing platform be set up and that you be worked on 24 hours a day until full recovery is achieved. In cases of chronic illness, conserve your sexuality a little more than you normally would to use this energy for healing. An overuse of sexual energy can be depleting.

Lesson 23
Don't coddle yourself too much physically and become a hypochondriac, however on the other side of the coin don't be too much of a pusher and super trooper at the expense of the physical vehicle. Both extremes can be damaging to your physical and spiritual health.

Lesson 24
A person with extreme sensitivities to pills, herbs, and/or homeopathics may try radionics. I am one of these sensitive types, so I have two radionic machines that I use to send myself all the homeopathics, herbs, vitamins, and minerals energetically. I honestly don't understand how these simple machines work but they do. I keep myself in perfect health using them and I never have to take a single pill or take any remedies orally. It is an absolutely mind boggling science and I have proven its effectiveness a million times over.

If you want more information on this call Susan and Sandy. They can do the radionics for you and/ or might be able to show you how to set up a simplified system for yourself! The two radionics machines I have are called a "black box" and a more modern machine called an "SE-5." This is truly the technology of the future. One day everybody will have a radionics machine as they do a television. It is the ultimate self-healing machine. It can be programmed to send energy through words, through numerical codes, or through energetically sending products. Instead of ingesting the physical substance, one's aura is bombarded with the energetic substance.

If you are interested in this, there are many easy to read good books about this at your local metaphysical bookstore.

Lesson 25

Every night as you are falling asleep and as you are waking up in the morning give yourself a self-hypnotic suggestion or auto suggestion that you are in perfect radiant health. Take advantage of these hypnotic states where suggestions slip into the subconscious mind more easily. Also do this whenever you are meditating and a have achieved an altered state of consciousness. I would also recommend making a health focused sleep tape that you can play on an auto-reverse tape recorder all night long at a barely audible sound level.

Lesson 26

Contact a Science of Mind practitioner and have them help you write up a "health treatment" which you are to say every day religiously. Stay positive at all times, and keep yourself focused at all times on spiritual pursuits for "an idle mind is the devil's workshop."

Lesson 27

Forgive yourself for all mistakes from this life and past lives in regards to your health. Forgive yourself and just start a completely brand new fresh cycle, like your life is completely starting over.

Lesson 28

Every night before bed pray to God directly in a most sincere and humble and non-attached manner for a miraculous healing if it be God's will.

Lesson 29

Every morning and every night pray for protection from Archangel Michael in the form of a golden dome that only the energies of the Christ frequency may touch you.

Lesson 30

Practice all the ascension techniques and meditations in *The Complete Ascension Manual*, the *Beyond Ascension* book, and in the *Soul Psychology* book over a one year period. If you do this you will have so much light and advanced Christed technology in your field there is no way on Earth that you will not feel physically better. Be patient in your practice and don't do too much all at once. Pace yourself, in other words. Trust your intuition as what to practice when.

I do have ascension activation tapes that can be obtained from me directly, which I would highly recommend getting. I have recorded these so you can just kick back and receive the activations with my voice. There are eleven tapes in the series, which can be ordered individually or as a complete set. The set costs $180.00 including postage. This is an incredibly comprehensive set. Call the phone number listed at the back of this book for further information and ordering.

Lesson 31

When you begin to explore homeopathy, radionics, naturopathic medicine, and bioenergetic medicine, health becomes a lot more than a positive report on a blood test. Western medicine, in truth, is still operating in the Dark Ages. To achieve good health and a healthy, functioning immune system all the physical toxins must be cleared. Most of these things Western medicine has no awareness of and couldn't cleanse if their life depended on it.

In dealing with chronic illness and/or the desire to really obtain good health, the following are some of the things I would recommend exploring to make sure you have cleared:

Removal of mercury fillings and homeopathic cleansing of mercury from your body

Balancing of yeast and bacteria from use of antibiotics

Removal of all vaccines which are totally toxic to the immune system.

Removal of all parasites

Removal of all viruses

Removal of all fungus

Removal of all improper bacteria

Removal of all radiation from color televisions

Removal of electromagnetic toxicity from powerlines and the like

Removal of all chemicals from body

Removal of all past drugs you have taken

Removal of all pesticides from vegetables, dairy products and other sources that are in the body

Balancing of the bioenergy fields

Cleansing of the liver and kidneys

Upgrading of the glandular system

Removal of negative emotions through Bach Flower remedies

Immune system building

Removal of environmental poisons

Proper balance of vitamins and minerals

Energetic check of physical diet

Blood cleansing

Cleansing of lymph system residual toxin

Clearing of tuberculosis

Clearing of all sexually transmitted diseases

It must be understood that very often we carry these things sublimi-nally in our system but this does not mean we will ever get these diseases. For example, tuberculosis toxin can be picked up by drinking milk or breathing the air in an airplane. I am speaking here of subclinical toxins that lodge in our system that deplete our immune systems. The medicine of the future works on a much more subtle level then Western medicine. The fact is a person can be dying of cancer and may still have normal blood. Western medicine worships science, which leaves out literally 90% of what is really going on within a person's reality.

Just as I have spoken in this book about the need to remove implants, elementals, negative imprints, astral entities, core fear, mental toxins, and emotional toxins, there are also subtle physical toxins which Western medicine does not have a clue about. Just as traditional psychology is missing entirely the psychic and spiritual realm of what is going on, Western medicine is doing the same but even worse. It is only when you go to a New Age homeopathic, or bioenergetic or naturopathic doctor that these residual toxins will be addressed. To be honest even a lot of them don't address it so you must find someone good.

What I am speaking of here is the cutting edge new age work in the field of holistic medicine. In my books I have tried to bring forth the cutting edge work that is going on in the spiritual or ascension movement, the cutting edge work going on around the planet in the field of psychology. In this chapter, I am speaking very briefly on the cutting edge work in the field of holistic health.

Other Things to Clear And Cleanse

All past medications. An interesting story on this point. As an adolescent, I took a great deal of antibiotics for some acne problems I had around the age of 15 or 16. Can you believe a doctor recommending antibiotics for acne? Is that barbaric or what? Anyway over 25 years later I was seeing a psychic nutritionist by the name of Eileen Poole who one day told me I was cleansing tetracycline from my field. I told her that was impossible for I had not had a single antibiotic in almost 15 years. It turned out that I was still cleansing the drugs from 25 years ago.

Now remember I am and have been a health food fanatic and exercise fanatic, as well as eating one of the purest diets on the planet. Yet 25 years later I was still cleansing. With a lot of these toxins without homeopathics or herbs one may never be able to cleanse the system.

Make sure all Epstein-Barr virus is cleansed. Very often, we carry this on subclinical levels that would never ever be detected on a blood test.

Make sure all staph and strep bacteria are cleared from the subclinical field. (Really, what we are speaking of here is the whole field of "subclinical medicine").

Stop using all drugs and use homeopathics and herbs which are not toxic for the body.

Never give your children or yourself any vaccines, for they are absolutely poisonous to the body.

Clear all herpes virus on a subclinical level

Clear all cold and flu medications, aspirins, pain killers, all the medication you have ever taken are stored in the liver and poison the body and deplete the immune system.

In essence, ask the bioenergetic specialist, or homeopathic doctor, or Susan and Sandy using a pendulum, or a naturopath to do a complete work-up using energetic testing to check your entire program and to cleanse everything. The spiritual path is the path of purification. You want your physical, etheric, astral, mental, and spiritual bodies cleared.

Cleanse all subclinical cancers, hepatitis, and mononucleosis that might be present on subclinical levels.

Remember all disease begins in the astral and etheric bodies first, as well as in the mental body. Western medicine has no way of testing or recognizing the diseases that are manifest on these levels let alone on subclinical physical levels below the surface of a blood test. A blood test is an incredibly gross level. Many people are walking around with walking hepatitis, walking mononucleosis, Epstein-Barr, or the likes and are being greatly debilitated.

Western medicine no matter how many tests they do will not be able to figure it out. The blood test is just the tip of the iceberg. The other 90% of the iceberg Western medicine has no way of scientifically detecting. The new technology that is now being invented and worked with is in the field of homeopathy, and naturopathic medicine. Such machines as the vega machine, and others like it, can scientifically detect the other 90% as accurately as a blood test on the gross level.

Of course, Western medicine rejects this as quackery when, in truth, the reverse is true. I would never ever go to a regular medical doctor unless it was for emergency procedures, which is the only thing they are good at. Western medicine with its focus on drugs and invasive testing is still in a very "barbaric stage." They reject homeopathic medicine, they never use herbs, they have no understanding of diet, and they reject acupuncture. They have absolutely no cure for viruses of any kind, when homeopathics and herbs can knock out any virus within a week to ten days and does not poison the body.

I can knock out any bacterial infection within a couple of days using homeopathics while the doctors prescribe antibiotics like candy for everything even though it only works on bacteria. The doctors being so backwards and behind the times don't even tell the person to take extra acidophilus to replace the friendly bacteria. People really have no idea how barbaric Western medicine really is.

Once you have been exposed to the New Age holistic cutting edge field of medicine and how everything can be tested through energy rather than invasive measures you will never consider going back except in emergency situations like a broken leg or car accident when immediate help is instantly needed. True preventive medicine and true healing is something that the traditional medical profession knows little about. Very often, they actually interfere in the process, for example, by giving a patient Valium for emotional distress. Antibiotics are given like candy for every known problem under the sun when homeopathics are just as effective and a thousand times better for the body.

Other things that need to be cleansed from the body are caffeine, traces of former drug use, alcohol, nicotine, metal poisoning, aluminum, lead, car exhaust, insect bites, malathion poisoning, and salmonella (75% of all chickens have salmonella poisoning according to the FDA). This again is what I am talking about when I say we all carry this stuff on subclinical levels. We all must clear all the preservatives we have eaten, weed killer, bug spray, measles vaccine, chicken pox vaccine, past influenzas, mumps, and polio vaccine.

All these things I have listed here get stored in the liver, kidneys, and in different areas of the body. Most of these residual toxins will never get removed from the physical body without homeopathics and specialized herbal remedies. All of these residual toxins and thousands of other ones I have not mentioned here deplete the functioning of your immune system. The biggest one probably being all the food poisons we have eaten in our life.

Going on prolonged and occasional fasts is an essential key to retaining good health. For people with chronic health lessons and for that matter really for every person who wants to become Self-realized I recommend that you get checked for all these things so you can become as purified in your energy fields as you possibly can on physical, etheric, astral, mental and spiritual levels. This book has been dedicated to help give you the tools and understanding to be able to do this to help you obtain perfect health on all levels and to help you realize God!

Lesson 32

This next lesson for people with chronic health lessons or occasional health lessons is to call in the "Acupuncture Inner Plane Healing Team." This is a phenomenal method, for the Inner Plane healing team will give you "etheric acupuncture" in the comfort of your own home any time you want. You have your own personal acupuncturist that costs you nothing out of your wallet. The only thing it costs you is your love and gratitude to the wonderful beings that perform these services on our behalf!

Lesson 33

The next method for people dealing with chronic health lessons is a new one, which Djwhal Khul recently told me about. Call in the inner plane Healing Masters and your own Mighty I Am Presence. Then request that a radionics machine be set up on the inner plane to send you the energies you need on an ongoing basis 24 hours a day to correct what ever type health lesson you are dealing with. This is a phenomenal method for I am basically giving you a radionics machine right now that again costs you nothing, but, in truth, is maybe more effective then even a real physical earthly radionics machine.

You can request at different times that it be programmed for different things. If you want energy and wakefulness request this. If you want immune system building, request that. If you want to work on a long term basis on a specific problem, request that. The other thing you request is that it send you whatever energies you need to keep you in balance with no specific focus.

The best method is probably a combination of all of these. The radionics machine can be used even to send you vitamins and minerals you need. The list is truly endless. This machine can be used for anything a real radionics machine can be used with and more. Look at the amount of money I am saving you with these last two methods and tools! I do have one request for payment however. Tell your students, friends, family, and local metaphysical bookstores about my books, if you like them. In doing this all can share in God's generosity and care for his beloved sons and daughters.

Lesson 34

One other healing tool for people with chronic health lessons or as a preventive tool which again will save you a ton of money in health care bills is to call the inner plane Healing Masters and request to be given the vitamin and minerals you need as inner plane shots to remain in perfect physical health. Ask for all inner plane shots to be given to you over the next month that will keep your physical and etheric body in perfect energetic and chemical balance.

For example, lets say your family is sick, and you want to build up your immune system, you might request an inner plane vitamin C shot every day to boost your immune system. You can also just request to the inner plane Healing Masters to give you any shot or substance that they feel you need to bring you back to balance.

With all the tools in this chapter, there is no way that even people with chronic illness are not going to start feeling better. The most important thing in dealing with chronic illness is to have a fighting spirit and to not give up. As long as you are assertively attacking the problem with all these tools and methods the illness will not be attacking and depressing you. This chapter is your spiritual battle plan, so to speak, to win this war.

The using of these tools will not only help you to feel better physically, but will also serve to give you good practice working on the inner plane, and will accelerate your spiritual growth tremendously. It will also help you to develop more of a conscious relationship of working with the Ascended Masters. It will thin the veil, so to speak, and help you to recognize that you are never alone. It will also demonstrate to you in infinite ways how much God loves you, and the bountiful blessings He has bestowed upon you for the asking. Everything in God's infinite universe is literally available to you for the asking. My service is nothing more than sharing with you some of the incredible things that are available. It is up to you, however, to ask. Ask and you shall receive, knock, and the door shall be opened.

Lesson 35

This lesson contains four meditations involving your solar angels that were synthesized and condensed from a book called *Healing Yourself with Light*, by Launa Huffines. I have not read the book myself, however, one of my main assistants in Djwhal Khul's ashram, Janna Shelley Parker, thought they might be helpful to my readers, so I have added them here for your enjoyment, healing, and light activation.

Meditation #1: Entering the Room of Inner Stillness
Relax, relax, relax, and breathe deeply and rhythmically. Allow yourself to get ready to enter into a room of utter stillness, tranquillity and

harmony. Bathe in a cleansing shower of colors and then enter a room–your room of Peace.

Completely free from the world, you are totally relaxed in your special place, your special room beyond the worries of the world, beyond the barriers of illness, for you are in a sanctuary of healing.

Find your position of comfort and let every cell float into relaxation. Think only of peace, serenity, harmony, wholeness, and balance. Let everything become soft.

Invite your Solar Angel, for whom your Guardian Angel is but a mere reflection. Your Solar Angel is with you until you have completed your rounds of incarnation. It is itself, yet totally at one with our higher purpose. Solar Angels work for evolution, and when you invoke your own Solar Angel you will be bringing this Divine Presence into you, filling you with Light, healing and expansion.

In your private place, your quiet space, focus the eyes upward and invoke this Angel. Allow yourself to believe you can be healed. Invite your Solar Angel to come to you like a sphere of golden light. Allow this light to circle your head, your thought-field with its healing energy. This will form a subtle halo around your head.

Now ask the Solar Angel for help in the area that needs healing. Stay in silence and trust, enwrapped, enveloped by the healing, soothing energy of the Angel of the Presence. Feel the new sense of balance it brings, the optimism. Feel and take note of your inner sense of feeling that are beyond mind.

When you are through, give thanks and quietly leave, knowing that this room is ever available to you. Record each experience in your journal. You can now monitor your progress, what works best, how you come to a state of relaxation, as well as wisdom learned and your attitude towards your healing.

Remember, you create the room and the stillness. It is always there for you.

Meditation #2: Entering the Room of Light

Begin with your imagination. Get a sense of this room and the wisdom there-in. Be sure to bathe in a shower of Light in the courtyard of the temple of healing. Bring the colors of light over you individually, drops of liquid light in orange, gold, yellow, and rose. Then use shades of green, blue and violet.

Cleansed, enter into your room to again meet your Solar Angel. Find a place to relax. Everything in the room glows, but the brightest point is where *you* are. You are surrounded by White Light and that White Light enters you. It is a living, intelligent Light, and makes offerings of wisdom. You sense the essence of Self and the essence of whatever else comes to mind. The mind calms, the emotions still and there is nothing but the radiance of your Solar Angel. Its essence of Love fills your heart and being.

The Solar Angel brings its light into the room from the heart of the sun. Its rays bring elements that are necessary for your life. To tap into these Solar Beings imagine the rays of Solar Light around your head. The more you allow the Solar Light to enter your mind and heart, the greater the illumination you bring. Think upon spiritual qualities and they are yours to experience.

Solar Light is also an agent of rejuvenation. Invite it into your body to heal and rejuvenate. The Light evolves your cells. It dissolves toxins as it filters into your cells and transmutes them. Through this connection, this column of Light, the Solar Light continues to restore your body cells. As you connect your inner sun with Solar Light, the two merge and distribute great Light throughout your body.

Use imagination to facilitate this reality. Picture your breath drawing healing light into every part of you. Look at the glorious morning sun. Think about the solar entities in these rays that can help you solve any health problems for that day. See in your mind's eye solar rays entering your body, healing each cell, vitalizing you with renewed life.

These are, in truth, living energies which heal, strengthen, and evolves your body. Breathe into your heart with love and breathe out from your heart loving gratitude and feel renewed.

Meditation #3: Healing in the Room of Love

Bathe in a shower of liquid gold and rose. See each color rinse the dense frequencies from your energy field. Now enter the Room of Love and find your comfortable position in the room's center.

Breathe in the Healing Angelic Presence and the sweetness of the rose and white flowers about you. Through the open skylight above luminous particles of Love Essence flow down into the room. Open up any and all places in your four lower bodies that need more love.

Create a rose-colored triangle between your Solar Angel, your soul, and your four lower bodies. Through the energy of your rose triangle comes the Angels of Divine Love. This Love contains wondrously healing life energy. Ask that any emotion that has created a block or problem in your emotional/astral body be released. If your problem is specifically of a physical nature, call upon the Love of these Angels to intone their specific healing sound in that direction.

Chant "Ah" slowly and open your heart even more. Remember the rose filled triangle and connection with your Solar Angel.

Chant "El" (as in bell), calling to the One Creative Force. The note will travel up a column of Light to the top of the head. Visualize it. "E" is for serenity and "L" uplifts the soul. Peaceful concentration will lift you up to the angels of Love Divine.

"I" (pronounced "ee" as in see), takes you right into the center of healing. Place sound between and above your eyes as it vibrates between the eyebrows, feel the soul resonation.

As you say "O" (as in oh), bring a line of lighted energy from above into your head and down the spinal cord. Visualize the Angels of Divine Love bringing healing into every nerve in your body.

Chant or intone the full vibratory sound A-El-I-O seven times and imaging it ringing in your temple of healing. The response will resonate in your heart. Each syllable calls in more Angels of Divine Love.

Now bathe in the frequencies of their energies. It is love and joy which purify your heart and neutralize all past suffering. As they recharge you with Divine healing love so are you drawn even closer to the Healing Angels.

See this love flow through your four lower bodies, refining and purifying all density from the past. Tell your cells it is OK to accept this wonderful healing love. Fill up on it.

After this process and intoning the healing syllables your cells will vibrate with love from the Spiritual Dimension. Give your four lower bodies time to absorb this Divine Gift. Sit quietly, play beautiful or spiritual New Age music, or look at beautiful art or nature. Stay within the serenity and peace of Love Divine.

Meditation #4: Color Baths

Healing Angels use specific colors in their healing. They weave the needed colors into your energy field to offer protection from disease. For vitality, they use rose or orange hues. A clear hue of green is very helpful for general healing needs. It cools down the center of the atoms in order to bring them back into balance.

It is important to work within the triangles of your Solar Angel, your soul, and your self (four lower bodies). Then you will receive the best healing colors for your purposes.

In general, for the physical body: for lung congestion, an iridescent orange is called into the area. For infections, sapphire blue might help by acting as a disinfectant. Sapphire blue might be used for poison ivy or rashes as well. A rich green or a green tinged with yellow is often used for inflammation. For higher energy, they use stimulating color, such as a bright or golden orange or yellow.

For emotions: different hues of yellow, gold, orange, or rose are great for inducing cheerfulness, confidence, and optimism. Hues of rose from intense to pastel can create an inner feeling of Love. One needs to experiment for oneself to find just the right color to help generate the desired mood.

For thoughts: color is also invaluable to calm your mind. You can surround yourself with luminous green. For clear thinking and mental stimulation, you might try a shower of bright yellow over and around your head. A tint of yellow-orange may very well get you out of a mental fog. If your will to live is not very strong, try rose. Two or three shades of rose will build your will to live.

Color is already used to create healing and restful environments. Colors are energy and use by the angels and man. It is well to take note of and make use of color for health evolution and purification.

Final Summation

In concluding this chapter, I asked Djwhal Khul to eloquently give me a statement as to health and disease from the perspective of the Spiritual Hierarchy and Ascended Masters. The simplicity of what he said surprised me. Djwhal said that, "Ill health is basically misdirected thinking."

Ill health then is the physicalization of negative ego thoughtforms. Health is the physicalization of Christ/Buddha Consciousness and thinking. Lack of health is not a bad thing, but a good thing, being nothing more than a neutral indicator of an imbalance or misdirected thought in the psyche. If we didn't have health lessons, we would never learn. It is our ultimate teacher to help us align our minds and emotions with God's Laws. Instead of cursing your body for getting sick, bless your body for being your neutral and objective guide, which does nothing more than mirror your state of consciousness.

If our bodies never gave us these signals, we would never achieve liberation and true God-consciousness. Our bodies in essence force us to remain on our spiritual path. God is balance, and it is our bodies that force us to hold to this ideal. God's sons and daughters can often be quite rebellious and disobedient, like little children. Health lessons are nothing more than the body communication with us and they should not be judged or looked at as a bad thing. It is through our suffering and health lessons that most of us have found God and our spiritual paths. This is an extremely difficult school and it is amazing that people's bodies hold up as well as they do given all the abuse they take. When they do break down have great compassion and love and understanding for self and others. Let the physical body teach you to remain balanced, integrated, and attuned to the Mighty I Am Presence at all times!!!

21

The Restructuring of the Ego

Lord Maitreya, Melchizedek, and Djwhal Khul told me that there was a focus during a certain two-week time frame of restructuring the ego, during a certain phase of work I was doing on this book. I found this comment to be quite interesting and I knew there was something new in this statement beyond that which I had previously understood. This whole book has been focused on how to consciously restructure the conscious and subconscious mind from negative ego thinking. All light-workers must do this work.

What I began to understand, however, through some digging and prodding from the Masters, is that there is a new technology that could make the process of restructuring the negative ego a lot easier. Before I explain this, I want to explain what I mean by restructuring the negative ego. This means first off, of course, learning to think with your Christ Mind and not with the negative ego mind. It also means learning to integrate the twelve archetypes in a balanced and appropriate manner. A great many lightworkers are over-identified with certain archetypes and are caught in certain complexes I spoke of many of these in the chapter on archetypes.

The restructuring of the negative ego also has to do with learning to parent oneself properly and to not be run by the inner child. Another factor is balancing the four bodies and three minds. As I have spoken about in great detail in this book, these psychodynamics are often imbalanced and off-kilter. Consciously working and studying this book and the *Soul Psychology* book is essential to make the appropriate attitudinal adjustments in your thinking to have a healthy psychoepistomology and a healthy ego. Here I am speaking of a spiritualized ego and not a negative ego.

In one particular meditation, I began questioning Djwhal about the possibility of using the Tree of Life as a tool and model for clearing the negative ego. Asking this question seemed to be the key to unlock a new technology that Djwhal Khul said he wasn't planning to unveil for at least another six months. Once catching wind of this I put on my Sherlock Holmes hat and would not let go until Djwhal blessed us. As usual, he blessed way beyond my wildest imaginations. He told me that the science that I was using to achieve our goals in restructuring the ego although being the most advanced on the planet was still in the dark ages from his perspective. Djwhal said there is a more advanced technology that could be used in conjunction with one's basic conscious studying that could greatly enhance this process. He had been using it all week on me, however, I had no conscious awareness of this until I pretty much accidentally stumbled into it, which is usually the case.

What Djwhal said is that there is a fifth, sixth and seventh dimensional technology that could be used to greatly accelerate this process of restructuring the negative ego. He referred to this as a process that could greatly enhance the re-establishing of a person's "energy signature." Asking to be taken to Djwhal Khul's ashram and requesting to enter his holographic computer room does this process. In previous chapters, I have begun to discuss the holographic computer, however its uses cover an expanse that is far beyond our wildest dreams.

I recently asked Djwhal Khul how he spends most of his time in the inner plane ashram. What he told me is that most of his time is spent working with the holographic computer. If an Ascended Master such as Djwhal Khul spends this much time on such a project, you know it must be incredible!

The Holographic Computer and The Twelve Archetypes

What Djwhal Khul said is that there is an advanced technology that can be used using the holographic computer whereby the twelve archetypes can be divinely imprinted upon the core of one's being along with the proper pranic energy flows that re-establish each person's monadic energy signature. This work, done in conjunction with the conscious work of studying this book and the *Soul Psychology* book and others like it, would be the one-two punch to completely restructure the ego back into its divine blueprint.

It must be understood here that each person's energy signature and archetypal pattern is completely different. This is why the holographic computer is needed in conjunction with each person's soul and monadic records. God creates each person differently, and each person has a different ray configuration, a different astrological configuration and a different archetypal mission and purpose. All these factors and more must be taken into account in the archetypal pranic imprinting process.

I asked Djwhal if this holographic computer could be used in the same way for divine ray imprinting, divine astrological imprinting, divine Tree of Life imprinting, as well as archetypal pranic imprinting. Djwhal said it most definitely could, however he said that when one does this process with the archetypes and pranic energy flows it automatically does the other systems I mentioned. The other systems are just other forms for doing similar work except for the divine ray and pranic flow imprinting which could be a second procedure that could be done in conjunction with the archetype imprinting procedure. He said that doing them all would just be repetitive. Studying them all, however, is not.

Updated Information on Universal Archetype Attunement

Djwhal Khul began to give us more information, which greatly began to expand our understanding of this process. The first thing he said is that we should call this process the Universal Archetype Attunement. He said that in reality, this was a one time imprinting process that could be asked for in the future, but this was more for the personality rather than the etheric body. You, my readers, will also be pleased to hear that we received a divine dispensation for this to be something that you can ask for in meditation telepathically from Djwhal Khul in his ashram. For those coming to the Wesak Celebrations put on each year this attunement and another attunement called the Yod Spectrum Attunement will be done en masse at these celebrations. The Yod Spectrum Attunement is one I am not allowed to speak of at this time and is only for seventh degree initiates; however, because of the 1000 people in attendance at Wesak it will be allowed to be given out to everyone. The Universal Archetype Attunement and the Yod Spectrum Attunement will be done together.

One of the purposes of these attunements among many is to connect each person to their mayavarupa body or perfect monadic blueprint body in terms of greater realization. It is the individual Ascended Master body for each person.

The Universal Archetype Attunement Djwhal said is to bring into balance all past life archetypal themes and future lives into the present. The idea here is to bring each person into the universal archetype, which of course is the twelfth dimensional level. This is the archetype of the Master in their fully realized mayavarupa body. As was stated in my book *Cosmic Ascension*, there are three stages to realization of these different chakra grids, bodies, and levels.

These are installation, activation, and actualization. The ultimate ideal for Ascended Masters is to not just achieve the fifth dimensional level, which is the beginning of the Ascended Master consciousness. But to install, activate, and actualize all the way up through the twelfth dimensional level, which includes the group soul, group monadic, level, solar level, galactic level, and universal level. It is the full actualization of the twelfth dimensional level that allows one to teleport, and develop other such advanced Ascended Master abilities.

This universal archetype energy attunement will integrate the archetypes and pranic energy flows up through this level. This does not mean that you have achieved fully this level, but it is most definitely a step in the right direction. You will have achieved this permanent imprinting on the etheric, psychological, and energetic levels. This, of course, must be supported by one's own psychological work on this level with the archetypes and transcending negative ego consciousness, or it won't hold psychologically and energetically even though the imprinting is permanent etherically.

Each mind and each body in a sense has its part to play to achieve perfect realization and integration. This particular attunement is a new dispensation now given to humanity that has never been available before. This archetype attunement is not just a planetary, solar, galactic archetype attunement, but a universal archetype attunement hence it is given by the grace of Lord Melchizedek himself, the Universal Logos, who is president of the universal level. This attunement is given at this time because of the mass waves of ascension that began at Wesak 1995 and will continue through the year 2000 and beyond.

Djwhal Khul said it is an attunement that, in truth, is for those who are just completing their fifth initiation and about to ascend or take their sixth initiation. For those receiving this attunement at Wesak from the third initiation and above, it will serve to be a greater accelerator on their path of initiation and ascension. It will fit each person into the perfect archetypal energy alignment, and pranic energy flow. Each person's archetypes will be brought together and centered. For those below the sixth initiation, it will plant a seed and help them to develop their future Ascended Master body.

The Actual Process

Ask to be taken to Djwhal Khul's ashram and ask him to be taken to the holographic computer room for a Universal Archetypal Energy Attunement. You are requesting to raise the light quotient and to bring in the pranic energy flow for the universal archetypes. The first station will be the crown chakra. The crown chakra will bring in the quality of "grace." The second station will be the third eye and this will bring in the quality of "wisdom."

The next station will bring in the quality of "unconditional love" in the heart chakra, and will serve to open the heart beyond the wounds of all other lifetimes. The solar plexus will be the station to anchor the quality of "universal will." This will then be grounded into the Earth.

In review, we have the universal grace, wisdom, love and will that will be imprinted into the core of your being, along with corresponding universal energy flows that are perfect for your matrix, so to speak. This will serve to allow each person to stand in the truth of their mastery.

Then a protective shield will be placed around you, which is in harmonic vibration of the love of all life, and non-separateness. Djwhal Khul referred to grace as standing alone in the crown and the three-fold flame of love, wisdom, and power standing together. The addition of the protective field then creates an integrated effect of peace and joy, which is a releasing of all ancient sorrow. Then an invocation is done to release the collective karma of all past lives into the light of mercy and compassion, to anchor in universal archetypes for humankind.

Again, I now mention that it is permissible to call for this attunement telepathically from Djwhal Khul directly, however, I have been given the authority to facilitate this for people. If you would like to have this done by one of us, please call and it will be arranged. It will be a permanent imprinting, however, Djwhal said that you might periodically go back into the energy and feeling of the experience. He said because of the influence of the negative ego there is often the losing of emotion connection with this universal archetype energy attunement state. This will help the person to recover their balance, which is a nice tool to have in your tool kit, so to speak. As with everything in God's infinite universe it is there for the asking. Djwhal concluded this discussion by saying that this process of the Universal Archetype Attunement is the energetic signature of the Ascended Master in the physical world.

22

How to Clear the Negative Ego
through the Science of the Tree of Life

As I was coming to the completion of writing this book Djwhal Khul requested that I discuss using one other system to clear the negative ego. So far, we have discussed the sciences of the archetypes, rays, and astrology. To this, we now add the science of the Kabbalah and the Tree of Life. For those of you who have never studied the Kabbalah or Tree of Life, I would highly recommend reading the easy-to-read chapter I wrote on the subject in my book called *Hidden Mysteries*. This chapter will give you a quick and profound foundation in this most incredible science. In my personal opinion, it is one of the most profound spiritual sciences I have ever come across.

To begin this discussion on the Tree of Life I have enclosed a couple of the charts from *Hidden Mysteries*.

The Tree of Life is composed of ten sephiroth or ten spiritual centers. There is actually an eleventh spiritual center called Daath, which refers to the hidden wisdom that is opened when one attains higher initiate status. Each of these ten sephiroth embodies a certain psychospiritual quality. For the purposes of this chapter I am not going to review what I already wrote about in the *Hidden Mysteries* book; however, there is a new sequence of information that Djwhal Khul asked me to write about in this book that is not contained in my other one. This has to do with how the Tree of Life can be used to help clear the negative ego.

Djwhal Khul told me that each sephiroth has a higher and lower expression. Sound familiar by now? This is exactly what I have presented in the chapters on the archetypes, rays, and astrology. The same is true of the Tree of Life. Each sephiroth has a spiritual expression and what might be called a lower psychic expression.

Kether or Crown Sephiroth

We will begin our discussion with the sephiroth called Kether or the crown. The crown or Kether sephiroth deals with the unmanifest level of the Tree of Life. It is the sephiroth that is embodied by the Archangel Metatron. It is connected to the Ain Soph and Ain Soph Aur, or the Limitless Light and Love. Djwhal said that this spiritual center deals with the type of person who puts spirituality as their top priority. They live a very in tune life spiritually and have spiritual practices and sadhana. They are also able to keep their physical life in balance and are able to move forward. Their heavenly and earthly life has a good balance.

Djwhal Khul said the lower expression of the Kether sephiroth is too top heavy or over-identified with heavenly energies at the expense of their physical body and earth life. This type of person is so into the ephemeral they don't live properly on the Earth. They haven't learned the lesson of bringing heaven to earth. Ascension as we all know is really descension. It is anchoring your soul and monad into your physical body on Earth and being of service on here.

This is a very common theme among many lightworkers. They often don't take care of their physical bodies properly. They often can't find work and they often don't do well in emotional relationships because they are too cosmic. There is nothing wrong with being cosmic. I happen to like this in myself. However, balance must be found among all chakras, all bodies, and fusion of heaven and earth must be achieved for true Self-realization. One might say in the lower expression the psychological and earthly levels are not integrated properly due to an imbalanced mindset.

Chokmah or Wisdom Sephiroth

The next sephiroth on the Tree of Life on the right side of the tree as one looks at it on a piece of paper, is Chokmah or wisdom. The higher expression of the sephiroth is connected to Lightworkers who have a learned or just innate connection to Divine wisdom and who are realizing their potentials. They are not necessarily very metaphysical in realizing this. The higher expression has a strong connection, Djwhal said, to the proper will/wisdom balance. This type of person has the wisdom to know where to be at the right time.

Djwhal Khul said that this sephiroth often tends to be a person who is very religious, since this sephiroth is connected to the Divine Father as opposed to the Divine Mother. It is connected to a little more of the male aspect of divinity. The Jewish religion might be a good example. A great emphasis on the law, academics, and education. Will and academic knowledge make up the wisdom. Djwhal Khul said that in the higher expression they are emotionally balanced, and are quite steady and evenminded.

The lower expression of this sephiroth, Djwhal said, has a weak will function. Wisdom is taken down into lower more materialistic endeavors, functioning just on the concrete mind and wisdom rather than the Higher Mind and abstract esoteric or philosophical mind. In religion that might mean they have to follow the letter of the law, instead of the higher meaning of what is really intended. What this leads to is that their scope of potentiality is unmanifested. Things have to be a certain way and have become more limited in scope. They might be too conser-vative, and limited in certain subconscious and conscious patterns. Wisdom has hence taken a small frame of reference instead of a large frame of reference. Wisdom has become strictly organized and limited by the things they have studied or experienced, as opposed to really tapping into the unlimited Source. The negative ego or fear has come into much greater play. This in truth is true of all the lower expressions of all ten sephiroth. Here we might say we have wisdom with a little "w," rather than a big "W." It is wisdom more of the personality rather than the progressing wisdom of the soul and monad.

The Sephiroth of Binah or Understanding

The sephiroth of Binah or understanding, on the left side of the Tree is connected more with the Divine Mother Principle as opposed to the Divine Father in the Chokmah. It has a focus upon understanding and receptivity. In its higher expression, Djwhal Khul said, we think of one who carries the Divine Mother. It also might be the great mystic where Chokmah would be more the great occultist psychologist or master spiritual teacher. The Divine Mother of course, is the embodiment of receptivity, love, compassion, and under-standing. Djwhal said that in the higher expression of Binah there is still the strong expression of the Divine will underlying this more feminine sephiroth.

In the lower expression of Binah we have the person who is always taking on too much. Here is the person who is not just compassionate but is too empathic. Also, here the mother is a codependent rather than a divine expression of unconditional love and non-attachment. We also have over-mothering, too selfless, not knowing how to take care of self. The person often needs to mother the world and hence puts on too much weight.

Djwhal went on to say that people often end up identifying with one of the ten sephiroth just as people often end up doing this with the twelve archetypes. The ideal is to integrate and utilize all ten sephiroth in their higher expressions in a balanced and appropriate manner. The Tree of Life hence is another wonderful method, tool, and system for understanding archetypes. Each of these tools can be a bit repetitive, however each person will attune to the system or systems that work best for them. The studying of them all in an eclectic and universal manner just helps to deepen the overall understanding and helps in the refinement and purification process. The ideal is to identify more with the top of the tree, but be well-balanced and integrated in all of them.

One can imagine the Tree of Life as superimposed over the physical body and etheric body much like a chakra system. When one sephiroth is not integrated properly this will prevent the prana from flowing properly through the etheric body. Our programming acts like a groove in a record, or like etheric pipes, which govern the flow of this energy. When archetypes, rays, or sephiroth are not integrated properly in their higher expression, the flow of energy will be imbalanced which will create physical and psychological symptoms. Every person, when they come into this world, is usually predominate in one sephiroth. This is the great psychological work that needs to be done.

This again is where the holographic computer room and the studying you are now doing can correct these imbalances in thinking and prana flow in a most amazing and complex manner. I think you can see that you would need the ultimate computer to work this out for each person. This is also a type of technology the Arcturians are so well versed in.

Djwhal Khul said that Binah, or understanding, really means compassion. This actually might be a better word to describe it than understanding as the touchstone. So, in review, we have Kether being the pure Spirit that contains all. Chokmah is the spiritual knowledge and Binah is the spiritual compassion and understanding when manifest in their highest expressions.

The Sephiroth of Chesed and Mercy

The sephiroth of Chesed on the right side of the Tree of Life deals with the soul level of the Tree as opposed to the monadic level which we were just speaking of previously. Chesed deals with emotions, and the feelings of unconditional love and compassion. Djwhal Khul said the upper expression would be someone like St. Francis of Assisi, or Mother Teresa. These two great saints are different than the sephiroth Binah for they don't mother the world as this previous sephiroth did. St. Francis and Mother Teresa administer mercy in a very balanced way. The term mercy, Djwhal said, deals also with the Christ quality of justice and fairness.

In the lower expression the person feels like they have never been treated fairly or justly and that they are victims of mercilessness. They often think they are giving mercy, but, in truth, what they are doing is victimizing themselves.

Geburah and The Sephiroth of Serenity

Geburah is the balance to Chesed. Where Chesed is unconditional love, compassion, and mercy, Geburah is discernment and self-control, and divine will. It is the will with the wisdom hence blended with the love. In the higher expression this type of person is always centered and in the middle path, as Buddha would say. They are always in inner peace within themselves and at inner peace with other people. They are serene and are very much the peacemaker in a very positive sense of the term. They are good in political situations for they have the serenity and strength of will to remain clear and centered. They are excellent mediators and arbitrators.

In the lower expression of Geburah is a person who is undiscerning in life. They have a problem making decisions. They are not decisive. They don't know how to retain their personal power. They are in essence out of balance and are always struggling. They do not have mastery over their emotions and are victimized by the outside world and other people. They talk about the importance of being strong but have not learned how to do it yet.

The Sephiroth of Tiphareth or Beauty

The sephiroth of Tiphareth has as its key quality that of beauty. In the higher expression it is the person who sees beauty in everything, rather like the fourth ray type in its higher expression. They not only see beauty in everything, but also create beauty all around them. This is beauty in nature, beauty in life, in environment and surroundings. They also have the strength of beauty about themselves.

The lower expression of Tiphareth is vanity. Instead of selfless interest in beauty, this is tainted by a self-interest in beauty beyond the quality of Godliness. They want everything to be beautiful for themselves not as a service for God and humanity.

The Sephiroth of Netzach and Victory

Netzach has to do with the personality level. The key word is victory and has to do with the feeling state. On the higher level, Djwhal said that this is the person who sees justice and triumph. If a person is just in this sephiroth it may manifest only on a personality level of self-actualization and not necessarily at the soul or monadic level of victory. We see here how when many sephiroth blend together in function, higher levels of victory and triumph can be achieved. At the personality level of victory, we might have the great athlete, conqueror, or successful psychologist who has not entered the realm necessarily of soul psychology, but is very successful in personality level psychology. Here we are speaking of personality level of mastery rather than soul or spirit mastery.

The lower expression would be the tyrant or dictator. Here we have the person who always needs to win and be the "top dog," and is extremely competitive. They have not yet learned to transcend the negative ego game of superiority/inferiority complex. This type of person always needs to be right and is hence very self-righteous. They strive for victory at all costs, even at the expense of their own soul. They make bad decisions when in a leadership role because of the negative ego. They always need to hide any sense of weakness or vulnerability because of their need to the best!

The Sephiroth of Hod or Splendor

Hod is the opposite of Netzach. Its key word is splendor and is focused not on the feeling state, but on logic, thinking, and analytical perception on the personality level. In the higher expression, this is a person who is a great organizer. Since we are still focused here on the personality level, if not blended with other sephiroth it will remain more on the level of the concrete mind. They can organize great splendid banquets, conferences, political campaigns, or weddings.

In the lower expression, we have the person who is totally disorganized and their house and life is a mess. They would like to have it together but are not well-developed yet in this sephiroth. They are often very limited in their perspective, and see life through a very small selfish lens and hence do not see the bigger picture. They are often striving for splendor, but it is done in service of the negative ego rather than the true splendor of Spirit. This reminds me of what Jesus referred to in *A Course In Miracles* as grandeur versus grandiosity. In the lower expression, we have misjudging self and others. Much projection, for the head is not screwed on straight, so to speak. The weakness of the mental function allows the emotional body to have too much sway.

Yesod, The Sephiroth of Foundation

Yesod again deals with the personality level, and focuses on the quality of foundation and the subconscious mind. This type of person has made the subconscious mind their servant, which, of course, is the ideal since it has no rational reasoning. In addition, the person has learned to tap and utilize the unbelievable abilities of the subconscious mind. This type of person is very strong in their convictions, has faith, and has mastered fear. They can go into the most difficult situations and handle themselves extremely well. They are often heroic and will take a job no one else will do. This is because they are so grounded and strong in their foundation. The foundation of all advanced spiritual work is a healthy psychology, which has its foundation in the relationship between a person's conscious and subconscious mind. This type of person might also be very psychic but not necessarily spiritual if not blended.

In the lower expression of Yesod is someone completely victimized by the subconscious mind. There are an enormous number of people in this world who suffer this malady. They are on automatic pilot and not conscious, vigilant and do not have personal power attached to the conscious mind. They are tormented souls who by no fault of their own have not been properly educated as to the workings of their mind. They feel great weakness and fear in all situations.

The Sephiroth of Malkuth or The Kingdom

Malkuth, or the Kingdom, has to do with the physical earth level of the Tree. It is the counterpart to Kether in the crown. It is like heaven and earth. Malkuth in its higher expression is a person who can live like a king on the Earth. When just developed in this one sephiroth they are physically very strong and healthy and function extremely well in earthly life. They may not necessarily be developed on the soul or monadic level but are very successful in an earthly sense. They are born with a very strong physical constitution. They are successful in their jobs and make a good living. They know how to live on the Earth and thrive. A person with very good physical capabilities. They often have great knowledge on how to fix physical things. The lesson of this type of person is then to learn to blend the soul level into this earthly function and then finally the monadic level into this function.

The lower expression of Malkuth is the person who is ridden with fears of physical illness or is a hypochondriac. A person who is fearful of money and physical survival. They are preoccupied with first chakra concerns. They are often very superstitious.

Tree of Life Summation

The ultimate example on this planet of the Master who fully embodies all sephiroth of the Tree of Life and much more is his Holiness the Lord Sai Baba. Here we would also have the hidden sephiroth of Daath in the upper center of the Tree coming into play. Daath is the sephiroth of hidden knowledge. Djwhal Khul told that there is no lower expression of this sephiroth, for it doesn't come into manifestation until the higher expression has come into play. In Sai Baba or Lord Maitreya on Earth, we have the fully realized Tree of Life where all sephiroth are integrated and balanced properly as God would have it be.

Again, the ideal is to integrate all ten sephiroth in a balanced manner as Sai Baba has so perfectly embodied. Superimpose now the Tree of Life upon your own body, and chakra system. The flow of prana throughout your seven basic chakras and through your entire etheric body will be governed by how well integrated you are in the Tree and/or where you are undeveloped. This will apply to specific chakras and also to the flow of energy on the right and left sides of your body. I think you can see here that there is probably no more perfect model for understanding creation and its manifestation on a macrocosmic and microcosmic level than the Tree of Life.

Do read and study the chapter on the Tree of Life and the Kabbalah in my book *Hidden Mysteries*. It is an interesting study then to see how the twelve rays fit in with the Tree and then how the Tarot Cards as another archetypal system of personality integration fits in. This study shows how the twelve signs of the Zodiac fit into this system, and the twelve archetypes. I do recommend that you call in Djwhal Khul, Lord Maitreya, Lord Buddha, and Lord Melchizedek for the anchoring and activation of your planetary and cosmic Tree of Life. Then do work with the holographic computer in Djwhal Khul's ashram under his tutelage to help integrate and imprint the actual archetypal pattern and prana flow that is perfectly precise for your energy signature and your personal Tree of Life configuration.

This, in truth, is the core and basis of all psychological and all psycho-spiritual work. It is the foundation for all advanced spiritual study. So you see that the archetypes can be balanced, and integrated through any of these systems be it archetypes, rays, astrology, tarot, or the Tree of Life. I have included all of them, as is my usual eclectic and universalistic style to try and give you the full scope and vision of the entire prism of light in this area. The study of all systems will deepen your understanding in a most profound way. Seeing how each of these systems correlates, further deepens this process. Djwhal Khul has referred to these sessions in the holographic computer room in his ashram as "archetypal attunements." The attunement being the divine archetypal imprint in conjunction with the perfect prana energy flow for each person's mission and purpose leads to the cementing in of each person's monadic energy signature being put perfectly into place.

23

My Spiritual Mission and Purpose
by Dr. Joshua David Stone

My Spiritual mission and purpose is a multifaceted process. Spirit and the inner plane Ascended Masters have asked myself and Wistancia (married since 1998), to anchor onto the Earth an inner plane Ashram and Spiritual/Psychological/Physical/Earthly Teaching and Healing Academy! This Academy is called the Melchizedek Synthesis Light Academy! We are overlighted in this mission by Melchizedek, the Mahatma, Archangel Metatron, the inner plane Ascended Master Djwhal Khul, and a large group of Ascended Masters and Angels such as the Divine Mother, Archangel Michael, Archangel Gabriel, Sai Baba, Vywamus, the Lord of Arcturus, Lord Buddha, Lord Maitreya, Mother Mary, Quan Yin, El Morya, Kuthumi, Serapis Bey, Paul the Venetian, Master Hilarion, Sananda, Lady Portia and Saint Germain, and a great many others who we like to call the "Core Group"!

I have also been asked by the inner plane Ascended Master Djwhal Khul, who again wrote the Alice Bailey books, and was also involved in the Theosophical Movement, to take over his inner plane Ashram when he moves on to his next Cosmic Position, in the not too distant future.

Djwhal holds Spiritual Leadership over what is called the inner plane Second Ray Synthesis Ashram. On the inner plane the Second Ray Department is a gigantic three story building complex with vast gardens.

The Ascended Master Djwhal Khul runs the first floor of the Second Ray Department in the Spiritual Hierarchy. Master Kuthumi, the Chohan of the Second Ray, runs the second floor. Lord Maitreya the Planetary Christ runs the third floor! When Djwhal Khul leaves for his next Cosmic Position, I will be taking over this first floor Department. The Second Ray Department is focused on the "Spiritual Education," of all lightworkers on Earth, and is the Planetary Ray of the Love/Wisdom of God. What is unique, however, about the Synthesis Ashram, is that it has a unique mission and purpose which is to help lightworkers perfectly master and integrate all Twelve Planetary Rays which is one of the reasons I love this particular Spiritual leadership position and assignment so much! For this has been a great mission and focus of all my work!

Wistancia and my mission has been to anchor the Synthesis Ashram and Teaching Academy onto the physical Earth, which we have done and are continuing to do in an ever increasing manner on a global Level. Currently there are over 15 branches of the Academy that have been set up around the world! The Academy actually first came into existence in 1996! This we have been guided to call the Melchizedek Synthesis Light Academy for the following reasons. It is called this because of the Overlighting Presence of Melchizedek (Our Universal Logos), The Mahatma (Avatar of Synthesis), and the Light which is the embodiment of Archangel Metatron, who created all outer light in our Universe and is the creator of the electron! These three beings, Djwhal Khul, and a very large Core Group of inner plane Planetary and Cosmic Masters help us in all this work.

I have also been asked by the inner plane Ascended Masters to be one of the main "High Priest Spokespersons for the Planetary Ascension Movement on Earth." I have been asked to do this because of the cutting edge, yet easy to understand nature of all my books and work, as well as certain Spiritual Leadership qualities I humbly possess. In this regard, I represent all the Masters, which works out perfectly given the Synthesis nature of my work. I function as kind of a "Point Man" for the Ascended Masters on Earth, as they have described it to me.

The Masters under the guidance of Lord Buddha, our Planetary Logos, has also guided us as part of our mission, to bring Wesak to the West! So, for the last six years we have held a Global Festival and Conference at Mt Shasta, California for 2000 People. This, of course, honors the Wesak Festival, which is the holiest day of the year to the inner plane Ascended Masters, and the high point of incoming Spiritual energies to the Earth on the Taurus Full moon each year! We invite all lightworkers to join us each year from all over the world for this momentous celebration which is considered to be one of the premiere Spiritual Events in the New Age Movement!

The fourth part of my mission and purpose is the 30 Volume Easy to Read Encyclopedia of the Spiritual Path I have written. So far, I have completed 27 volumes in this Ascension Book Series. The Ascended Master Djwhal Khul prophesized in the 1940s that there would be a third dispensation of Ascended Master teachings what would appear at the turn of the century. The first dispensation of Ascended Master teachings was the "Theosophical Movement," channeled by Madam Blavatsky. The second dispensation of Ascended Master teachings was the Alice Bailey books, channeled by Djwhal Khul, and the *I AM Discourses*, channeled by Saint Germain. My 30 volume series of books is, by the grace of GOD and the Masters, the third dispensation of Ascended Master teachings as prophesized by Djwhal Khul. These books are co-creative channeled writings of myself and the inner plane Ascended Masters. What is unique about my work is how easy to read and understand it is, how practical, comprehensive, cutting edge, as well as integrated and synthesized. Wistancia has added to this work with her wonderful book "Invocations to the Light."

The fifth aspect of our work and mission, which is extremely unique is the emphasis of "Synthesis." My books and all my work integrate in a very beautiful way all religions, all Spiritual paths, all mystery schools, all Spiritual teachings, and all forms of psychology! Everyone feels at home in this work because of its incredible inclusive nature! This synthesis ideal is also seen at the Wesak Celebrations, for people come from all religions, Spiritual paths, mystery schools and teachings. The Event is overlighted by over one million inner plane Ascended Masters, Archangels and Angels, Elohim Masters and Christed Extraterrestrials. Wesak, the books, the Academy and all our work embody this synthesis principle. This is part of why I and we have been given Spiritual Leadership of the Synthesis Ashram on Earth, and soon on the inner plane as well. This also explains our unique relationship to Melchizedek who holds responsibility for the "synthesis development," of all beings in our Universe. Our connection to the Mahatma is explained by the fact that the Mahatma is the Cosmic embodiment of "Synthesis" in the infinite Universe. This is also why the Mahatma also goes by the name, "The Avatar of Synthesis." Archangel Metatron who holds the position in the Cosmic Tree of Life of Kether, or the Crown, hence has a "Synthesis Overview," of all of the Sephiroth or Centers of the Cosmic Tree of Life! Djwhal Khul holds Spiritual leadership of the "Synthesis Ashram" on a Planetary, Solar and Galactic level for the Earth! The Core Group of Masters that overlight our mission are the embodiment of the synthesis understanding!

The unique thing about our work is that it teaches some of the most cutting-edge co-created channeled work on the planet, in the realm of Ascension and Ascended Master Teachings. This can be seen in my books *The Complete Ascension Manual, Beyond Ascension, Cosmic Ascension, Revelations of a Melchizedek Initiate,* and *How To Teach Ascension Classes.* Because of my background as a professional Psychologist and Licensed Marriage, Family, and Child Counselor, I also specialize in some of the most advanced cutting-edge work on the planet in the field of Spiritual psychology. In this regard, I would guide you to my books *Soul Psychology, Integrated Ascension, How To Clear The Negative Ego*, and *Ascension and Romantic Relationships*! Thirdly, I also have humbly brought forth some extremely cutting-edge work on the physical/earthly level in the field of healing, Spirituality and society, politics, social issues, Extraterrestrials, Spiritual leadership, Spirituality and business, Goddess work with Wistancia, and of course the annual Wesak Celebrations. This can be found in my books *The Golden Keys to Ascension and Healing, Hidden Mysteries, Manual for Planetary Leadership, Your Ascension Mission: Embracing Your Puzzle Piece, How to be Successful in your Business from a Spiritual and Financial Perspective*, and *Empowerment and Integration of the Goddess* written by Wistancia and myself, to name a few!

Adding to this, the eleven new books I have just completed and am completing: *The Golden Book of Melchizedek: How To Become an Integrated Christ/Buddha in This Lifetime, How to Release Fear-Based Thinking and Feeling: An In-depth Study of Spiritual Psychology, The Little Flame and Big Flame* (my first children's book), *Letters of Guidance to Students and Friends, Ascension Names and Terms Glossary, Ascension Activation Meditations of The Spiritual Hierarchy, The Divine Blue Print for the Seventh Golden Age, How To Do Psychological and Spiritual Counseling For Self and Others, God and His Team of Super Heroes* (my second children's book), and *How To Achieve Perfect Radiant Health From The Soul's Perspective*!

Currently I have completed 27 Volumes in my Ascension Book Series. Fourteen of these books are published by Light Technology Publishers. A new version of *Soul Psychology* has just been published by Ballantine Publishers which is owned by Random House, which I am quite excited about as well! The other books are in manuscript form and I am currently negotiating with various publishers for publishing rights! My books have also been translated and published in Germany, Brazil, Japan, Holland, Israel and this process continues to expand.

Spirit and the inner plane Ascended Masters have told me that because of this unique focus, that what I have actually done in a co-creative way and manner with them, is open a new Portal to God. This new portal opening stems out of all the cutting-edge Ascension Activations and Ascended Master Teachings, the totally cutting-edge Spiritual Psychology work because of my background as a Psychologist and Licensed Marriage, Family, and Child Counselor, and the unique ability to ground all the work into the physical/earthly world in a balanced and integrated manner. Spirit and the Masters have told me that this new Portal to God is on an inner and outer plane level, and continues to be built in a co-creative way with Spirit, the Masters, myself, and certain other Masters and High Level Initiates who are helping me on the inner and outer planes! I have Spiritual leadership, however, in spearheading this project, and it is one of the most exciting projects I am involved in.

In terms of my Spiritual initiation process as I have spoken of in my books, I have currently now taken my 14th major initiation. These are not the minor initiations that some groups work with, but are the major initiations that embody all the minor initiations within them. The Seventh Initiation is the achieving of Liberation and Ascension. The Tenth Initiation is the completion of Planetary Ascension and the beginning of Solar Initiation. The Eleventh Initiation, being the first Galactic Initiation. The Twelfth Initiation, being the first Universal Initiation from an Earthly perspective. Having taken my 14th initiation, what is most important to me is that these initiations have been taken in an "integrated manner," for, in truth, the Masters told me that they are not really into Ascension, which may surprise a great many lightworkers. The Masters are into "Integrated Ascension"! There are many lightworkers taking initiations, but many are not doing so in an integrated and balanced manner! They are taking them on a Spiritual level, but they are not being properly integrated into the mental and emotional bodies or psychological level properly. They are also not transcending negative ego fear-based thinking and feeling and properly balancing their four body system. They are also not integrating their initiations fully into the physical/earthly level addressing such things as: Healing, Grounding their Missions, Finding their Puzzle Piece Mission and Purpose, Prosperity Consciousness and Financial and Earthly Success, Integrating the God/Goddess, Embracing the Earth Mother and the Nature Kingdom, Properly Integrating into Third Dimensional Society and Civilization in terms of the focus of their Service Mission. This is just mentioned as a very loving reminder of the importance of an integrated and balanced approach to one's Spiritual Path. The grace to have been able to take these 14 major initiations and be able to have completed my Planetary Ascension process and to have moved deeply into my Cosmic Ascension process, I give to GOD, Christ, the Holy Spirit, Melchizedek, The Mahatma, and Archangel Metatron and the Core Group of Masters I work with. I have dedicated myself and my life to GOD and the Masters service, and I have humbly attempted to share everything I know, have used and have done in my Spiritual path and Ascension process with all of you, my beloved readers!

Melchizedek, the Universal Logos, has also inwardly told me, that because of the Cosmic work I am involved with, that I have taken on the Spiritual assignment of being one of the "Twelve Prophets of Melchizedek on Earth." I am very humbled to serve in this capacity, because Melchizedek is the Universal Logos, which is like the President of our entire Universe. In truth, all religions and Spiritual teachings have their source in Melchizedek and in the Great Ancient Order of Melchizedek. It is my great honor and privilege to serve GOD and Melchizedek in this capacity. This is something I have never spoken of before, although I have known of this for many, many years. I have been guided after all this time to share a little more deeply about my Spiritual mission on Earth at this time.

The Academy Website is one of the most profound Spiritual Websites you will ever explore, because it embodies this "synthesis nature," and is an ever-expanding, living, easy-to-read Spiritual encyclopedia that fully integrates all 12 Rays in design and creation! This is also embodied in the free 140 page information packet that we send out to all who ask who wish to get involved and know more about our work! The information in the information packet is also available by just exploring the Academy Website!

We have also set up a wonderful Ministers Ordination and Training Program, which we invite all interested to read about. I am also very excited about a relatively recent book I have written called *How to Teach Ascension Classes*. Because I have become so busy with my Spiritual leadership and global world service work, I really do not have the time to teach weekly classes, as I have in the past. I firmly believe in the motto "Why give a person a fish, when you can teach them to fish?" In this vein, the Masters guided me to write a book on how to teach people to teach Ascension classes based on my work. I humbly suggest it is a most wonderful channeled book that can teach you in the easiest way and manner on every level to teach Ascension classes in your home or on a larger level if you choose. These classes are springing up now all over the globe and have been successful beyond my wildest dreams and expectations. When I wrote the book I was so involved with the process of writing it, I never fully envisioned the tremendous success it would have on a planetary and global level. Using this book and my other books, I have really done the initial homework for you, which can and will allow you to immediately begin teaching Ascension classes yourself. I humbly suggest that you look into the possibility of doing this yourself if you are so guided!

One other very interesting aspect of our Spiritual mission is something the Masters have been speaking to us about for over ten years which is what they described as being "Ambassadors for the Christed Extraterrestrials"! We have always known this to be true! This was part of the reason I wrote the book *Hidden Mysteries*, which I humbly suggest is one of the best overviews and an easy-to-read and understand manner, of the entire Extraterrestrial movement as it has affected our planet. If you have not read this book, I highly recommend that you do so. It is truly fascinating reading! My strongest personal connection to the Extraterrestrials is with the Arcturians! The Arcturians are the most advanced Christed Extraterrestrial race in our galaxy. They hold the future blueprint for the unfoldment of this planet. The Arcturians are like our future planet and future selves on a collective level. Part of my work, along with the Ascended Master Teachings, that I have been asked to bring through, is a more conscious and personal connection to the Arcturians, the Ashtar Command, and other such Christed Extraterrestrial races. This year's Platinum Wesak, because of being in the year 2001, will have a special connection to these Christed Extraterrestrials, and we invite you all to attend for this reason and many others! I also encourage you to read my book *Beyond Ascension*, where I explore some of my personal experiences with the Arcturians and how you may do so as well!

Currently, behind the scenes, we are working on some further expansions of this aspect of our mission, which we will share at a later time! Wistancia has also been involved with White Time Healing, which is another most wonderful Extraterrestrial healing modality that she offers to the public!

One other aspect of our mission deals with having developed with help from the inner plane Ascended Masters, some of the most advanced Ascension activation processes to accelerate Spiritual evolution that has ever been brought forth to this planet. In this co-creative process with the Masters, we have discovered the keys to how to accelerate Spiritual evolution at a rate of speed that in past years and centuries would have been unimaginable! This is why I call working with the Ascended Masters "The Rocketship to GOD Method of Spiritual Growth." There is no faster path to God Realization than working with the Ascended Masters, Archangels and Angels, Elohim Masters, and Christed Extraterrestrials! What is wonderful about this process is that you do not have to leave your current Spiritual practice, religion, or Spiritual path. Stay on the path you are and just integrate this work into what you are currently doing! All paths as you know, lead to GOD my friends! This is the profundity of following an eclectic path, and path of synthesis! I humbly suggest I have found some short cuts! I share this with all lightworkers on Earth, for I love GOD with all my heart and soul and mind and might, and I recognize that we are all incarnations of GOD,and Sons and Daughters of this same GOD regardless of what religion, Spiritual path, or mystery school we are on. We are all, in truth, the Eternal Self and are all God! There is, in truth, only GOD, so what I share with you, I share with you, GOD, and myself,, for in the highest sense we are all one! What we each hold back from each other, we hold back from ourselves and from GOD. This is why I give freely all that I am, have learned and have, to you, my beloved readers, giving everything and holding back nothing! In my books and audiotapes, I have literally shared every single one of these ideas, tools, and Ascension activation methods for accelerating evolution that I have used and come to understand. My beloved readers, these tools and methods found in my books and on the audio tapes will "blow your mind as to their effectiveness," in terms of how profound, and easy-to-use they are! I would highly recommend that all lightworkers obtain the 13 Ascension Activation Meditation tapes I have put together for this purpose. Most of them were taped at the Wesak Celebrations with 1500 to 2000 people in attendance, with over one million inner plane Ascended Masters, Archangels and Angels, Elohim Masters, and Christed Extraterrestrials in attendance, under the Wesak full moon and the mountain of Mt Shasta. You can only imagine the power, love, and effectiveness of these Ascension activation audiotapes. I recommend getting all 13 tapes and working with one tape every day or every other day! I personally guarantee you that these tapes will accelerate your Spiritual evolution a thousand fold! You can find them in the information packets and on our Website. They are only available from the Academy! Trust me on this, the combination of reading my books, Wistancia's book, and working with these audio ascension activation tapes, will accelerate your Spiritual evolution beyond your wildest dreams and imagination!

One other extremely important part of my mission, which is a tremendous Spiritual passion of mine, is the training of lightworkers on Earth in the area of Spiritual/Christ/Buddha thinking and negative ego/separative/fear-based thinking! These are the only two ways of thinking in the world, and each person thinks with one, the other, or a combination of both. If a person does not learn how to transcend negative ego thinking and feeling, it will end up over time corrupting every aspect of their lives including all channeling work, Spiritual teaching, and even healing work! One cannot be wrong with self and right with GOD. This is because our thoughts create our reality, as we all know! I cannot recommend more highly that every person reading this read my books *Soul Psychology*, *The Golden Book of Melchizedek: How to Become an Integrated Christ/Buddha in this Lifetime*, and *How to Release Fear-Based Thinking and Feeling: An In-depth Study of Spiritual Psychology*! I humbly suggest that these three books will be three of the most extraordinary self-help books in the area of mastering this psychological area of life. They are extremely easy to read, very practical and filled with tools that will help you in untold ways. The last two books I have mentioned are only available through the Academy. Being a channel for the Ascended Masters and being uniquely trained as a Spiritual Psychologist and Marriage, Family, and Child Counselor, as well as being raised in a family of psychologists, has given me an extraordinary ability to teach this material through my books in a most effective manner. The combination of my books on Ascension, and these books on Spiritual Psychology, along with Wistancia's book on the art of invocation will literally revolutionize your consciousness in the comfort of your own home! The most extraordinary thing about all this work is how incredibly easy to read, and easy to understand it is. It is also incredibly comprehensive, completely cutting-edge, and totally integrated, balanced and synthesized. It contains the best of all schools of thought in the past, present, and channeled cutting edge future understanding that is available now! I humbly ask you to trust me in this regard and just read one of these books and you will immediately want to buy the others!

One other aspect of our work and mission is our involvement with the "Water of Life," and the Perfect Science products for the healing of our own physical bodies and the physical body of Mother Earth of all pollution in the air, water and earth. This is the miracle Mother Earth has been waiting for to bring her back to her "original edenic state" after so much abuse. This is not the time or the place to get into this subject in detail, however I invite you to check out the "Water of Life" and the Perfect Science information in the information packet and on the Academy Website! It is truly the miracle we have all been waiting for to help heal the Earth!

One other aspect of our work and mission is a project that the Ascended Masters have asked us to put together on behalf of lightworkers and people around the globe. It is called the "Interdimensional Prayer Altar Program"! The Masters have guided us to set it up in the Academy located in Agoura Hills, California on the property we live on. We have set up a "Physical Interdimensional Prayer Altar" where people can send in their prayers on any subject and we will place them on this Altar. In consultation with the Masters, Archangels and Angels, Elohim Masters, and Christed Extraterrestrials, we have set up an arrangement with them that all physical letters placed upon this Altar will be immediately worked upon by these Masters. We have been guided by the inner plane Ascended Masters to create 15 Prayer Altar Programs in different areas of life that people can sign up for. For example, there is one for health and another for financial help in your Spiritual mission. There are 15 in total, and two-thirds of them are totally free. There are five or six that are more advanced Spiritual acceleration programs where written material is sent to you to work with in conjunction with these programs to accelerate Spiritual. All letters we receive by e-mail, fax, or letter are placed on the Altar by myself or my personal assistant. It is kept 100% confidential and is an extremely special service provided by the inner plane Ascended Masters and Angels to help all lightworkers and people on Earth with immediate help for whatever they need, should they desire assistance. Other examples of Prayer Altars are: Building your Higher Light Body, Extra Protection, Relationship Help, World Service Prayers, Help for your Animals, Prayer Altar for the Children, Integrating the Goddess, Integrating your Archetypes, Integrating the Seven Rays and working with the Seven Inner Plane Ashrams of the Christ, Integrating the Mantle of the Christ, Ascension Seat Integration, and Light, Love, and Power Body Building Program! These Prayer Altar Programs have been co-created with the inner plane Ascended Masters as another tool for not only helping all lightworkers with whatever they need help with, but also as another cutting-edge tool to accelerate Spiritual evolution!

In a similar regard, the Masters have guided us to set up a Melchizedek Synthesis Light Academy Membership Program which is based on three levels of involvement. Stage One, Stage Two, and Stage Three! Stage One and Stage Three are totally free. Stage Two costs only $20 for a lifetime Membership with no other fees ever required. You also receive free large colored pictures of Melchizedek, the Mahatma, Archangel Metatron, and Djwhal Khul for joining. It is not necessary to join in order to get involved in the work; however, it has been set up by the inner plane Ascended Masters as another service and tool of the Academy to help lightworkers accelerate their Spiritual evolution! When joining the different Stages, the Masters take you under their wing so to speak, and accelerate your evolution by working with you much more closely on the inner plane while you sleep at night and during your conscious waking hours. The joining is nothing more than a process that gives them the permission to work with you in this more intensive fashion! Again, it is not necessary to join to get involved in the work, and it is really just another one of the many fantastic tools and services the Academy has made available to you to accelerate your Spiritual, psychological, and earthly/physical evolution in an integrated and balanced manner!

I had a dream shortly after just about completing my two new books, *The Golden Book of Melchizedek: How to Become an Integrated Christ/Buddha in this Lifetime* and *How to Release Fear-Based Thinking and Feeling: An In-depth Study of Spiritual Psychology*. In this dream, I was being shown the different Spiritual missions people had. My Spiritual mission was the embodiment of the Holy Spirit. I was clearly shown how other people within GOD, Christ and the Holy Spirit, had missions of being more detached off-shoots of the Holy Spirit, and continuing outward from there with all kinds of different Spiritual missions; however, mine was the embodiment of the Holy Spirit on Earth.

My beloved readers, I want to be very clear here that in sharing this I am in no way, shape or form, claiming to be the Holy Spirit. There is enough glamour in the New Age Movement and I am not interested in adding any more to it. What I am sharing in this chapter to more clearly and precisely share my Spiritual mission and purpose, is that which I am here to strive to embody and demonstrate. The Holy Spirit is the third aspect of the Trinity of GOD. I have always greatly loved the Holy Spirit, for the Holy Spirit is like the "Voice of GOD"! It is the "Still, Small Voice Within"! When one prays to GOD, it is the Holy Spirit who answers for GOD. The Holy Spirit is the answer to all questions, challenges, and problems. The Holy Spirit speaks for the Atonement or the At-one-ment! It teaches the Sons and Daughters of GOD how to recognize their true identity as God, Christ, the Buddha, and the Eternal Self! In truth, there are only two voices in life! There is the voice of the negative ego and the voice of the Holy Spirit! There is the voice of the negative ego/fear-based/separative thinking and feeling, and there is the voice of God/Spiritual/Christ/Buddha thinking and feeling! There is the "Voice of Love" and the voice of fear! There is the "Voice of Oneness" and the voice of separation!

I was given this dream after completing these two books because, I humbly suggest, this is the energy I was embodying in writing them and that I am striving to embody at all times in my Spiritual mission and purpose on Earth. This is not surprising in the sense that this has always been my Spiritual ideal and the dream was just an inward confirmation in that moment that I was embodying and demonstrating that Spiritual Ideal in the energy flow I was in. This is what I strive to do in all my work, be it my Ascension Book Series, Wesak Celebrations, Teaching, Counseling, Video Tapes, Audio Tapes and all my work, which is to strive to be the embodiment of a "Voice for God"! By the grace of GOD, Christ, the Holy Spirit, and the Masters, I provide a lot of the "answers" people and lightworkers are seeking! I teach people how to "undo" negative ego/fear-based/separative thinking and feeling and show then how to fully realize God/Christ/Buddha thinking and feeling! I show them how to release and undo glamour, illusion, and maya, and instead seek "Truth," as GOD, Christ, the Holy Spirit, and the Masters would have you seek it!

My real purpose, however, is not to just be the embodiment of the Holy Spirit on Earth, for I would not be embodying the Voice and Vision of the Holy Spirit if I just focused on this. The Voice and Vision of GOD, Christ, the Holy Spirit, and Melchizedek is that of synthesis! This is the other thing I feel in the deepest part of my heart and soul that I am here to embody! So my "truest and highest Spiritual ideal" that I am here to strive to embody is to try to embody GOD, Christ, the Holy Spirit, the inner plane Ascended Masters, he Archangels and Angels of the Light of GOD, the Elohim Councils of the Light of GOD, and the Christed Extraterrestrials of the Light of GOD. I feel in the deepest part of my heart and soul and what I try to embody every moment of my life is "All that is of GOD and the Godforce on Earth"! In this regard, it is my Spiritual mission and purpose to strive to be the embodiment of the "synthesis nature of God on Earth"! This is why I have been given Spiritual leadership of the Synthesis Ashram and Academy on Earth, and future leadership of the inner plane Synthesis Ashram that governs our Planet.

The other thing I strive to do in my Spiritual mission is to embody Spiritual mastery on a Spiritual, psychological, and physical/earthly level. What most people and lightworkers do not realize is that there are three distinct levels to God Realization. There is a Spiritual level, a Psychological level, and a Physical/Earthly level! To achieve true God Realization, all three levels must be equally mastered! Another way of saying this is that there are "Four Faces of GOD"! There is a Spiritual Face, a Mental Face, an Emotional Face, and a Material Face! To truly realize God, all four must be equally mastered, loved, honored, sanctified, integrated, and balanced! The "Mental and Emotional Faces of GOD" make up the psychological level of GOD. So, my Spiritual mission and purpose is to fully embody Spiritual mastery, unconditional love, and wisdom on all three of these levels and in all Four Faces of GOD! In a similar vein, my Spiritual mission and purpose is to embody self-mastery and proper integration of all "Seven Rays of GOD," not just one or a few. For the "Seven Rays of GOD" are, in truth, the true "Personality of GOD"! My Spiritual mission and purpose is to not only strive to embody all levels of GOD, but to also try and develop all my God-given abilities and Spiritual gifts; on a Spiritual, Psychological, and Physical/Earthly level, and in all Four Faces of GOD!

My beloved readers, all these things that I have written about in this chapter are what I strive to fully embody and demonstrate on the Earth every moment of my life, and is what I strive with all my heart and soul and mind and might to teach others to do as well!

As the Founder and Director of the Melchizedek Synthesis Light Academy along with Wistancia, with great humbleness and humility, it has been my great honor and privilege to share "my Spiritual mission and purpose in a deeper and more profound manner at this time." I do so in the hopes that all who feel a resonance and attunement with this work, and will get involved with the "Academy's Teachings" and all that it has to offer. I also share this so that all who choose to get involved might join this vast group of lightworkers around the globe, to help spread the teachings and work of the inner plane Ascended Master. The inner plane Ascended Masters and I, along with the Archangels and Angels, Elohim Councils and Christed Extraterrestrials, put forth the Clarion Call to lightworkers around the world to explore this work, integrate this work, and become Ambassadors of the Ascended Masters, so that we may at this time in Beloved Earth's history bring in fully now the Seventh Golden Age in all its Glory!

About the Author

Dr. Joshua David Stone has a Ph.D. in Transpersonal Psychology and is a Licensed Marriage, Family, and Child Counselor, in Agoura Hills, California. On a Spiritual level, he anchors *The Melchizedek Synthesis Light Academy and Ashram*, which is an integrated inner and outer plane ashram that seeks to represent all paths to God! He serves as one of the leading spokespersons for the Planetary Ascension Movement. Through his books, tapes, workshops, lectures, and annual Wesak Celebrations, Dr. Stone is known as one of the leading Spiritual Teachers and Channels in the world on the teachings of the Ascended Masters, Spiritual Psychology, and Ascension! He has currently written over 27 volumes in his "Ascension Book Series," which he also likes to call "The Easy to Read Encyclopedia of the Spiritual Path!"

For a free information packet of all Dr. Stone's workshops, books, audiotapes, Academy membership program, and global outreach program, please call or write to the following address:

Dr. Joshua David Stone
Melchizedek Synthesis Light Academy
28951 Malibu Rancho Rd
Agoura Hills, CA 91301

Phone: 818-706-8458
Fax: 818-706-8540
e-mail: drstone@best.com

Please come visit my new Website at:
http://www.drjoshuadavidstone.com

Printed in the United States
105428LV00003B/154-156/A